INTRODUCTION

In the frenetic whirl of modern media—where every glance is scrutinized, every word dissected, and every image immortalized—few figures have captivated the public eye quite like Melania Trump. As a journalist who has spent decades chronicling the powerful, glamorous, and polarizing, I've borne witness to countless personalities who flicker across the stage of history. Some dazzled briefly, their light extinguished by time or scandal; others carved their names into the annals with force or fervor. Yet, among this parade of luminaries, none have embodied the enigmatic blend of elegance, resilience, and timeless beauty quite like the 45th and 47th First Lady of the United States. This book is not a political treatise, nor a partisan cheer; it is an ode to a woman whose very presence has redefined what it means to be seen.

From the moment she stepped into the national spotlight, Melania Trump was more than a figure beside a president—she was a vision. Her statuesque poise, those piercing eyes that seem to hold a thousand untold stories, and a wardrobe that married sophistication with daring originality set her apart in a world often dulled by conformity. In newsrooms and studios, we whispered about her not just as a subject, but as a phenomenon. She was the Slovenian-born model who became a First Lady, yes, but she was also something more—a living testament to the power of beauty as both shield and sword in the unrelenting glare of public life. To watch her was to witness an alchemy of grace and grit, a woman who turned the harsh fluorescence of fame into a soft, radiant glow that defied easy categorization.

Melania Trump: Elegance in the White House seeks to peel back the layers of that beauty, not merely in the superficial sense (though her aesthetic perfection is undeniable), but in the way it has shaped her narrative. I've watched her glide through state dinners with the grace of a diplomat, command magazine covers with the ease of a seasoned icon, and weather storms of criticism with a quiet strength that left even her detractors in reluctant awe. As someone who has spent years behind the camera and the byline, I can attest: Melania's allure is not just skin-deep—it's a masterclass in composure, a silent rebuttal to a culture that often mistakes noise for influence. In an age of shouting matches and soundbites, she chose silence as her megaphone, elegance as her manifesto, and beauty as her enduring argument.

Here, through the lens of a media insider, we'll explore the moments that defined her—those crystalline images etched into our collective memory, the subtle gestures that spoke louder than words, and the undeniable artistry of a woman who turned every frame into a portrait. This is not a biography in the traditional sense; it's a celebration of Melania Trump as a muse of our time, a figure whose beauty transcends the fleeting headlines and reminds us of the enduring power of grace under fire. So turn the page, dear reader, and join me in admiring a woman who, in the chaos of our era, stood as a beacon of serenity and style. Melania Trump: the First Lady who didn't just occupy the role—she adorned it!

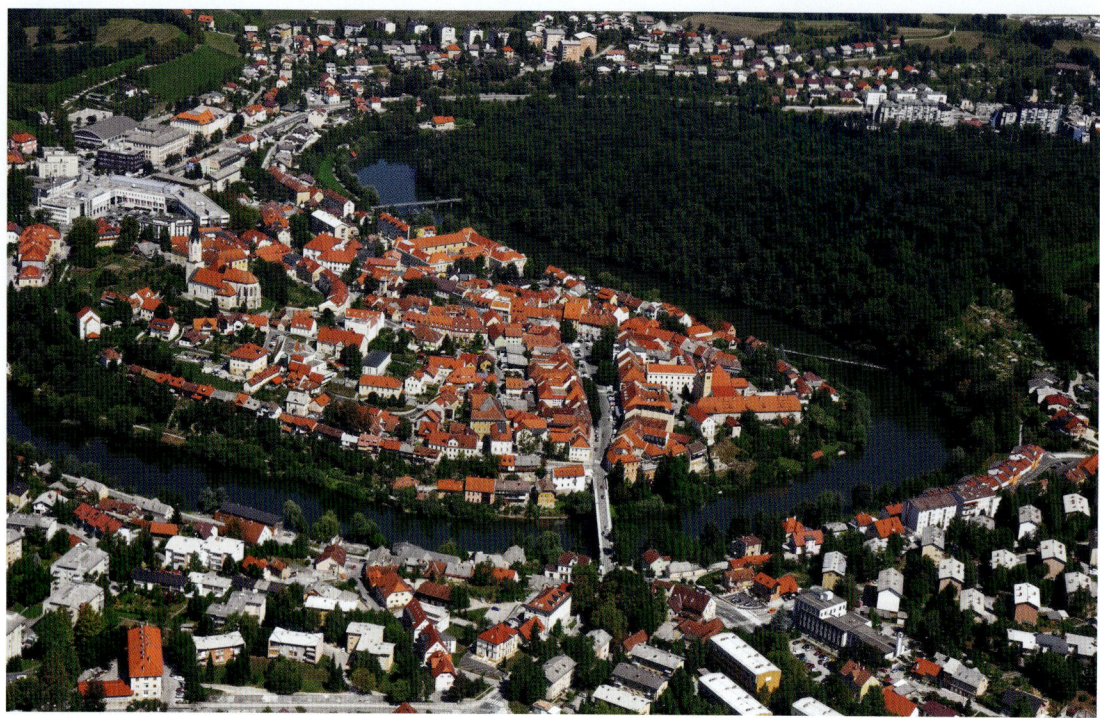

Novo Mesto, Slovenia[25]

THE MAKING OF A MUSE

To understand Melania Trump's singular place in the public imagination, we must begin where her story first intersected with the world's gaze: not in the White House, but on the glossy pages of fashion magazines and the catwalks of Europe. Born Melania Knauss in Novo Mesto, Slovenia, in 1970, she emerged from a modest upbringing in a then-communist country—a world of concrete and constraint—into the shimmering realm of high fashion. It's a journey that feels almost mythic: The small-town girl with striking features and an unyielding determination, crossing borders and oceans to chase a dream that most would deem unreachable. By the time she arrived in New York in the mid-1990s, she was already a seasoned model with a portfolio brimming with the kind of images that stop editors in their tracks—sharp cheekbones, a gaze that could pierce steel, and a presence that seemed to whisper of secrets untold.

Yet, it wasn't just her looks that set her apart; it was the way she wielded them. In an industry notorious for chewing up and spitting out its brightest stars, Melania navigated the chaos with a quiet confidence that belied her years. She wasn't the loudest voice in the room, nor the most flamboyant figure on the runway, but she didn't need to be. Her beauty was her currency, and she spent it wisely—securing contracts, building a name, and carving out a space in a city that rarely offers second chances. By the time she met Donald Trump in 1998 at a Manhattan fashion event, she was no wide-eyed ingénue; she was a woman who had already mastered the art of being seen on her own terms.

That encounter—fate, serendipity, or perhaps a collision of two larger-than-life trajectories—marked the beginning of a new chapter, one that would catapult her from the elite circles of fashion to the global stage of politics. When she married Donald Trump in 2005, in a ceremony dripping with opulence and attended by a who's-who of power players, the world took notice. The images from that day—a radiant bride in a John Galliano gown, her smile a blend of warmth and mystery—became a prelude to the icon she would become. But even then, as the tabloids buzzed and the cameras flashed, Melania remained an enigma. She didn't court the spotlight; she commanded it, with a stillness that made the world lean in closer.

A FIRST LADY LIKE NO OTHER

When Donald Trump announced his candidacy for president in 2015, Melania's role shifted once more. No longer just a model or a mogul's wife, she became a potential First Lady—a title steeped in tradition, expectation, and scrutiny. For those of us in the media, it was a tantalizing prospect: *How would this poised, private woman adapt to a role that demanded both visibility and vulnerability?*

The answer, as it turned out, was with a grace that defied precedent. From the campaign trail to the White House, Melania Trump didn't just step into the role of First Lady—she redefined it, infusing it with a modern elegance that felt both timeless and utterly her own.

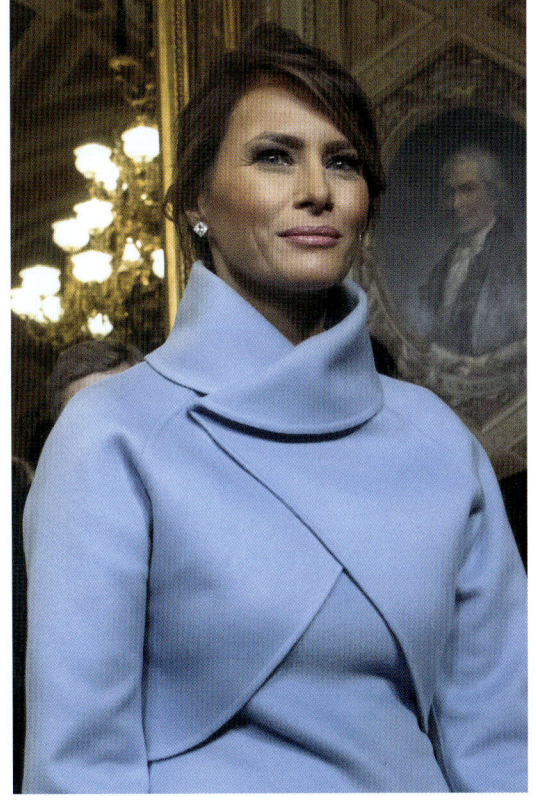

Consider the images that emerged during those years: Melania in a powder-blue Ralph Lauren ensemble at the 2017 inauguration, her silhouette a nod to Jackie Kennedy yet unmistakably contemporary; Melania in a crisp white suit during a state visit, her every step exuding a quiet authority; Melania in a flowing emerald gown at a diplomatic dinner, turning heads with the ease of a woman born to the spotlight. These were not mere fashion choices—they were statements, each one a brushstroke in the portrait of a First Lady who understood the power of visual language. In a political landscape often defined by bombast and bluster, she offered something different: a serene beauty that spoke volumes without raising its voice.

But it wasn't just her wardrobe that captivated us. It was the way she carried herself through the maelstrom of public life. The White House, with its endless cycle of crises and controversies, is a crucible that tests even the most seasoned figures. For Melania, it was a proving ground. She faced relentless scrutiny—over her accent, her past, her every word, and moment of silence—yet she emerged unscathed. Her composure became her shield against the slings and arrows of a polarized age. I recall watching her during a particularly tumultuous news cycle, as pundits debated her husband's latest outburst and critics parsed her latest speech. There she stood, at a White House event, her expression calm and her posture impeccable, as if to say: *This, too, shall pass*. It was a moment that crystallized her strength—not the loud, brash kind, but the quiet, enduring sort that weathers storms and leaves a mark.

BEAUTY AS ARMOR

To speak of Melania Trump is, inevitably, to speak of her beauty. It's a subject that has sparked endless debate: *Is it a gift? A weapon? A distraction?* For some, it's a shallow lens through which to view a complex woman; for others, it's the key to understanding her. As a journalist, I've grappled with this question myself, torn between the instinct to analyze and the impulse to simply admire. But after years of observing her, I've come to see her beauty not as a footnote, but as a force—a tool she has wielded with precision and purpose throughout her life.

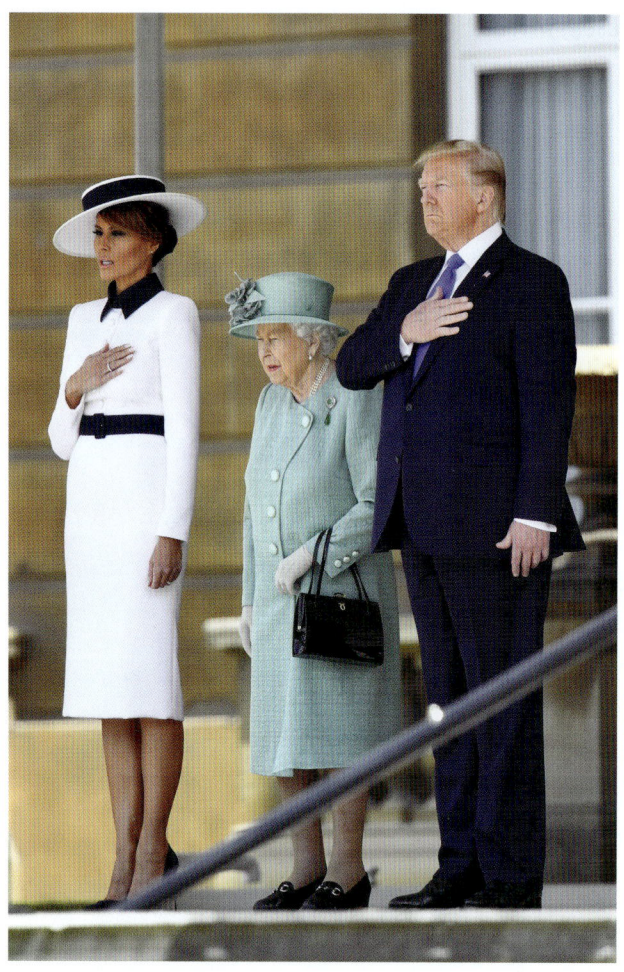

In the modeling world, her looks opened doors, securing her a foothold in an industry that thrives on the ephemeral. In her marriage to Donald Trump, the media elevated her from companion to equal, a partner whose presence amplified his own. And as First Lady, they became a kind of armor, deflecting the barbs of a media machine that often seeks to reduce women to caricatures. Consider the infamous "I Really Don't Care, Do U?" jacket she wore during a 2018 visit to migrant children at the border—a moment that ignited a firestorm of speculation. *Was it a misstep? A message? A defiance?* Whatever the intent, Melania wore it with the same unflappable poise she brought to every public appearance, turning a potential scandal into a study in resilience. The jacket became a Rorschach test for a divided nation, but she remained above the fray, her beauty a constant amid the chaos.

That beauty, though, is more than physical. It's in the way she moves—deliberate, measured, as if every step is choreographed. It's in the way she speaks—softly, with an accent that hints at her roots yet carries the weight of her journey. It's in the way she meets the camera's gaze, unflinching, as if daring the world to look deeper. To dismiss it as mere aesthetics is to miss the point: Melania's beauty is a narrative in itself, a story of transformation, survival, and quiet triumph. It's the thread that ties her past to her present, her private self to her public persona, her Slovenian origins to her American legacy.

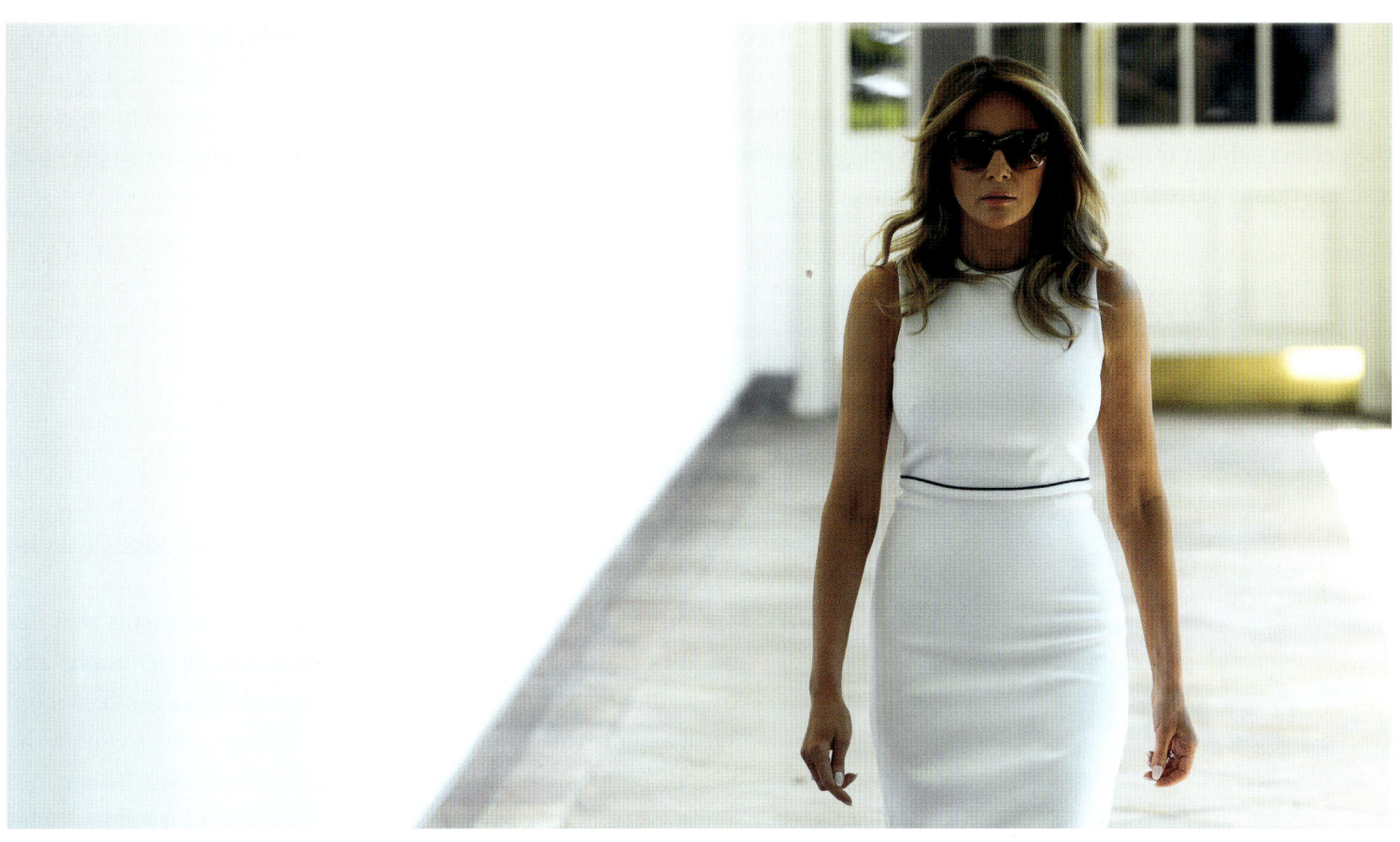

THE MEDIA'S MUSE

For those of us in the media, Melania Trump has been a perpetual fascination—a puzzle we've spent years trying to solve. In newsrooms, we debated her silence: *Was it aloofness or strategy?* On air, we parsed her style: *Was it vanity or vision?* In print, we chronicled her every move, from the Rose Garden she redesigned to the Christmas decorations she curated with an artist's eye. She was a subject who defied easy headlines, a woman who slipped through the cracks of our usual narratives. Where others shouted, she whispered; where others stumbled, she soared. And in doing so, she became more than a First Lady—she became a muse.

I remember the first time I saw her up close, at a White House event in 2018. The room was abuzz with the usual clamor of power and politics, but when Melania entered, it fell silent—not out of reverence, but out of sheer captivation. She wore a cream-colored dress that seemed to float around her, her hair swept back in a way that framed those arresting eyes. She didn't speak much that evening, but she didn't need to. Her presence was its own language, one that spoke of strength, mystery, and an unshakable sense of self. As a journalist, I scribbled notes, trying to capture the moment; as an observer, I simply marveled at the woman who could command a room without saying a word.

That ability—to captivate without conforming—has been the hallmark of her time in the spotlight. Whether posing for Vogue before her White House years or standing beside world leaders during them, Melania turned every frame into a work of art. Photographers loved her, not just for her features, but for the way she inhabited them. She was, in many ways, the perfect subject for an era obsessed with images: a woman who understood the power of a single glance, a single pose, a single moment frozen in time.

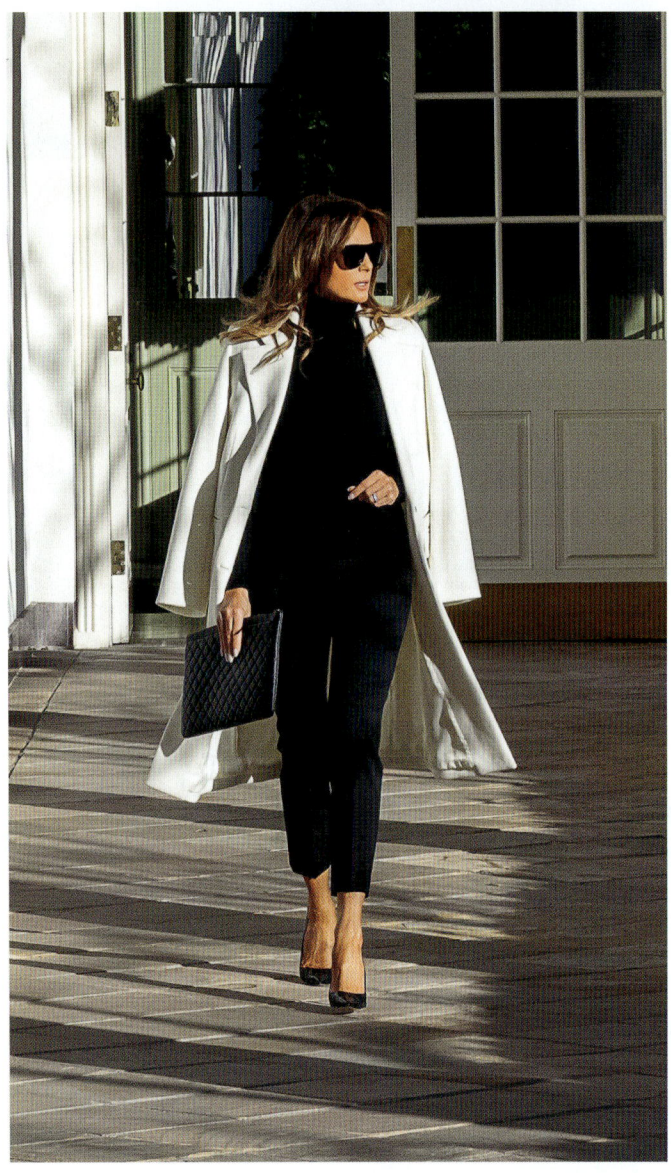

A LEGACY OF GRACE

As I write these words in March 2025, Melania Trump's tenure as First Lady is both a memory and a current reality whose impact lingers. This book is my attempt to capture that allure, to trace the arc of a journey that took her from Slovenia to the world stage, and to celebrate a beauty that transcended the noise of our times.

In the pages that follow, we'll revisit the moments that defined her: the campaigns and controversies, the triumphs and trials, the images and impressions that made her a modern icon. We'll explore the woman behind the mystique—not through the lens of politics, but through the prism of presence. This is not a story of policy or partisanship; it's a story of a woman who turned every challenge into a canvas, every spotlight into a stage, and every glance into a legacy. Melania Trump didn't just endure the glare of history—she adorned it, with a grace that will echo long after the cameras have turned away.

Let us step back from the clamor of the present and look anew at a figure who, in the chaos of our era, stood as a beacon of serenity and style. Let us celebrate Melania Trump: the First Lady who didn't just occupy the role—she transformed it into something unforgettable.

This new edition has been stunningly updated with photos from the remainder of the first term, as well as images from the start of her second tenure as First Lady. We hope you enjoy!

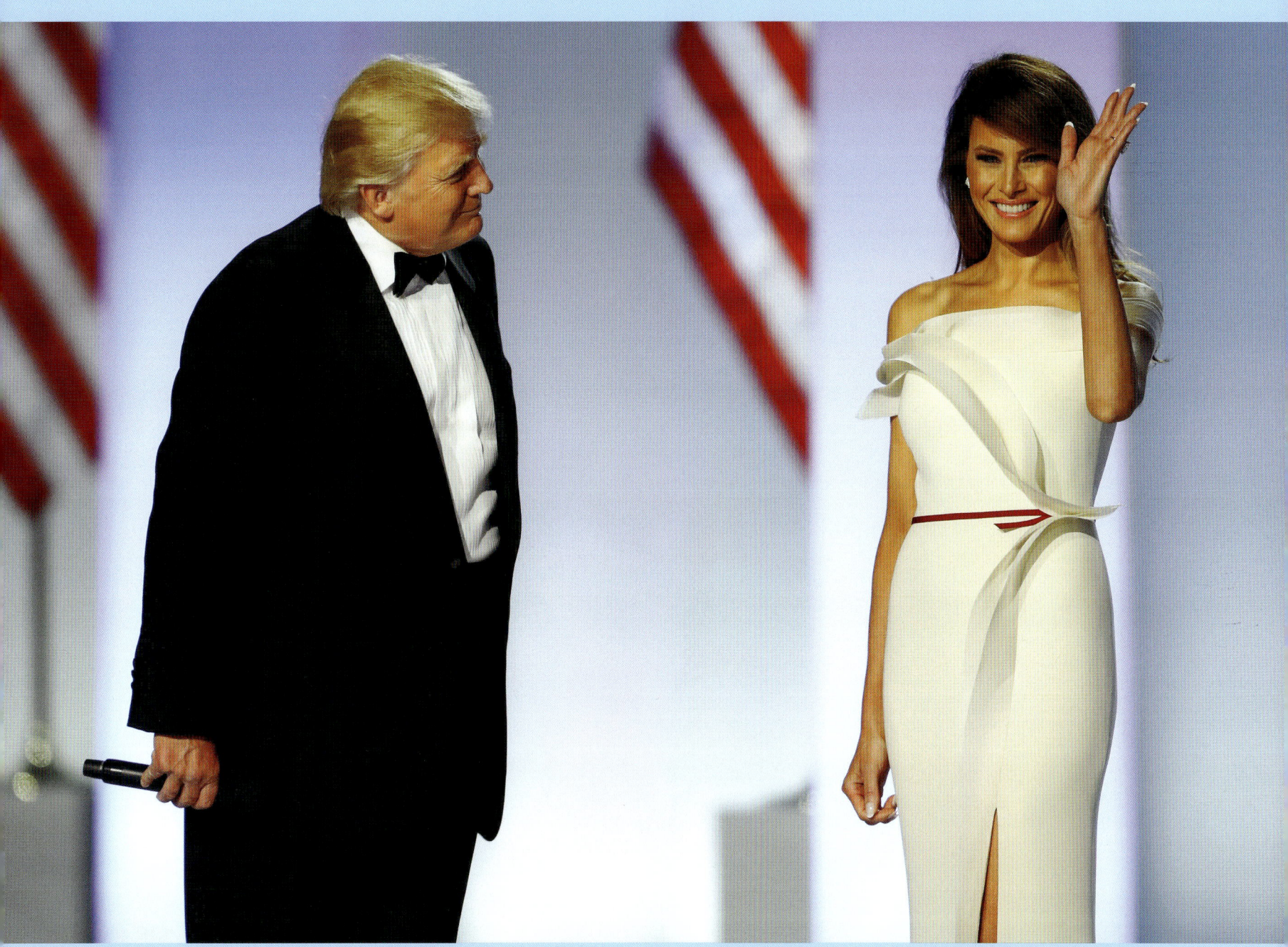

THE FIRST TERM

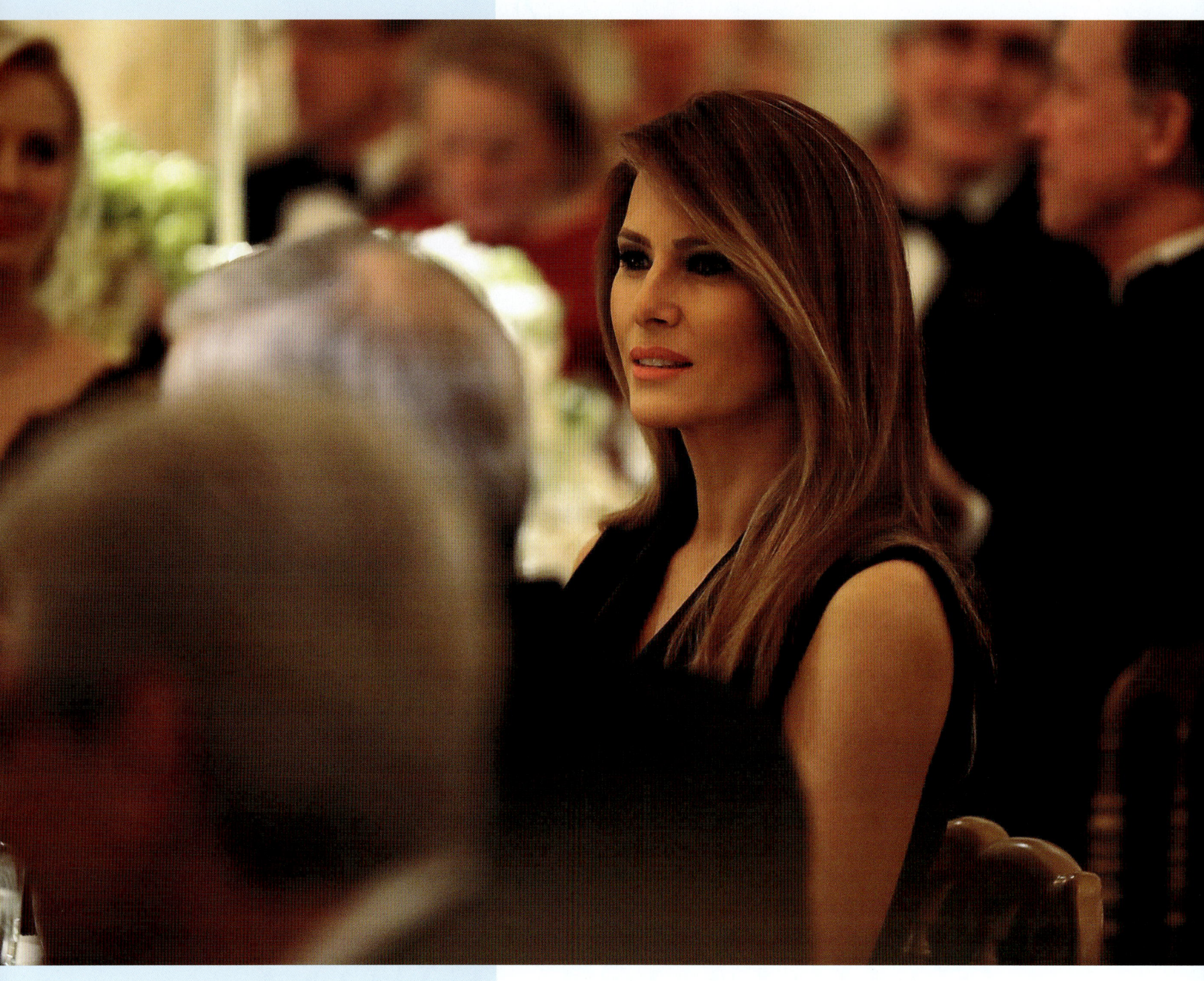

Melania Trump lights up the room while hosting the President's first black-tie event of Trump's new administration, the Governor's Ball, February 26, 2017.[3]

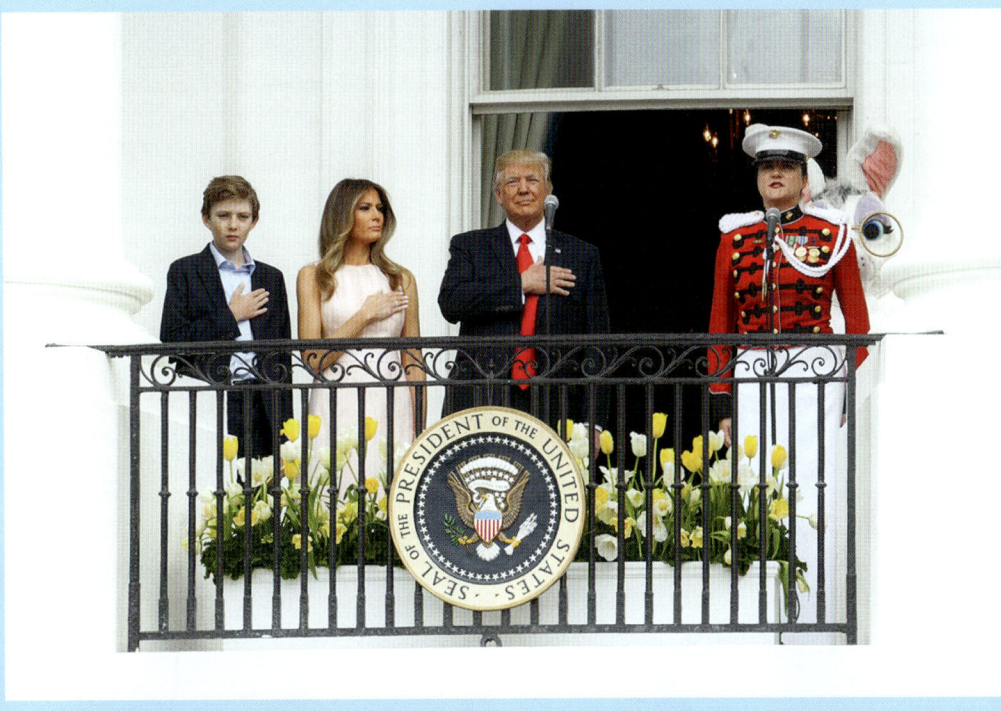

Melania Trump, her son Barron, and President Donald Trump stand at attention as the National Anthem is played at the first annual White House Easter Egg Roll of the new occupants of the White House. April 17, 2017.[4]

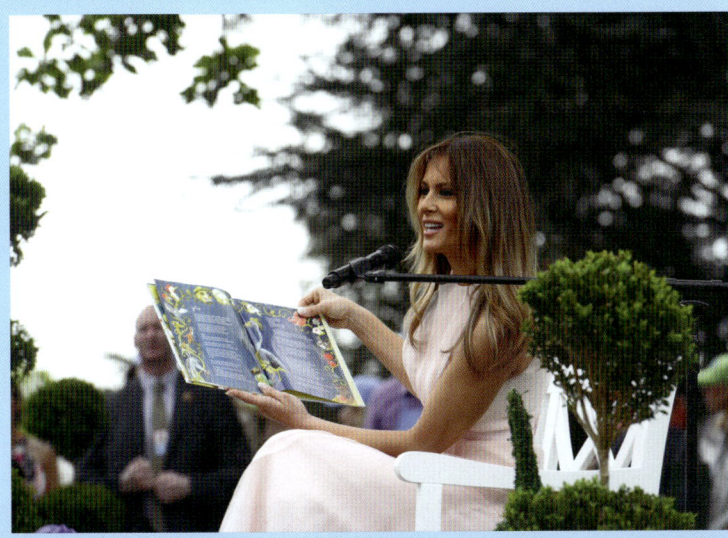

First Lady Melania Trump enjoys reading to children at the White House Easter Egg Roll, Monday, April 17, 2017.[4]

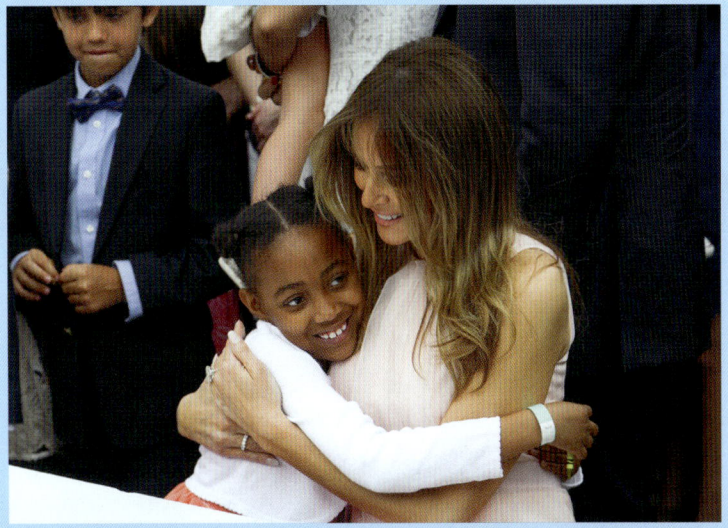

Melania Trump hugging a child while doing arts and crafts at the first Easter Egg Roll of the Trump Administration.[5]

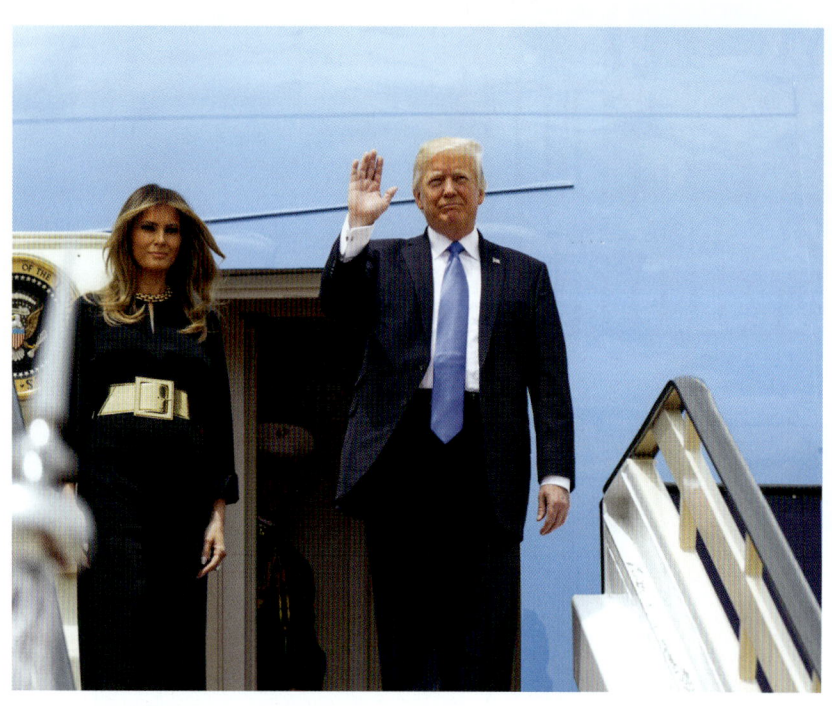

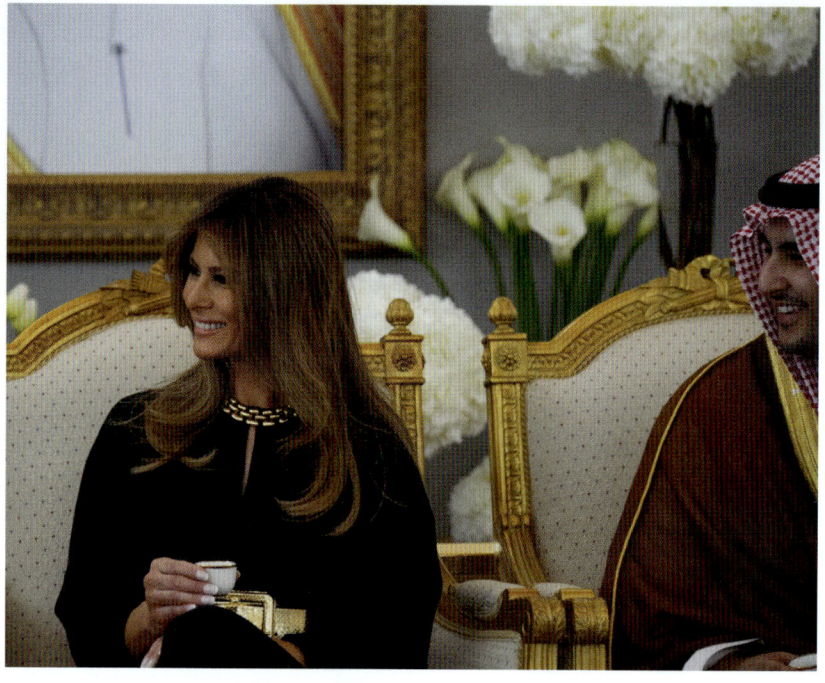

President Donald Trump and First Lady Melania Trump arrive on the tarmac, Saturday, May 20, 2017, to King Khalid International Airport in Riyadh, Saudi Arabia. Mrs. Trump is dressed conservatively to match Saudi Arabia's strict dress code for women.[5]

The First Lady is allowed a moment to relax and smile at a Saudi ceremonial welcoming tea, after exiting Air Force One.[6]

Right: Melania Trump exhibits elegance and style for her official White House Residency Photograph.[7]

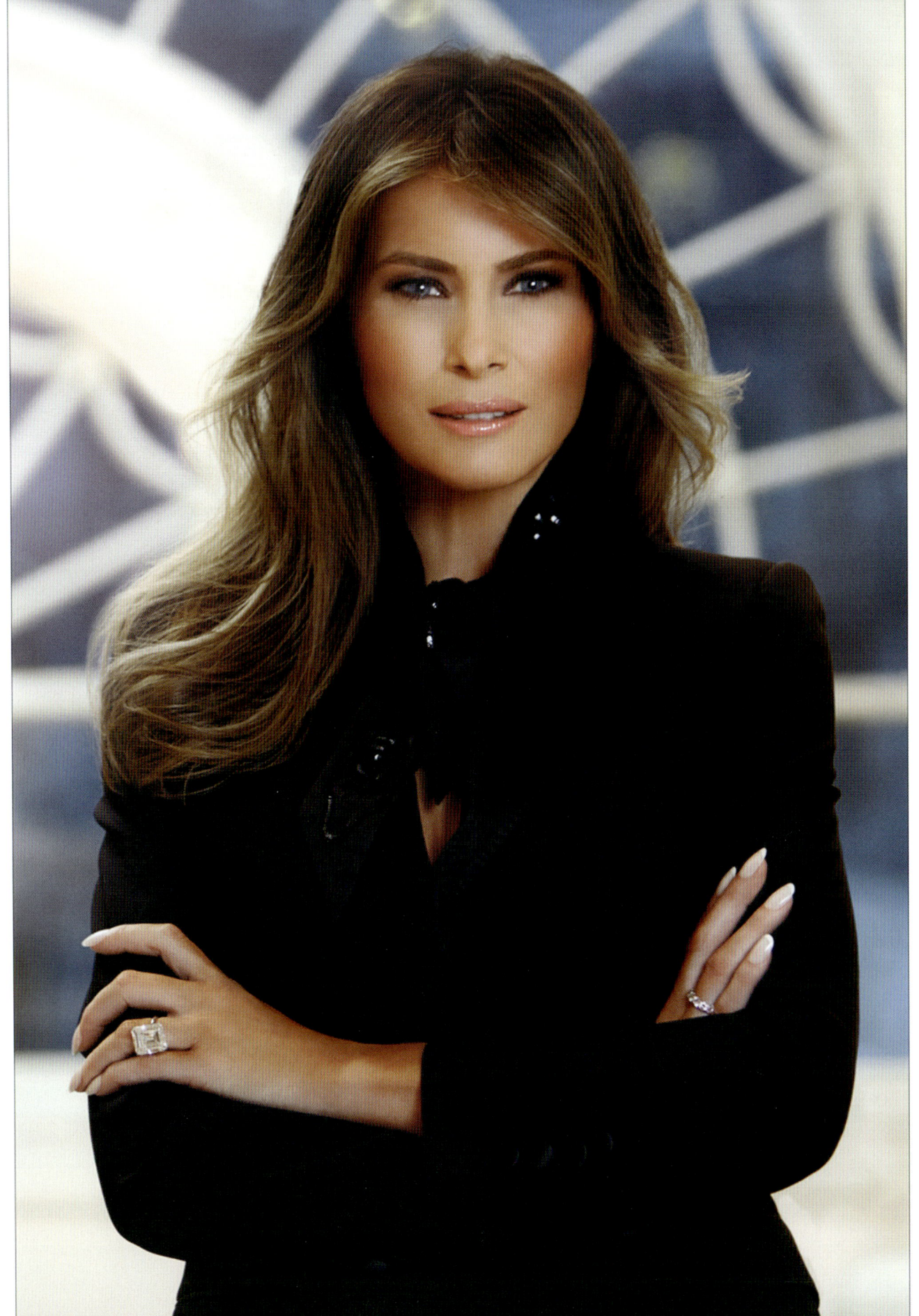

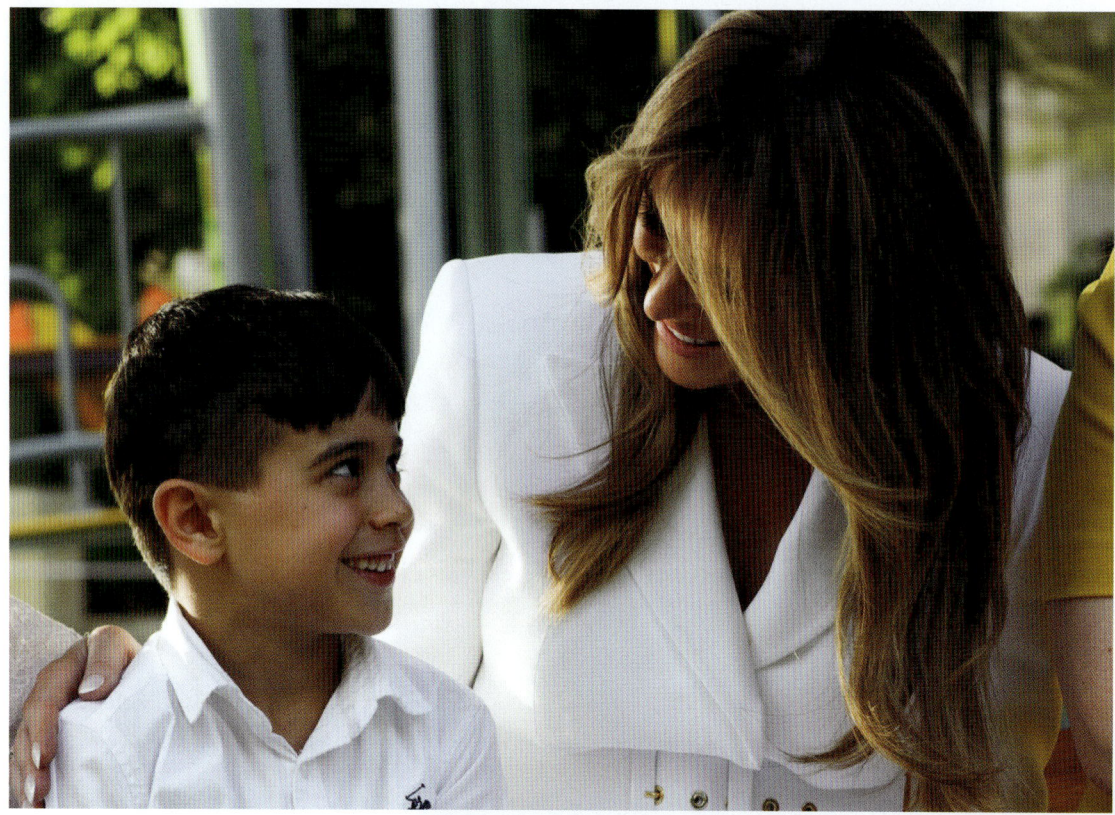

The First Lady makes new
friends while visiting the
Hadassah Medical Organization
facility in Jerusalem.
Mrs. Trump often visits medical
facilities for children.[6]

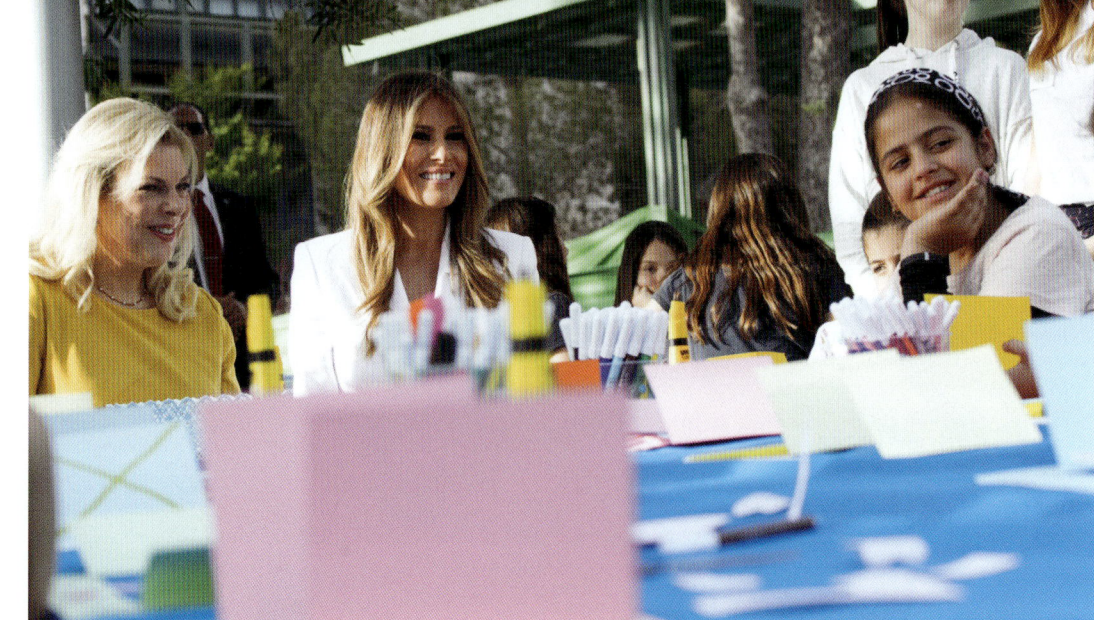

Mrs. Trump enjoys playtime
while at the Hadassah Medical
Organization facility.[6]

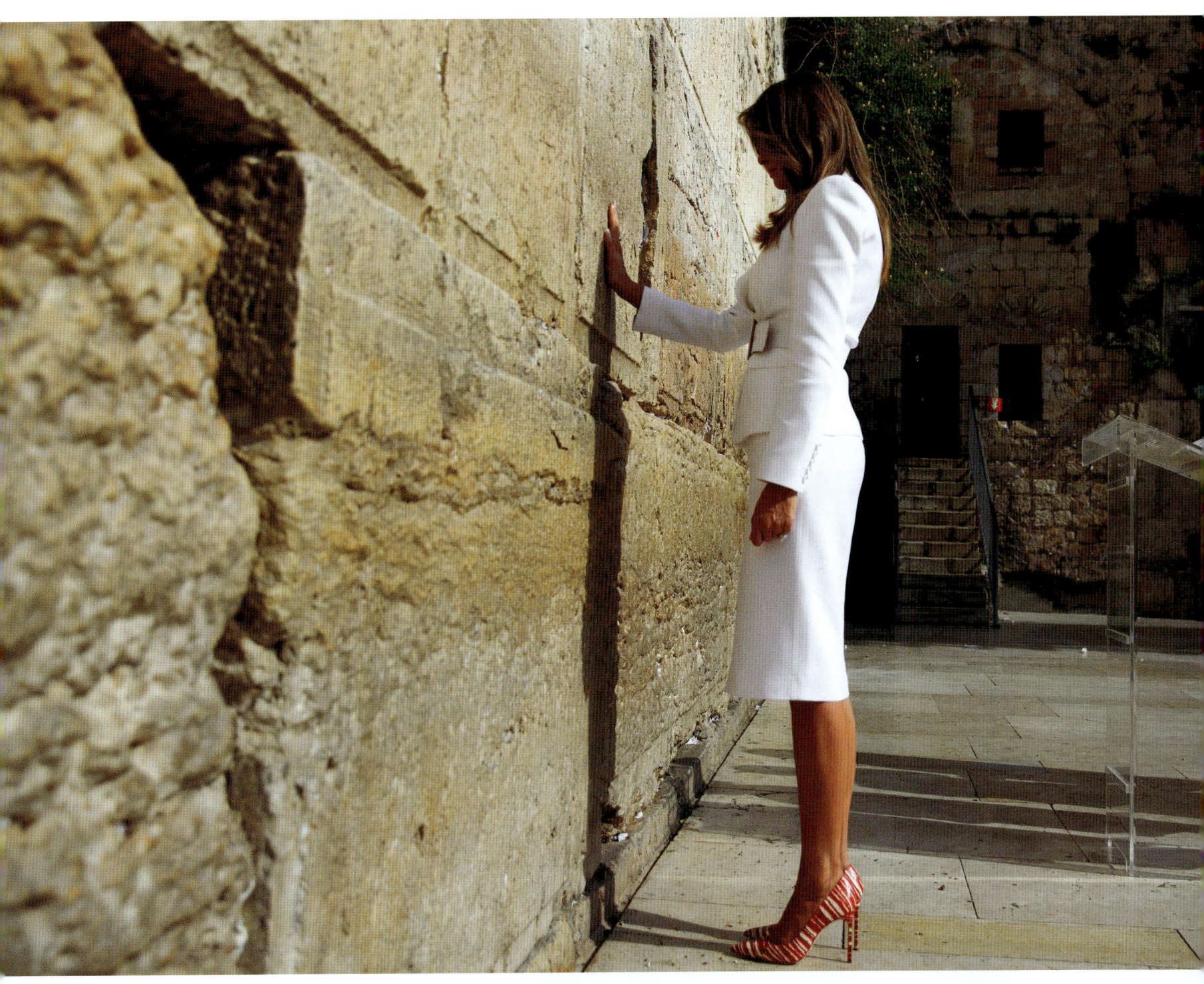

While visiting Jerusalem, the First Lady reverently prays at the Western Wall, the holiest site in Judaism. Rabbi Shmuel Rabinowitz, the rabbi of the Western Wall said that the Trump's visit "showed respect for the Jewish people and for tradition."[8]

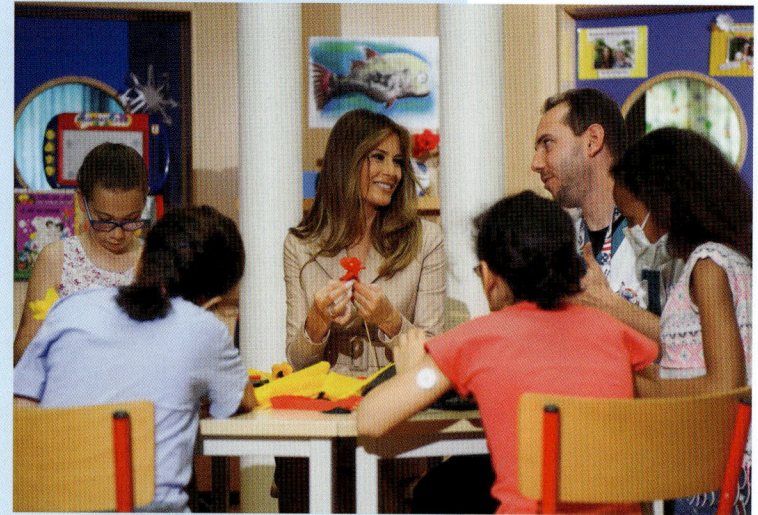

Here the First Lady visits the Queen Fabiola Children's University Hospital in Brussels, Belgium. The only university hospital in Belgium reserved for children's medicine.[6]

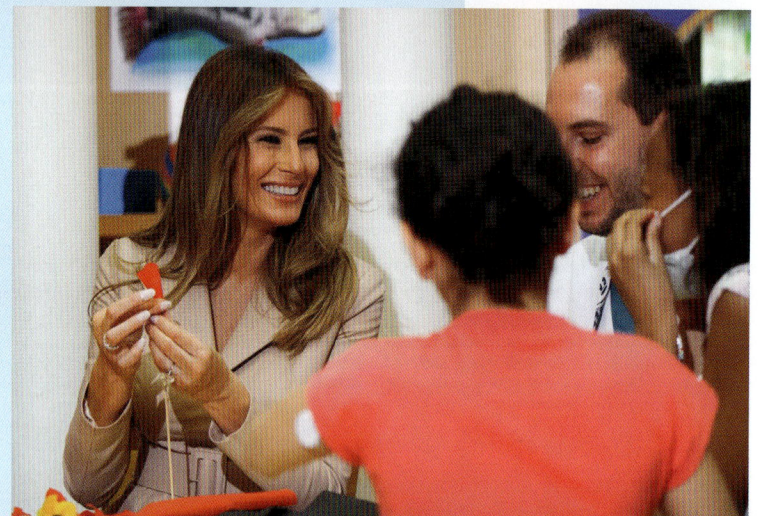

Making tulips at the children's hospital.[6]

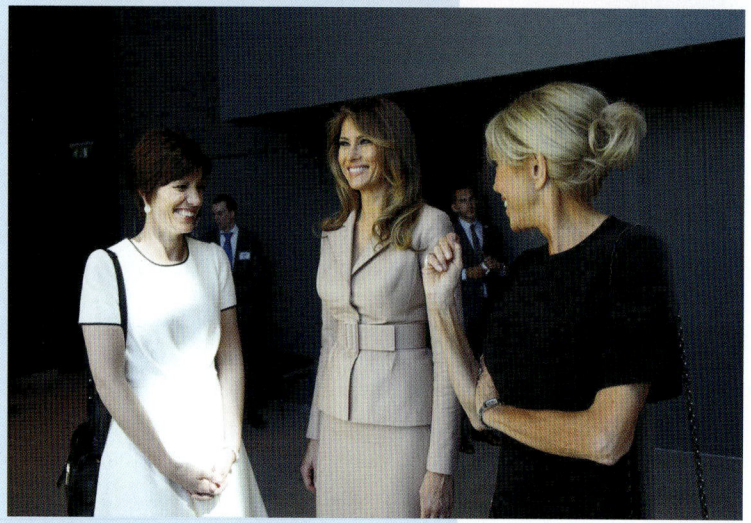

Mrs. Trump, the First Lady of France, Brigitte Trogneux, and Belgium's Amélie Derbaudrenghien, enjoy a visit to the Magritte Museum in Brussels, The Royal Museum of Fine Arts of Belgium.[6]

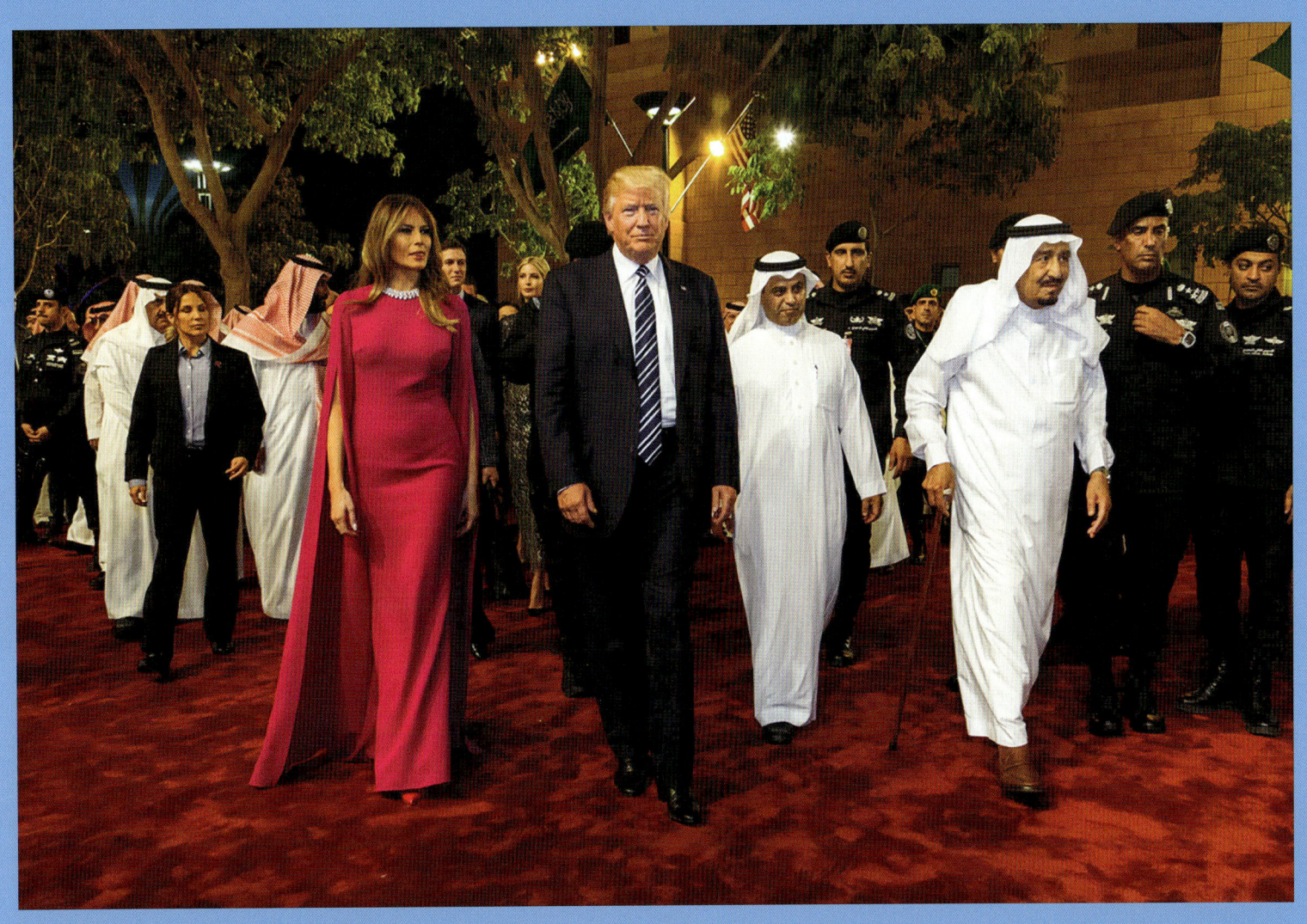

King Salman bin Abdulaziz Al Saud escorts the President and his wife to a banquet
in the Murabba Palace, in Saudi Arabia.[5]

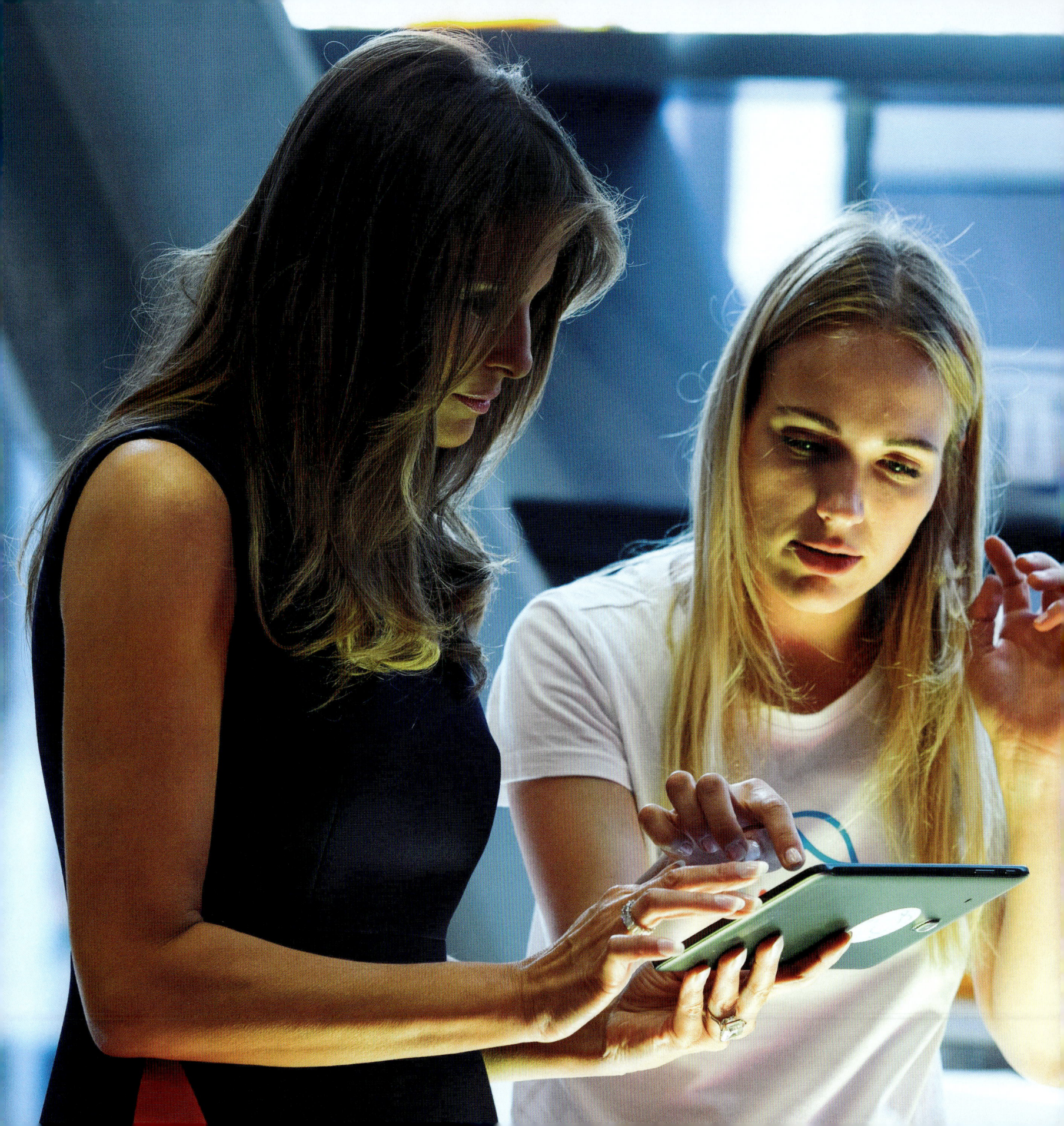

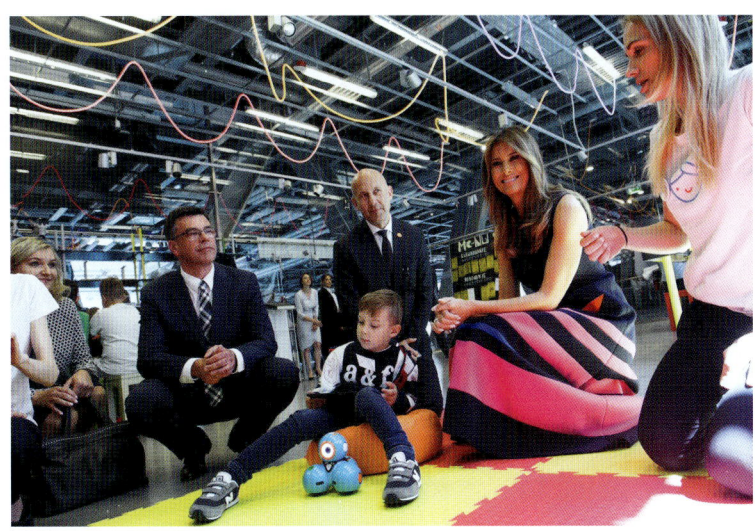

Robots in action and big smiles![6]

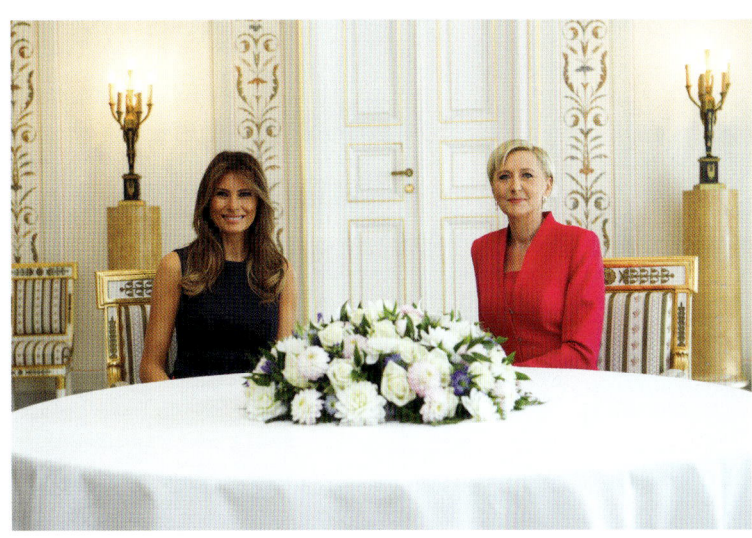

First Lady Melania Trump and First Lady of Poland Agata Kornhauser-Duda, July 6, 2017.[6]

Left: Learning about electro-fashion accessories at the Copernicus Science Centre in Warsaw, Poland. Mrs. Trump was hosted by the First Lady of Poland.[10]

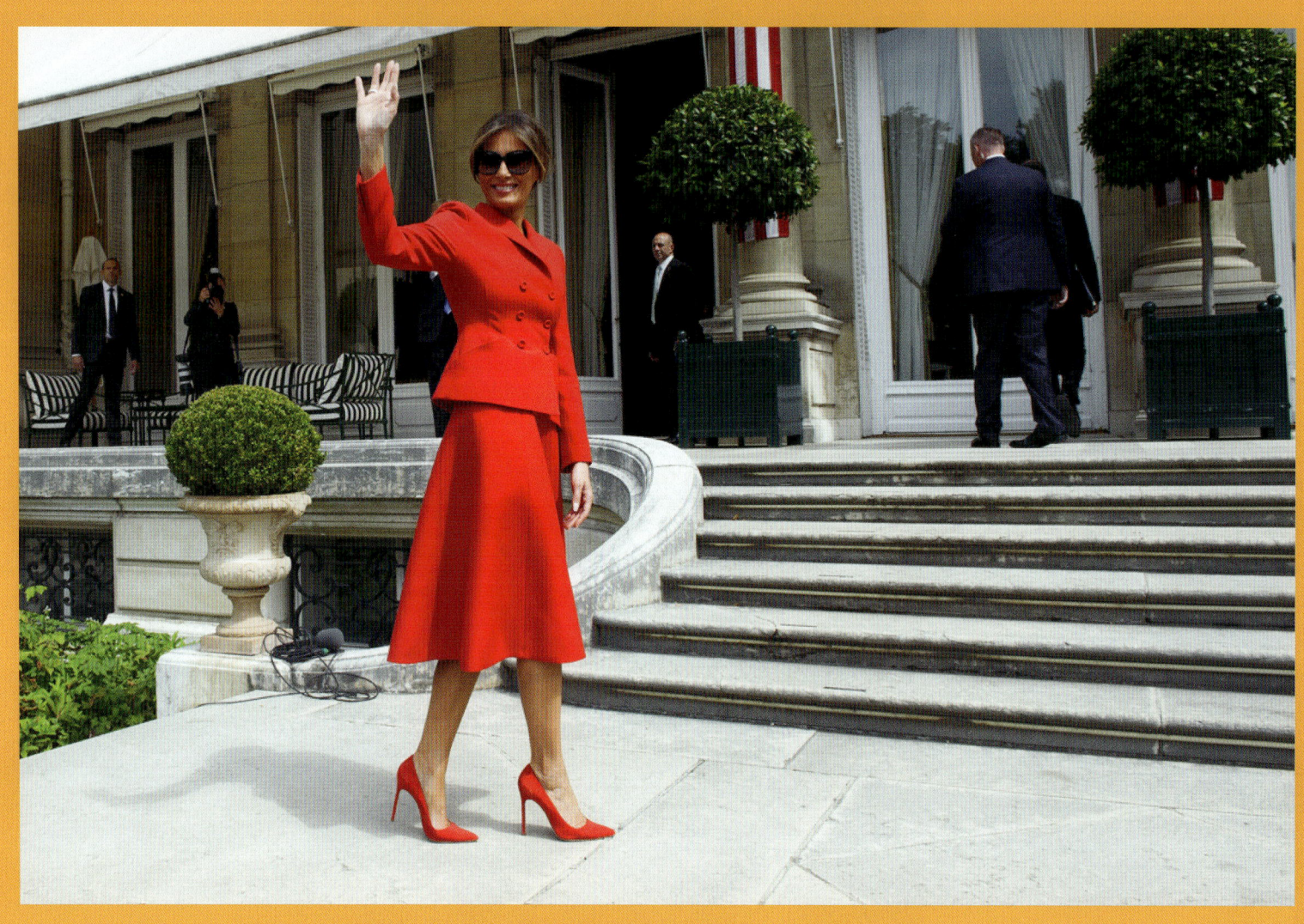

Melania Trump bringing elegance back to France as well![6]

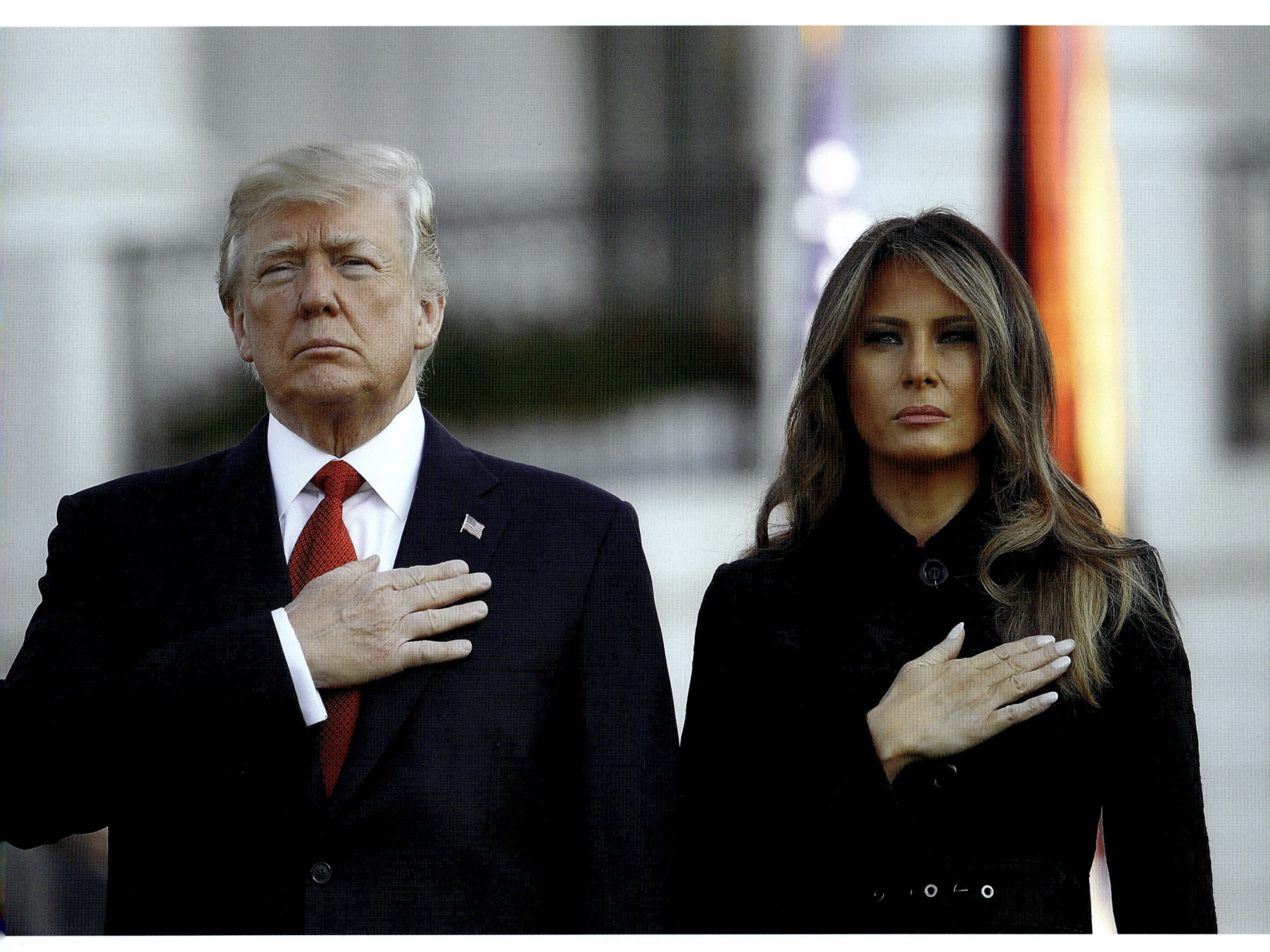

Taps plays in the background as the President and First Lady lead a moment of silence on the anniversary of the 9/11 assaults on the United States.[11]

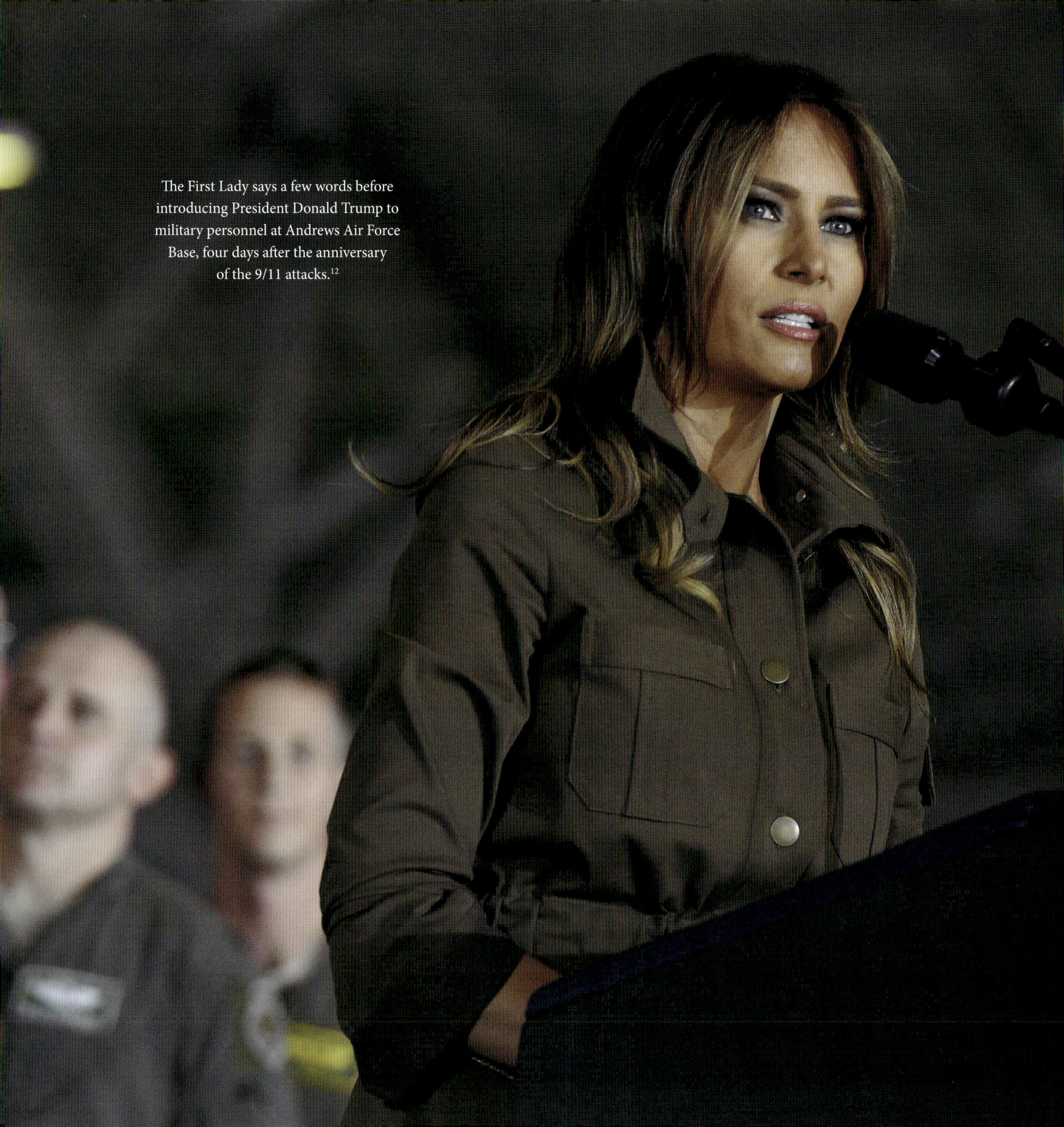

The First Lady says a few words before introducing President Donald Trump to military personnel at Andrews Air Force Base, four days after the anniversary of the 9/11 attacks.[12]

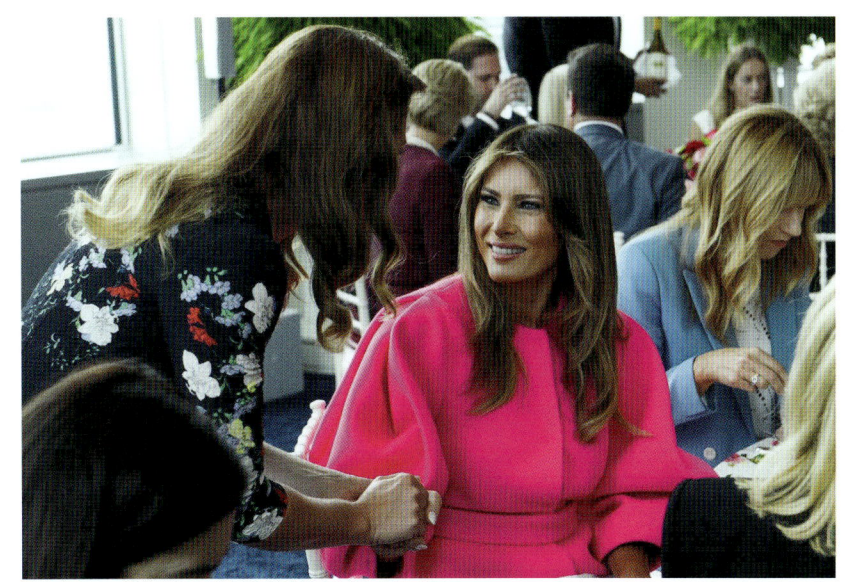

At the United Nations.[6]

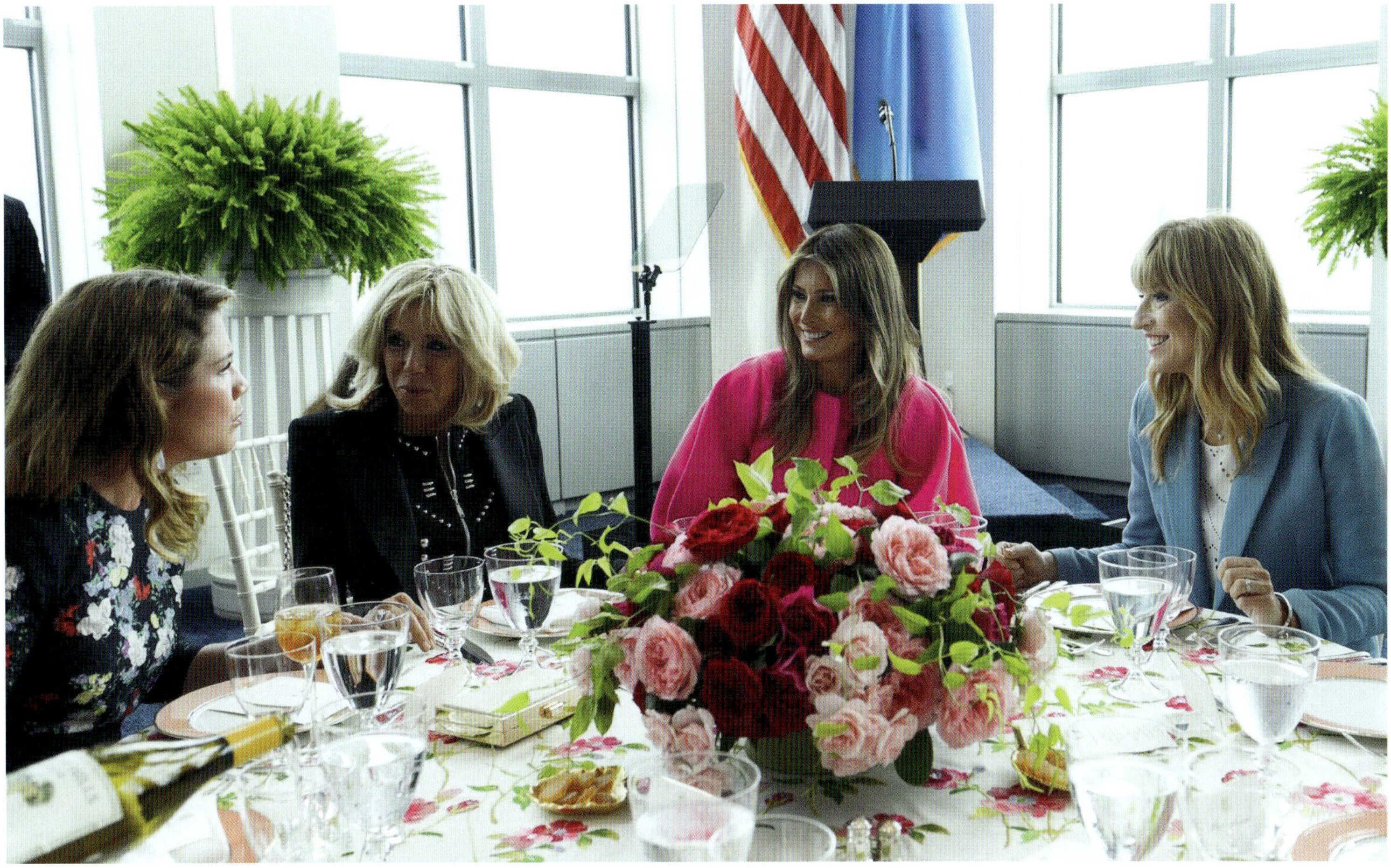

United Nations Luncheon.[6]

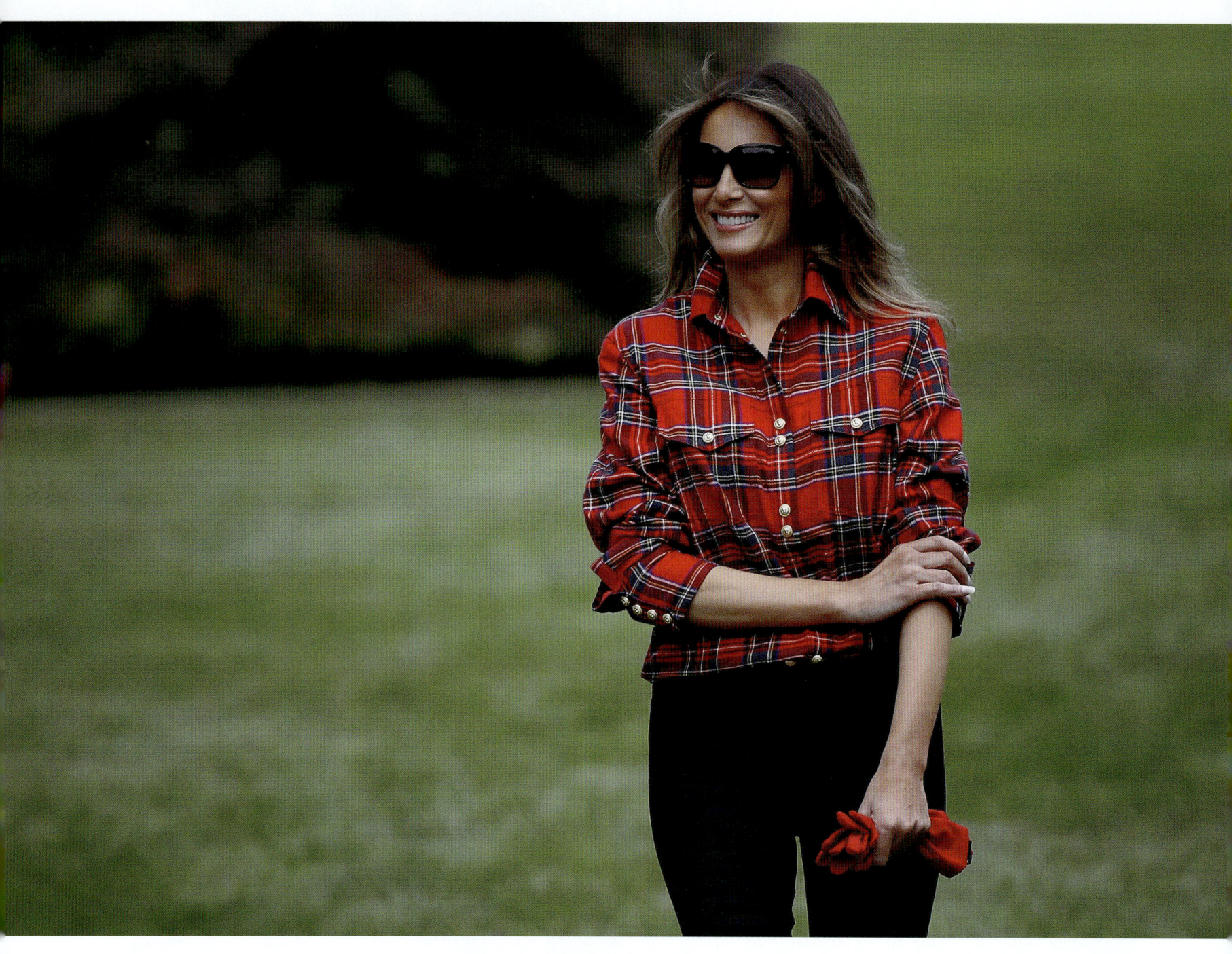

Following up on a tradition started by Michelle Obama, Melania Trump meets with the Boys & Girls Club of Washington to plant and harvest vegetables for the White House Kitchen Garden.[11]

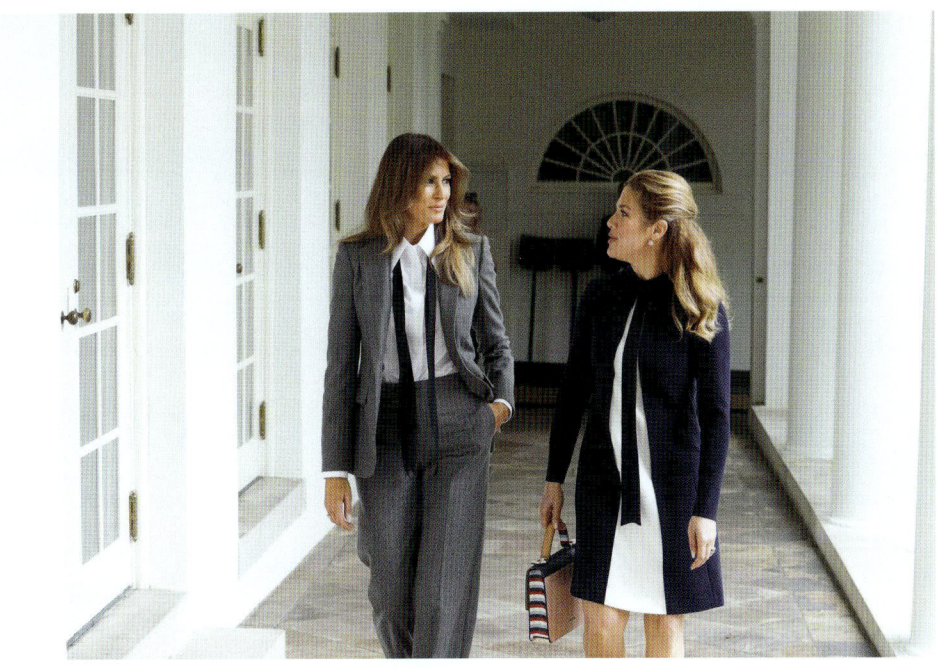

First Lady Melania Trump and Mrs. Sophie Grégoire Trudeau of Canada.[6]

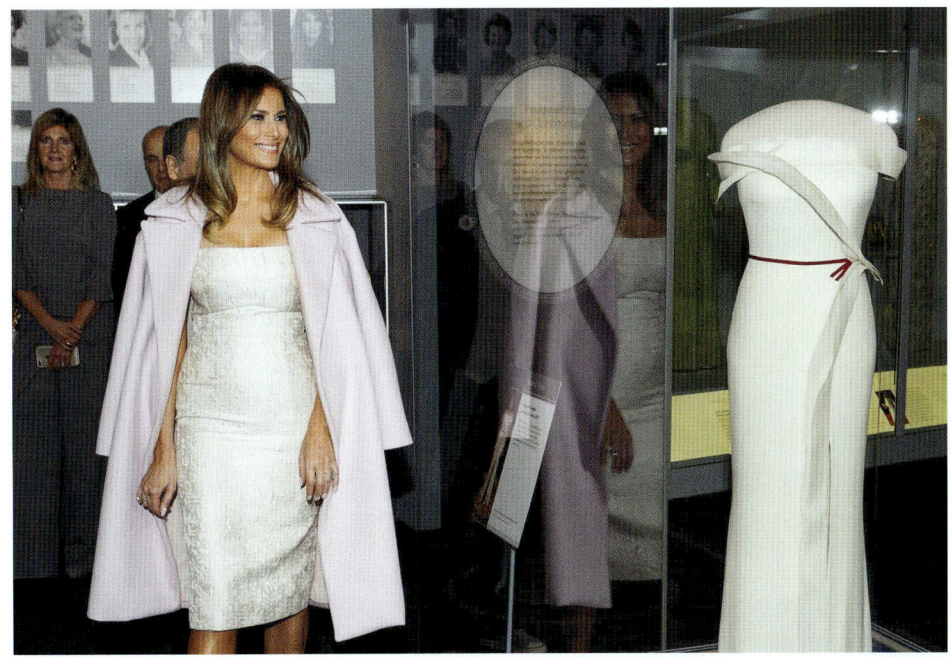

The First Lady presents her elegant inaugural gown to the
Smithsonian National Museum of American History.[6]

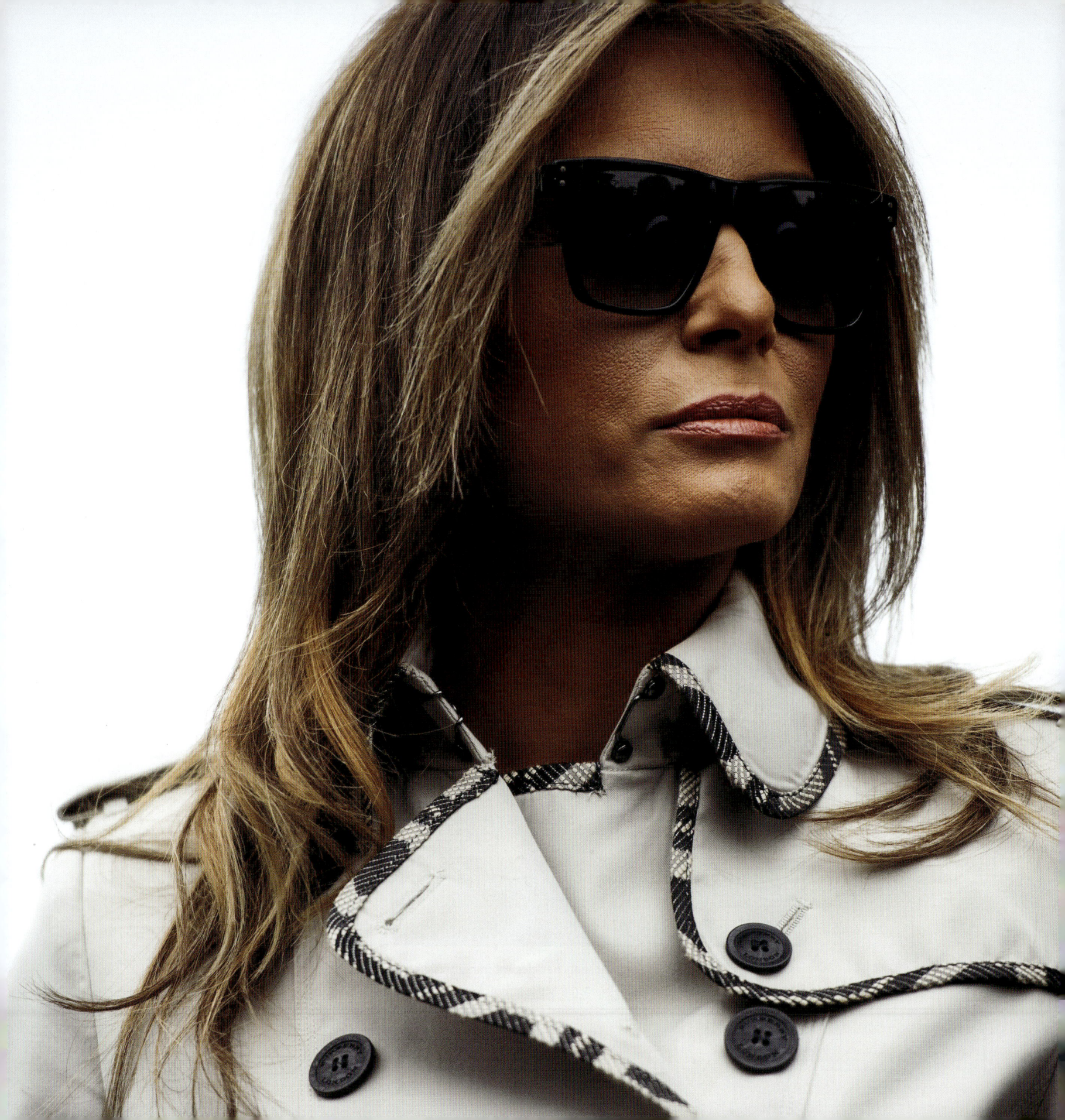

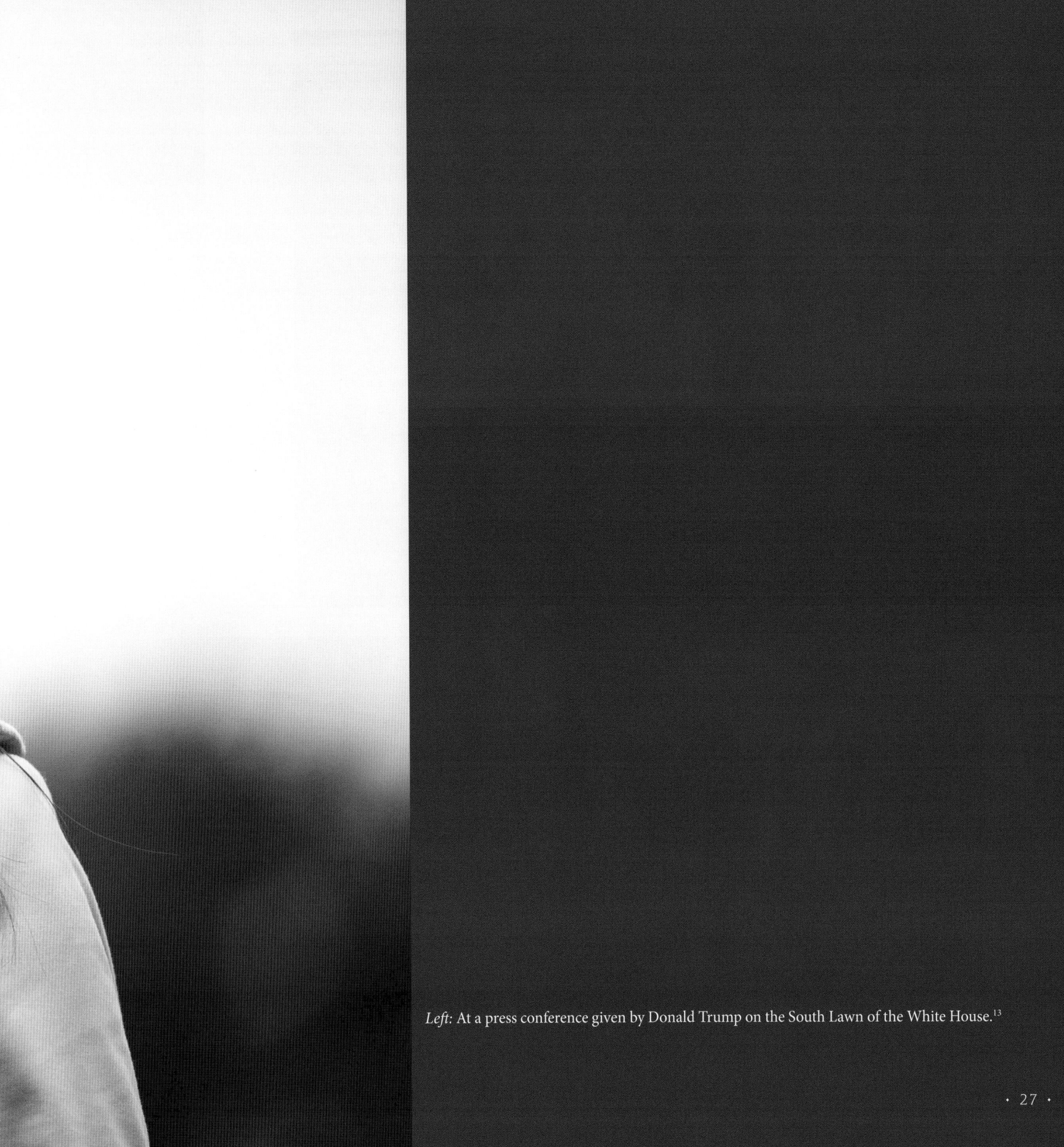

Left: At a press conference given by Donald Trump on the South Lawn of the White House.[13]

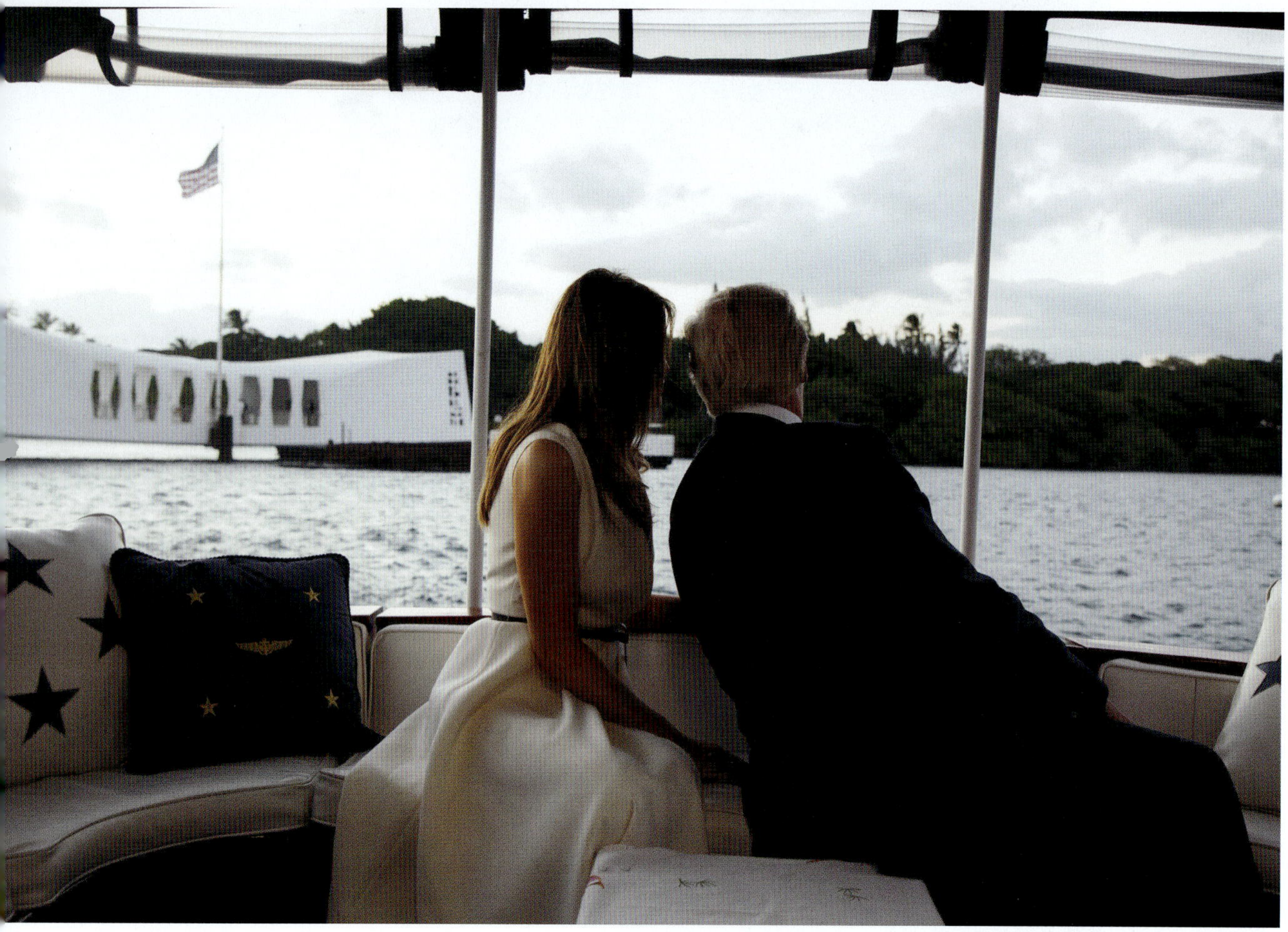

The first couple tour the USS *Arizona*
Memorial in Pearl Harbor, Hawaii.[5]

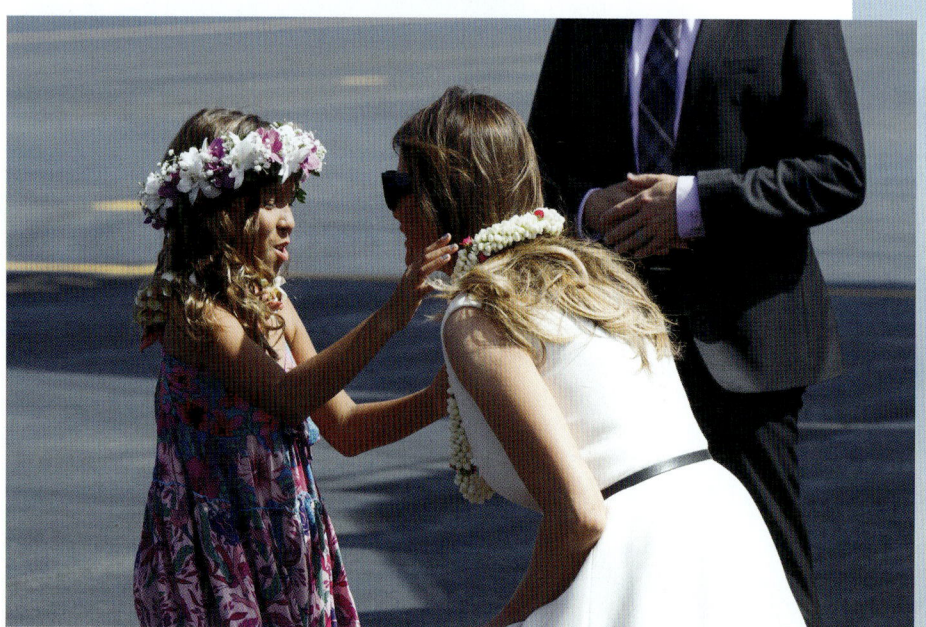

Aloha, Melania! As the Trumps
arrive in Hawaii.[6]

Right: Paying homage at the USS *Arizona*,
Pearl Harbor, Honolulu, Hawaii.[14]

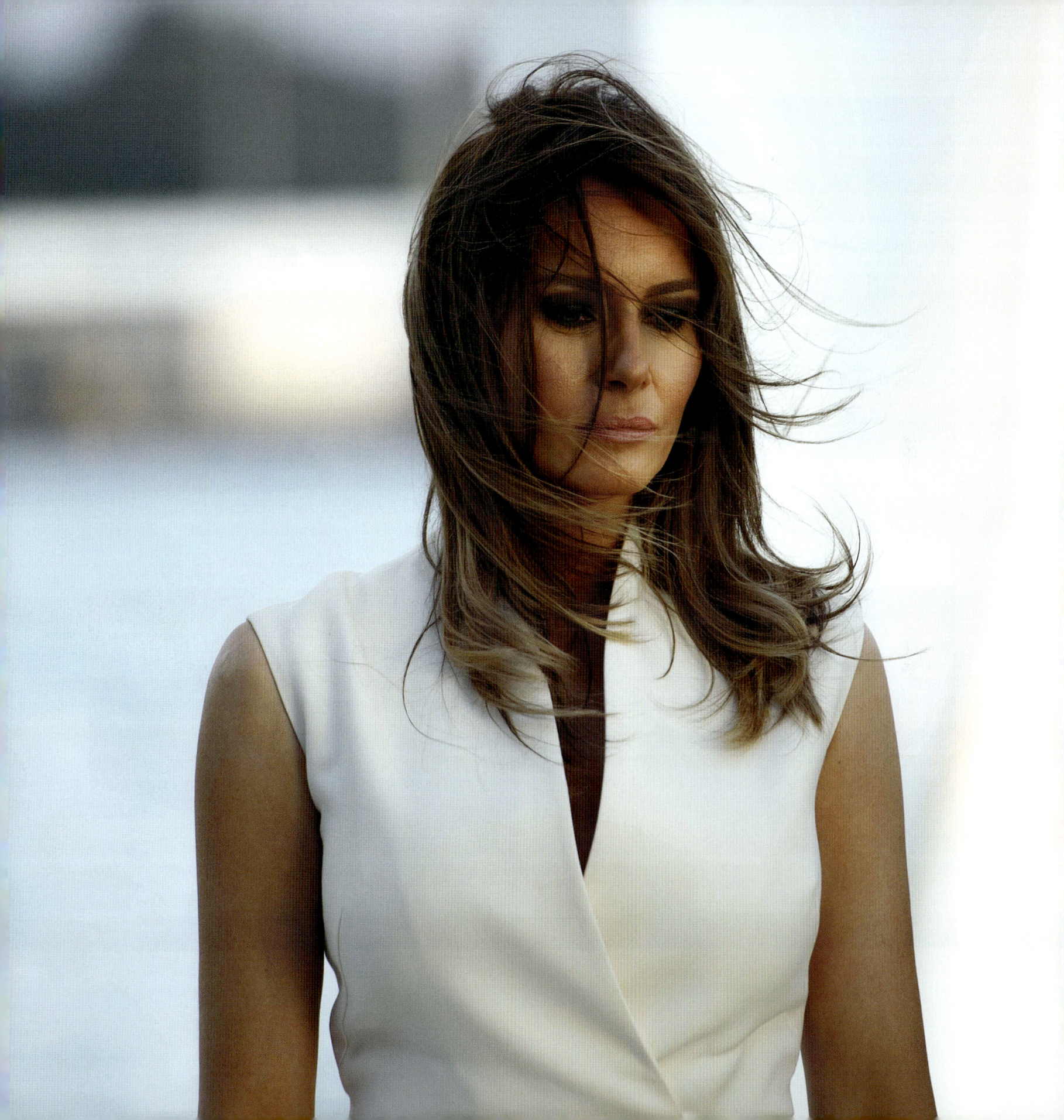

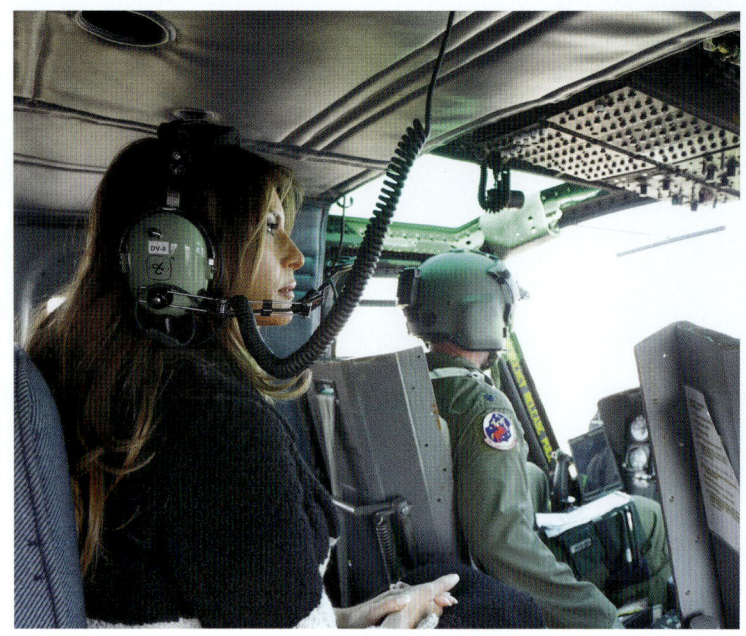

Harbor Chopper Rides![6]

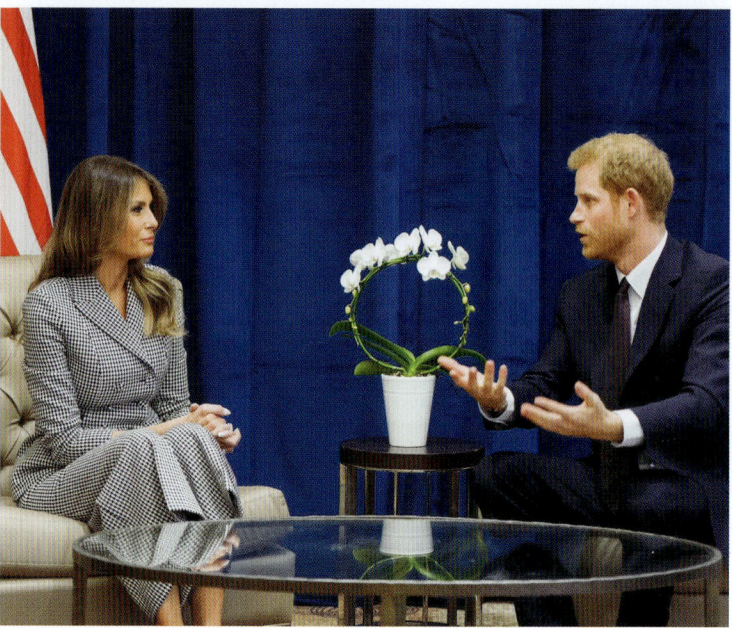

First Lady Melania Trump and Prince Harry at the Invictus Games, which were started by Prince Harry for wounded and ill soldiers from all over the world.[6]

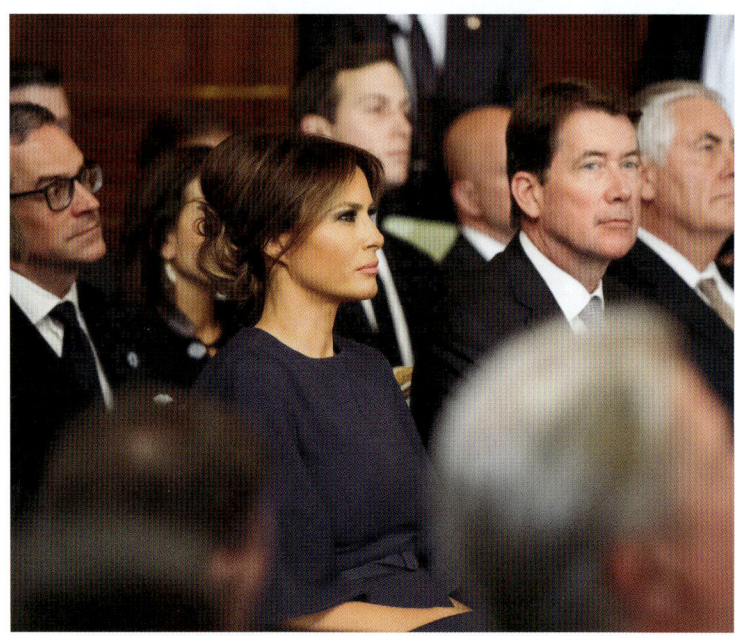

Sitting with dignitaries in Japan.[6]

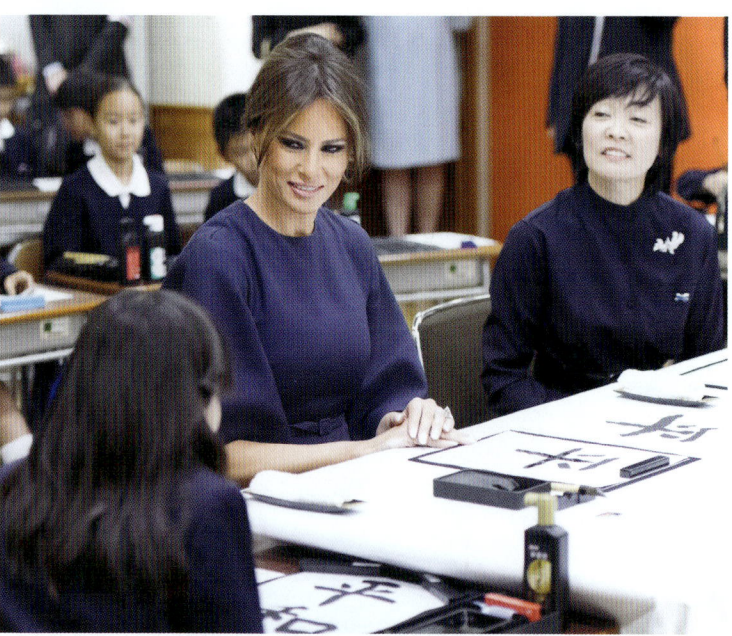

Melania goes back to school in Japan![6]

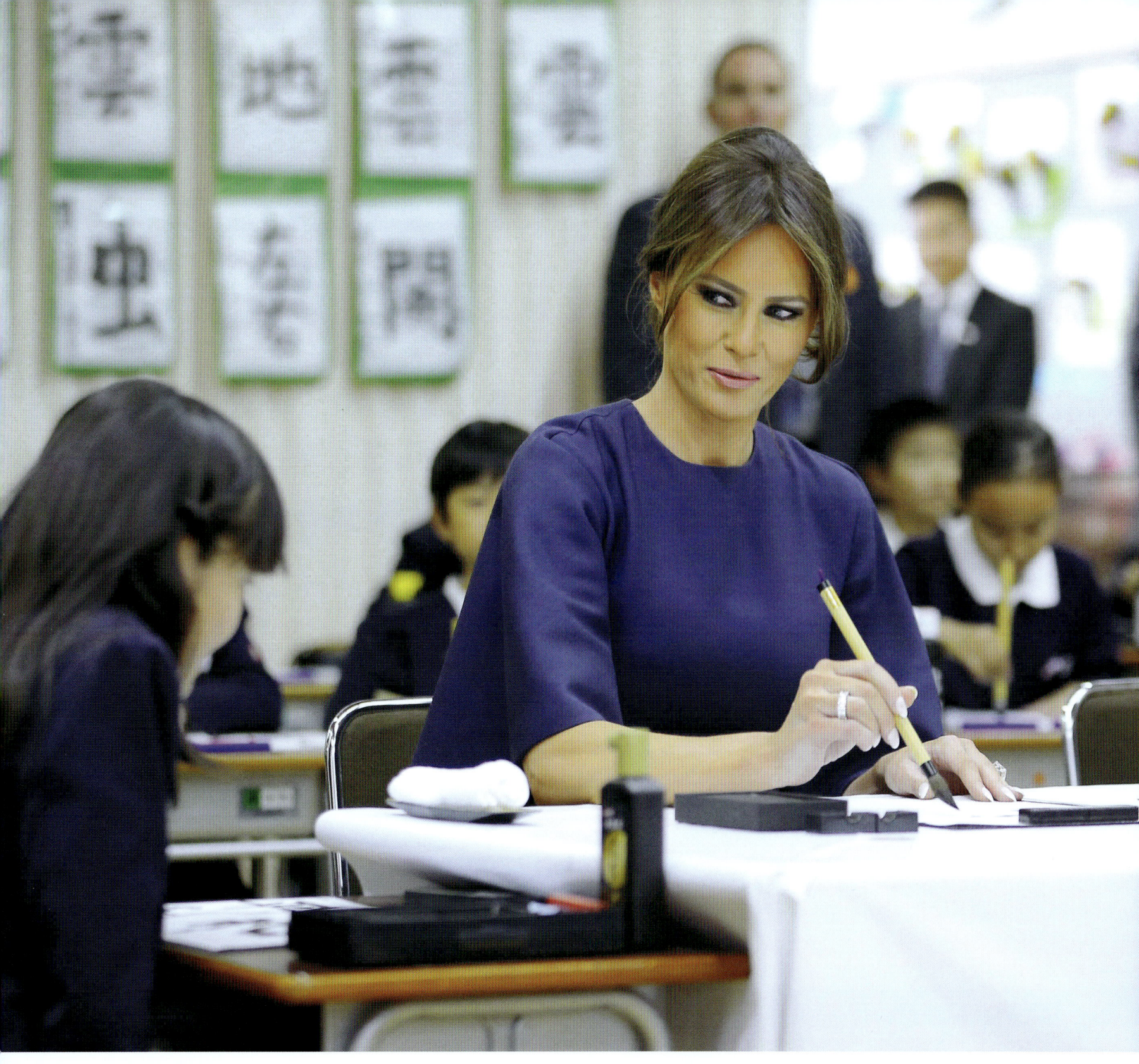

The First Lady learns calligraphy from students in Japan.[15]

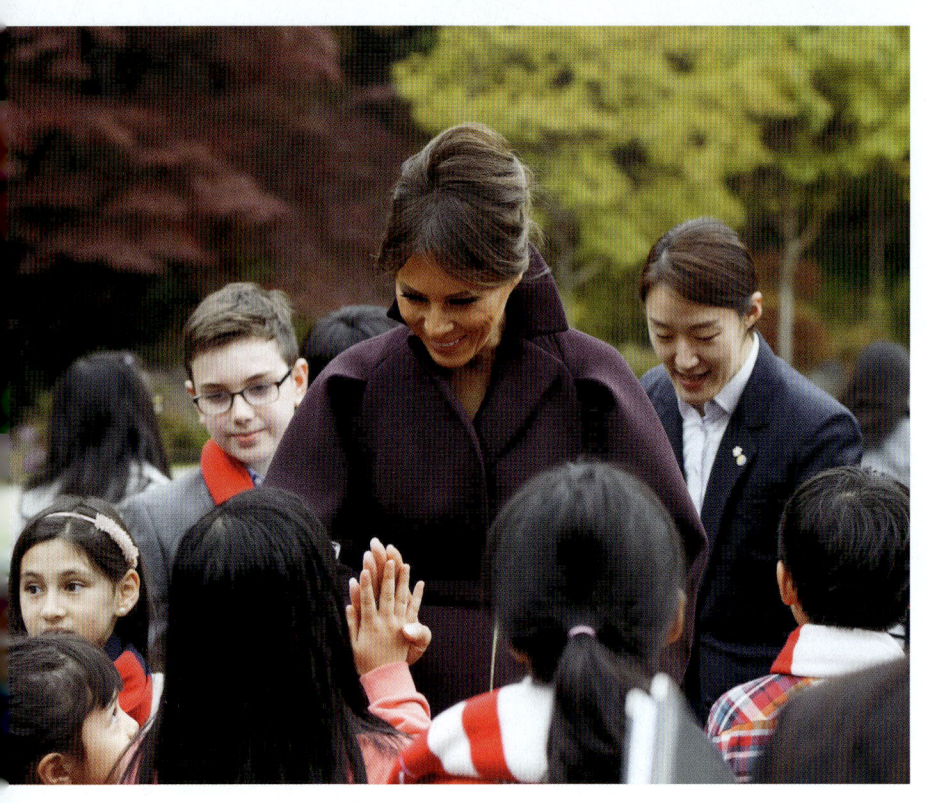

High fives and smiles with children in Asia.[6]

Melania visits China.[6]

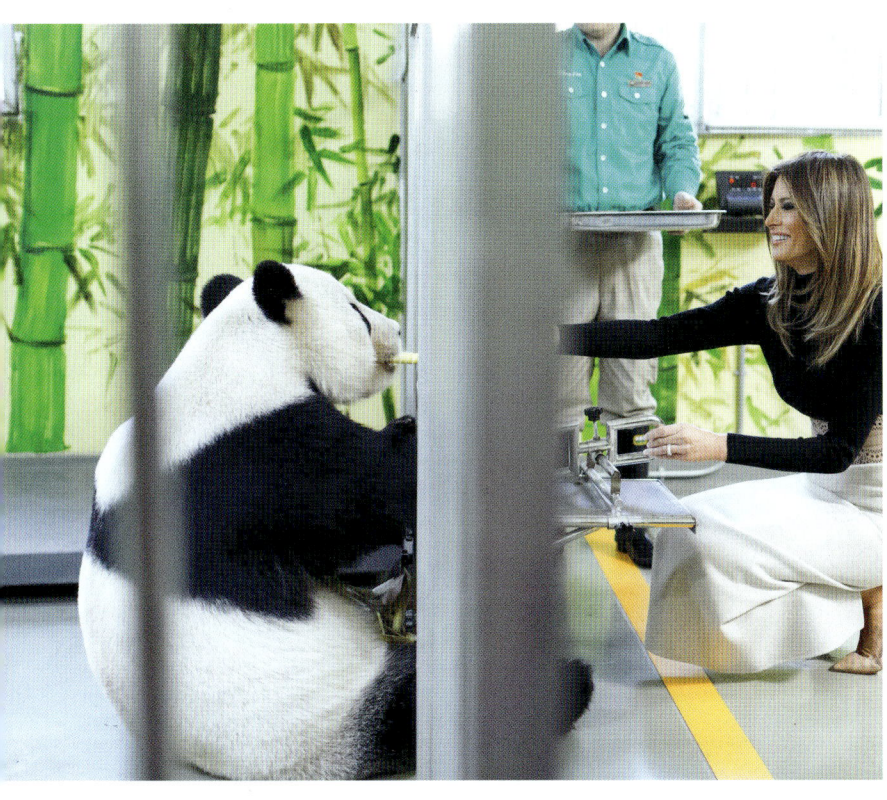

Party time with pandas.[6]

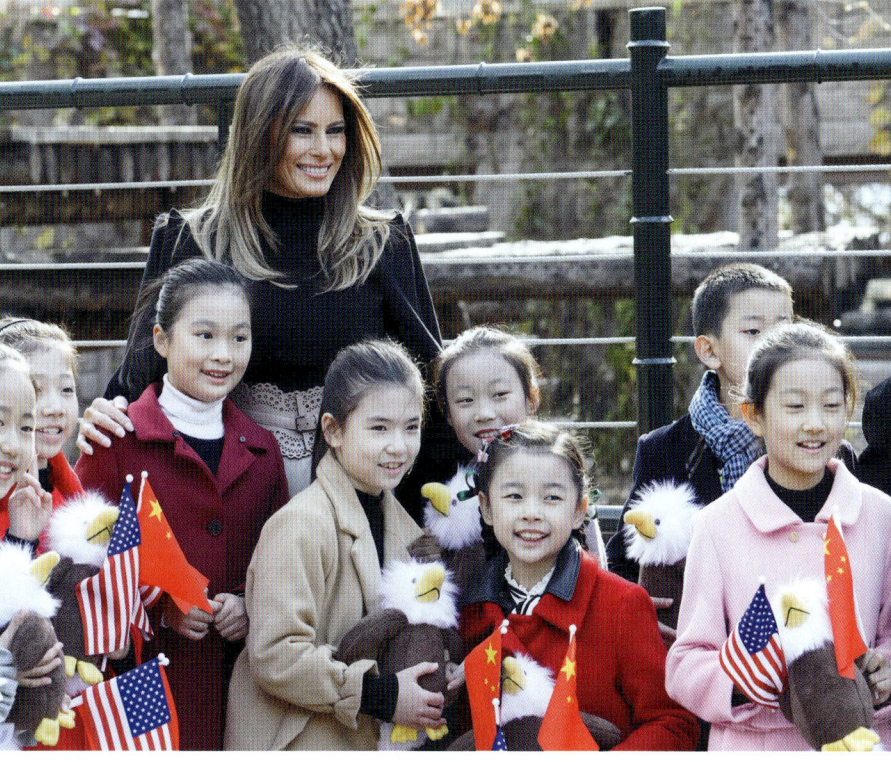

Eagles, smiles, and flags.[6]

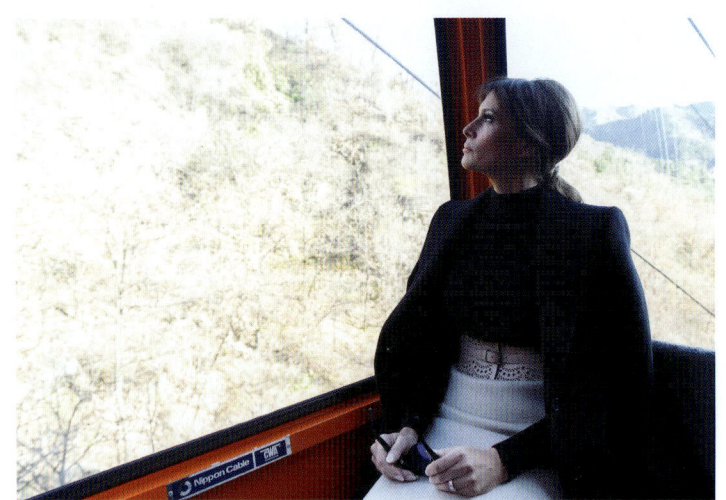
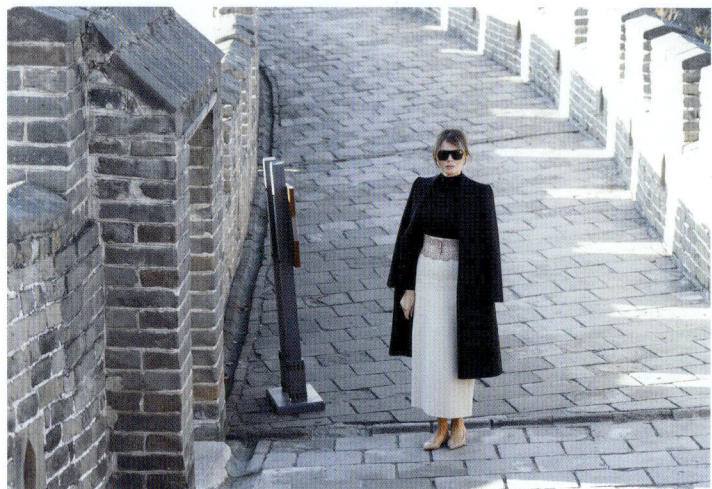

Contemplation.[6]

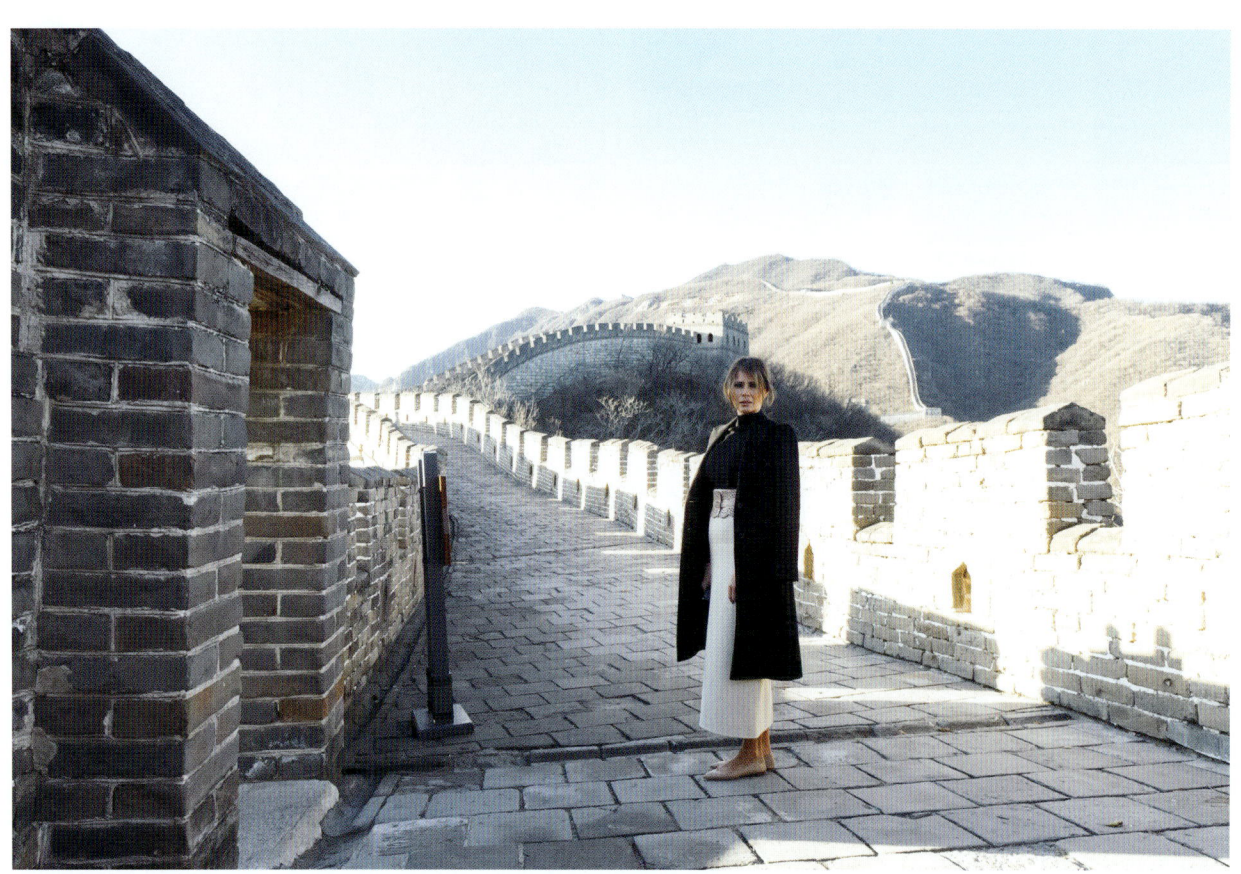

On the Great Wall.[6]

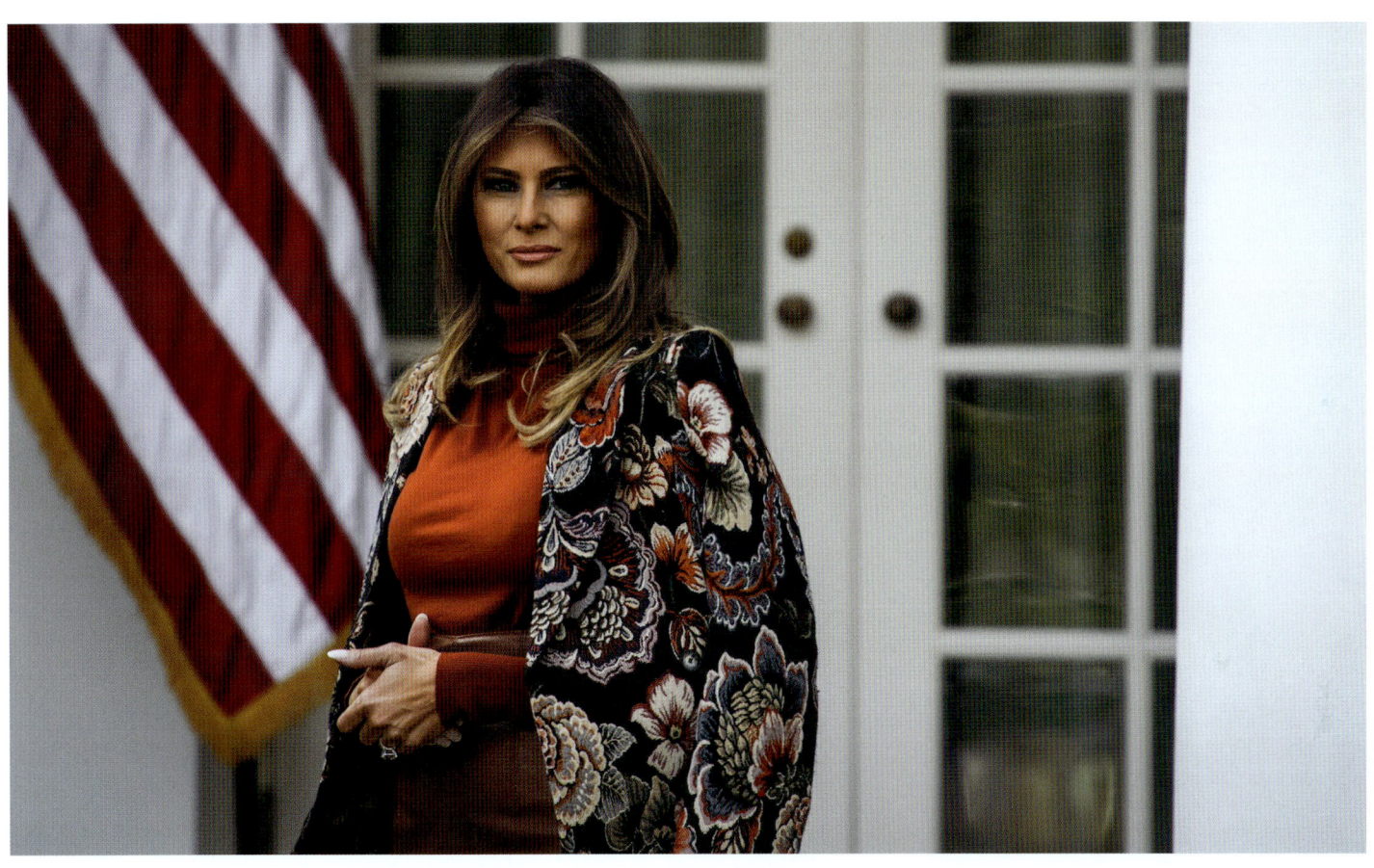

On Thanksgiving, a turkey is pardoned on Melania's watch during
the annual pardoning ceremony at the White House.[16]

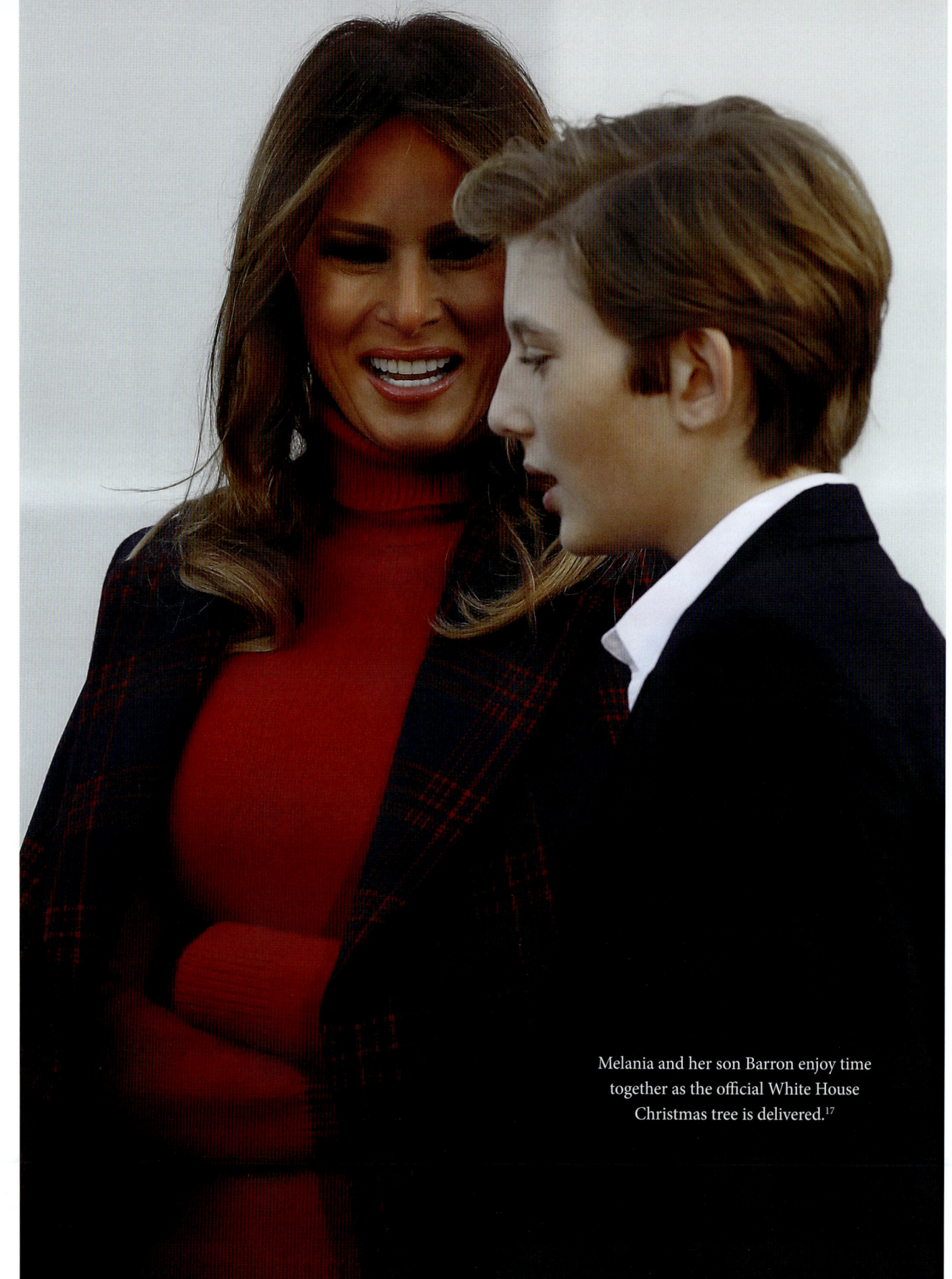

Melania and her son Barron enjoy time together as the official White House Christmas tree is delivered.[17]

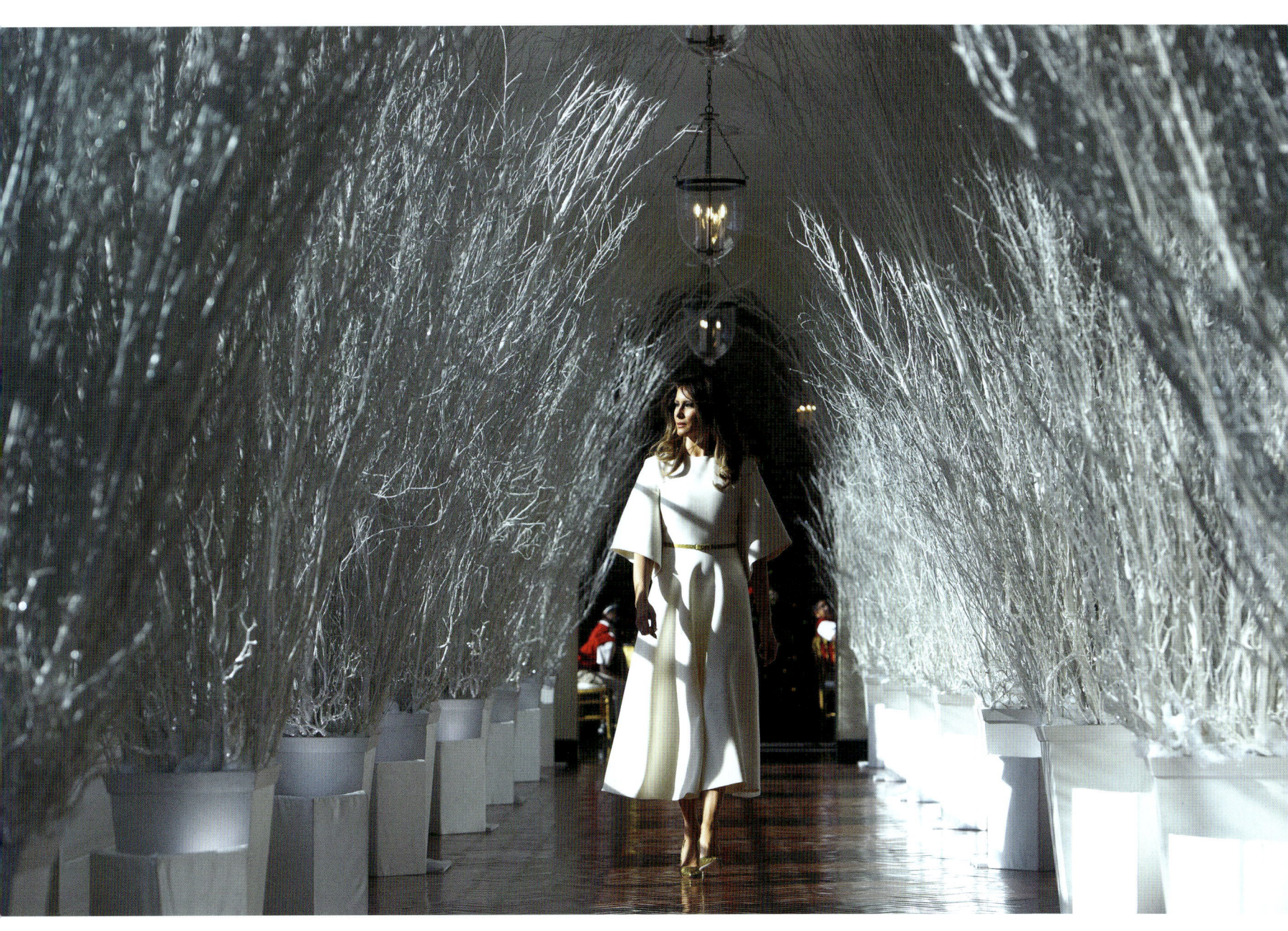

Mrs. Trump inspects the new Christmas decorations in the White House.[18]

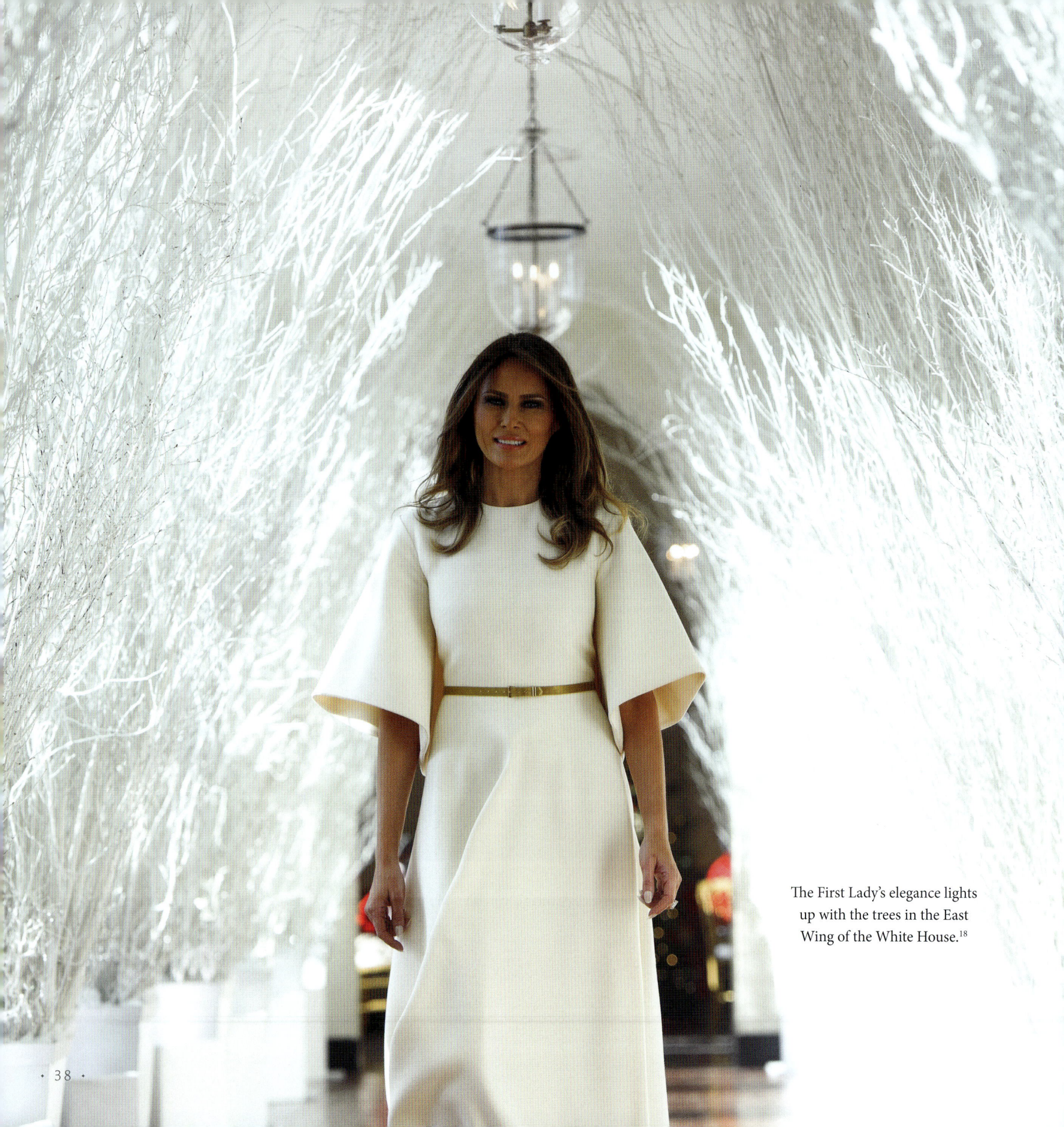

The First Lady's elegance lights up with the trees in the East Wing of the White House.[18]

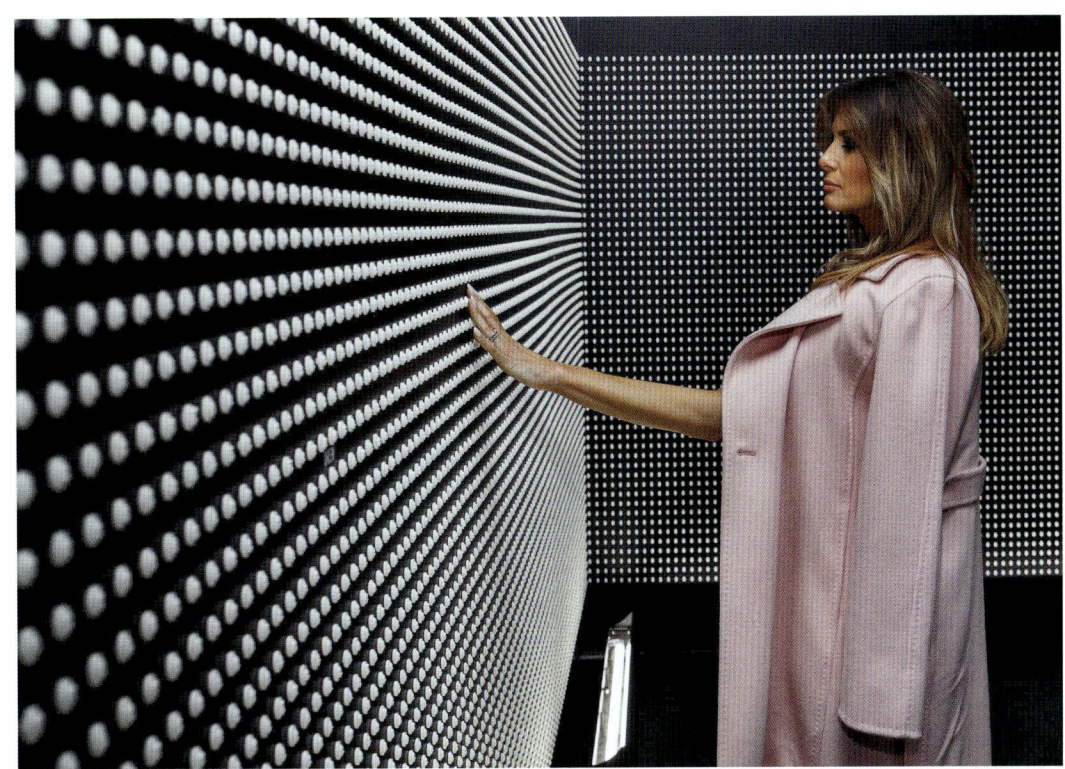

At the "Prescribed to Death" opioid memorial.[6]

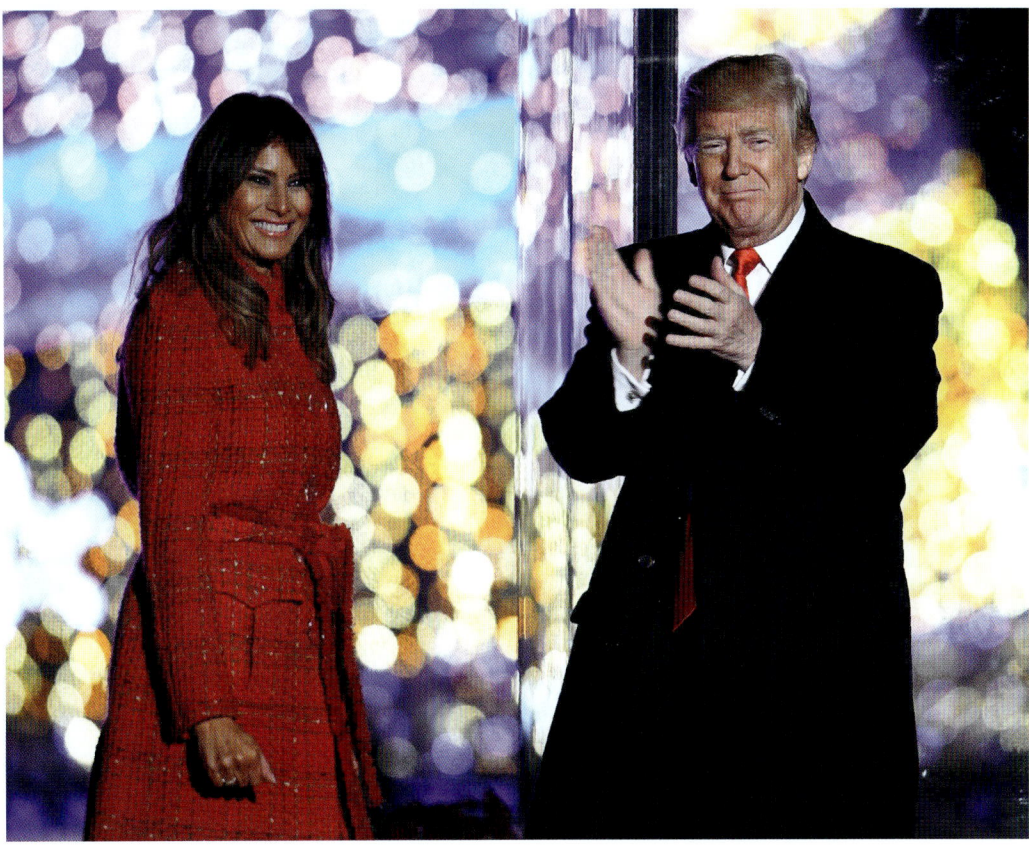

The President and First Lady preside over the annual Christmas tree lighting ceremony.[14]

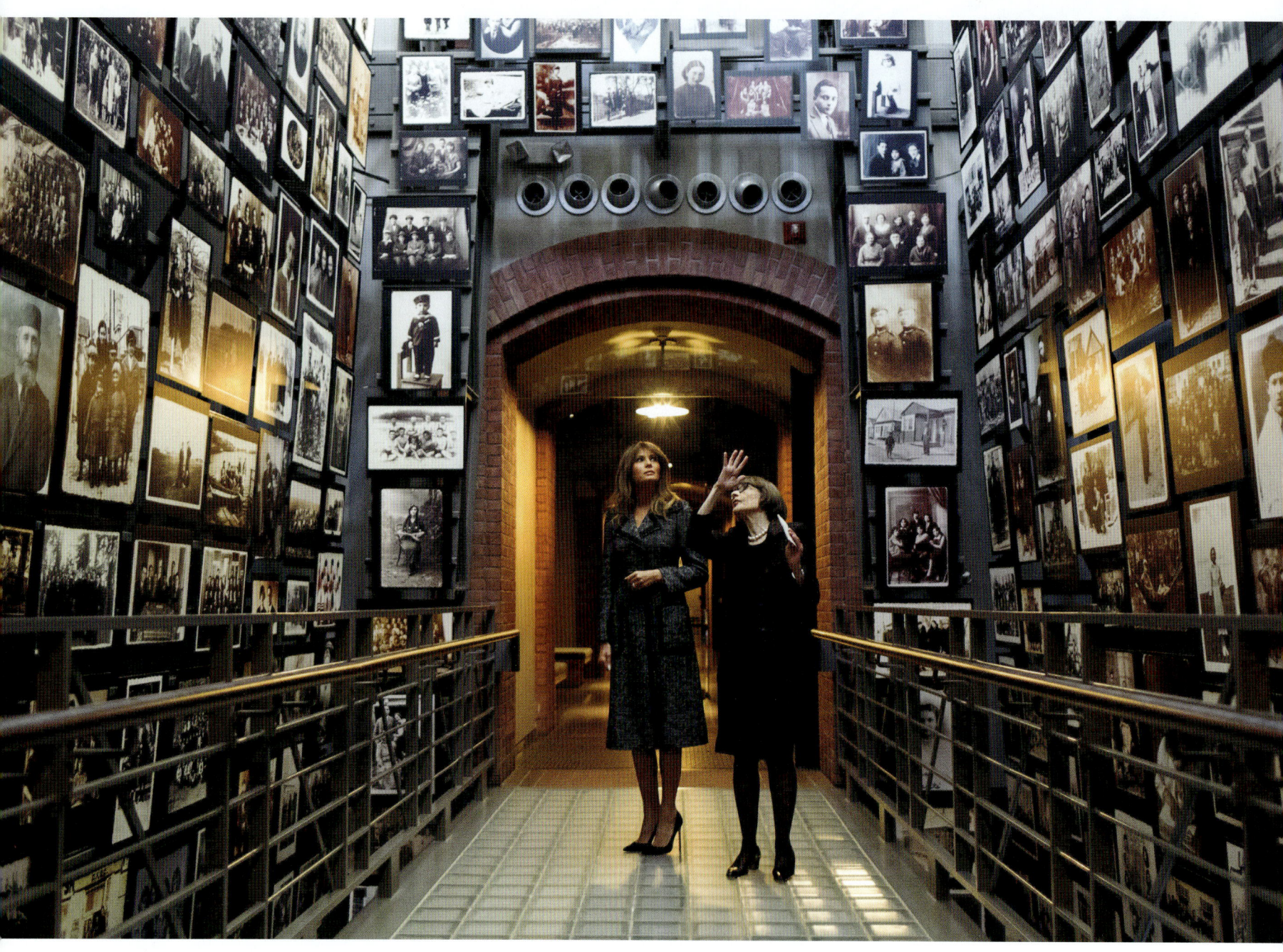

Visiting the Holocaust Memorial Museum.[6]

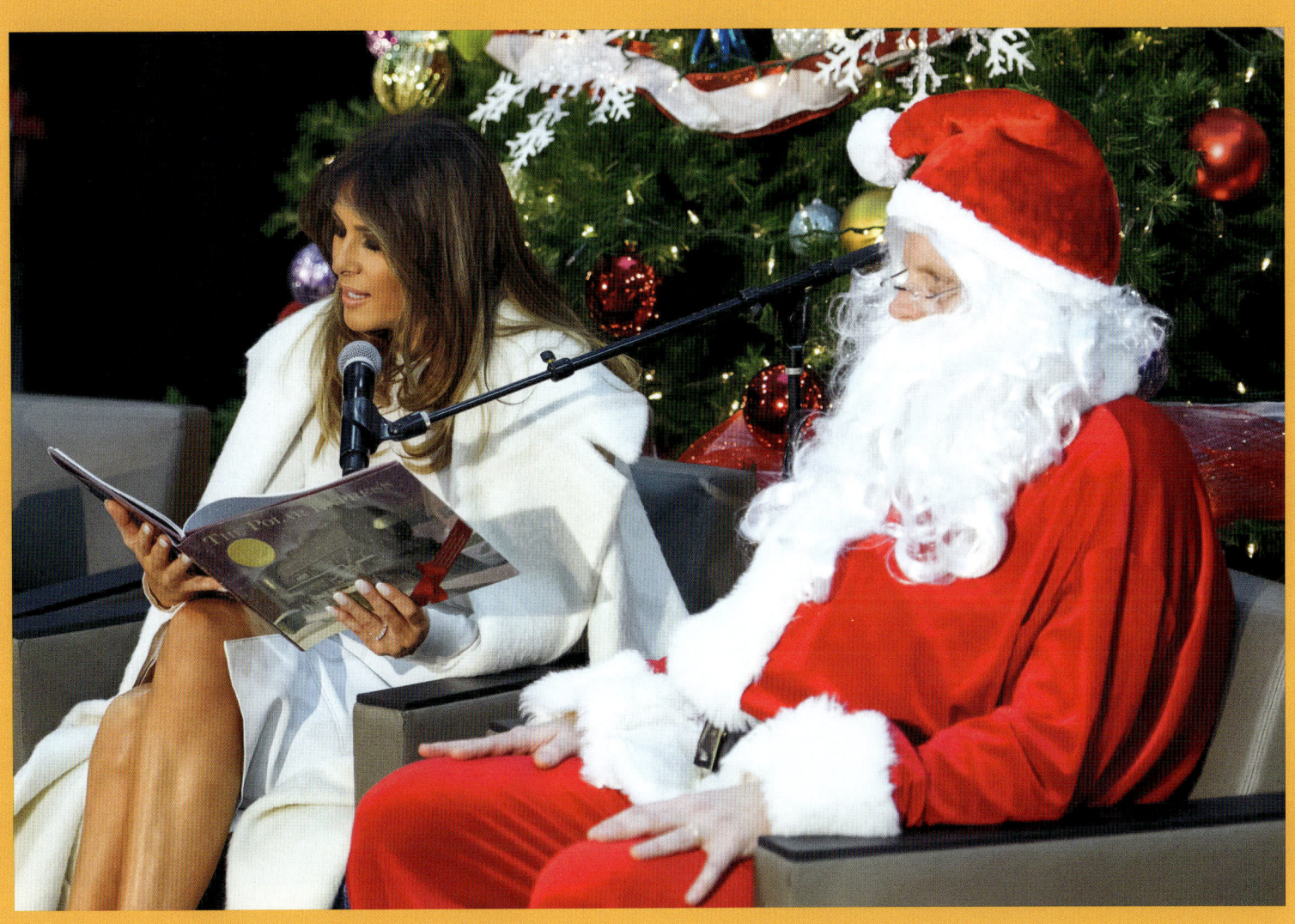

Reading *The Polar Express* with Santa Claus for Christmas at Children's National Hospital.[6]

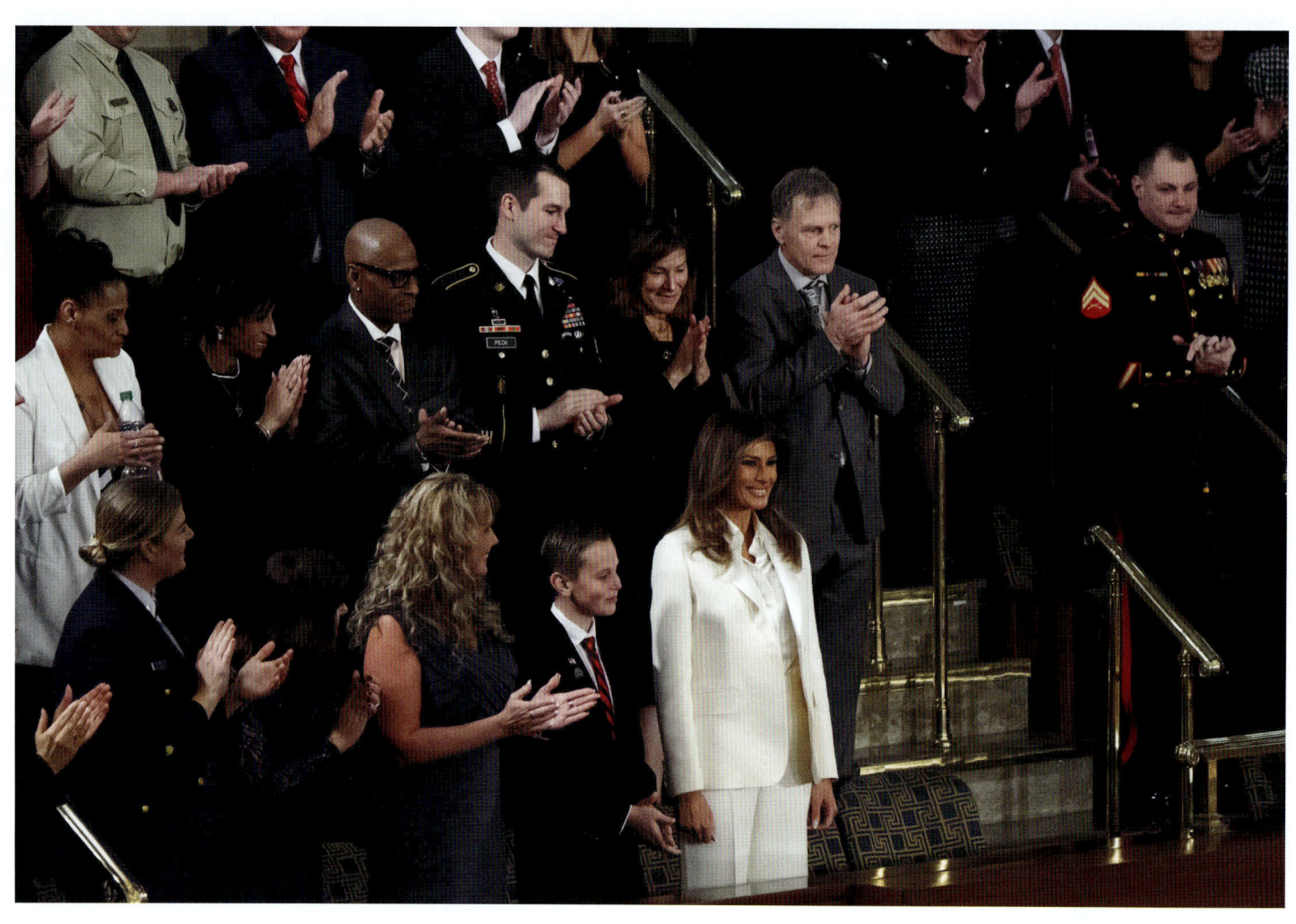

Elegance wears Dior and a tan at the 2018 State of the Union Address.[6]

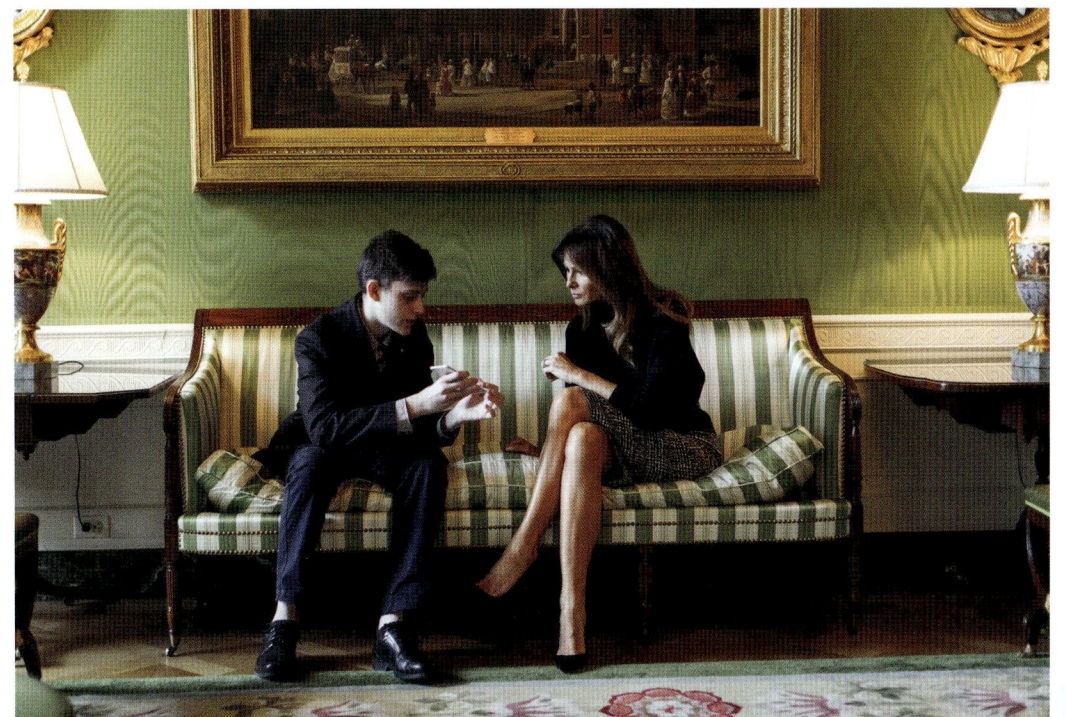

The First Lady and Marjory Stoneman Douglas High School shooting survivor, Kyle Kashuv.[6]

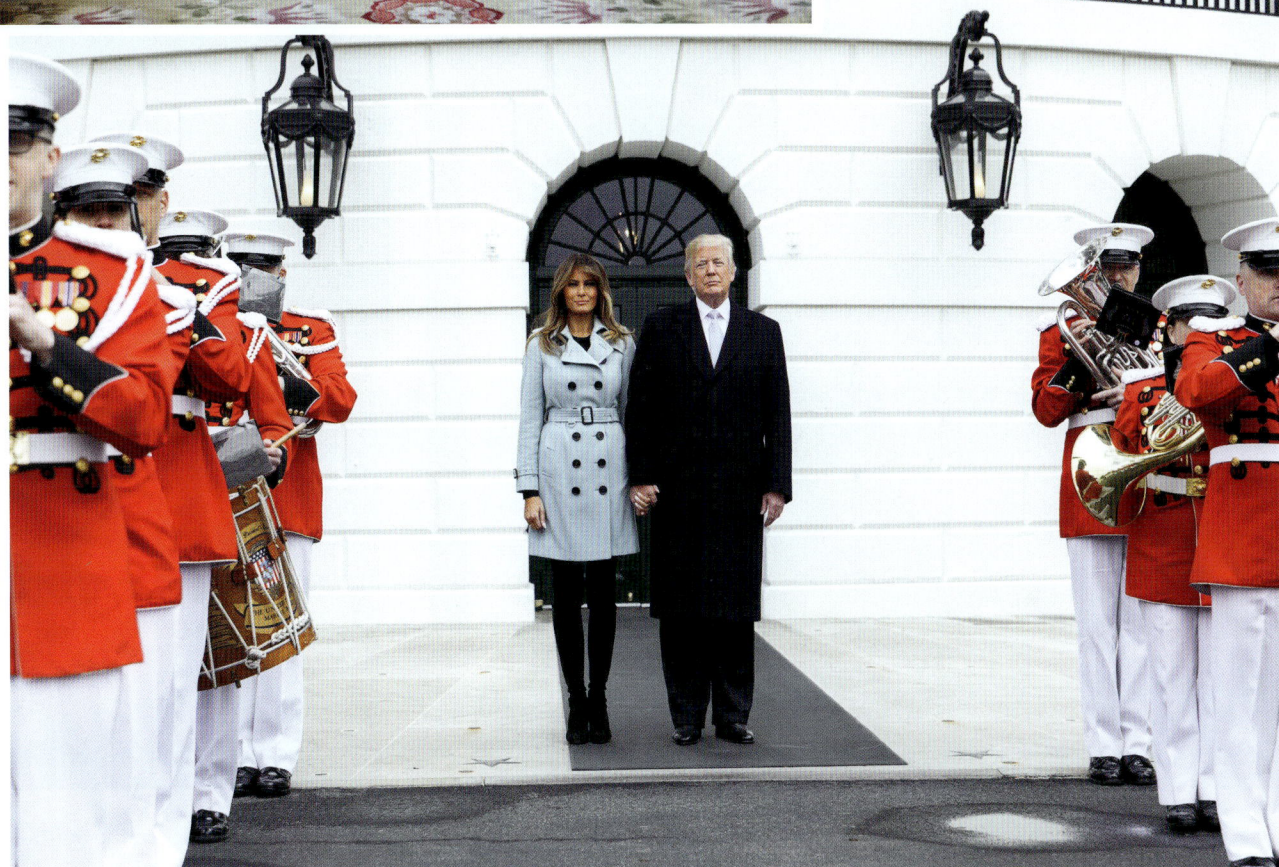

Another year of Easter Egg Rolling![6]

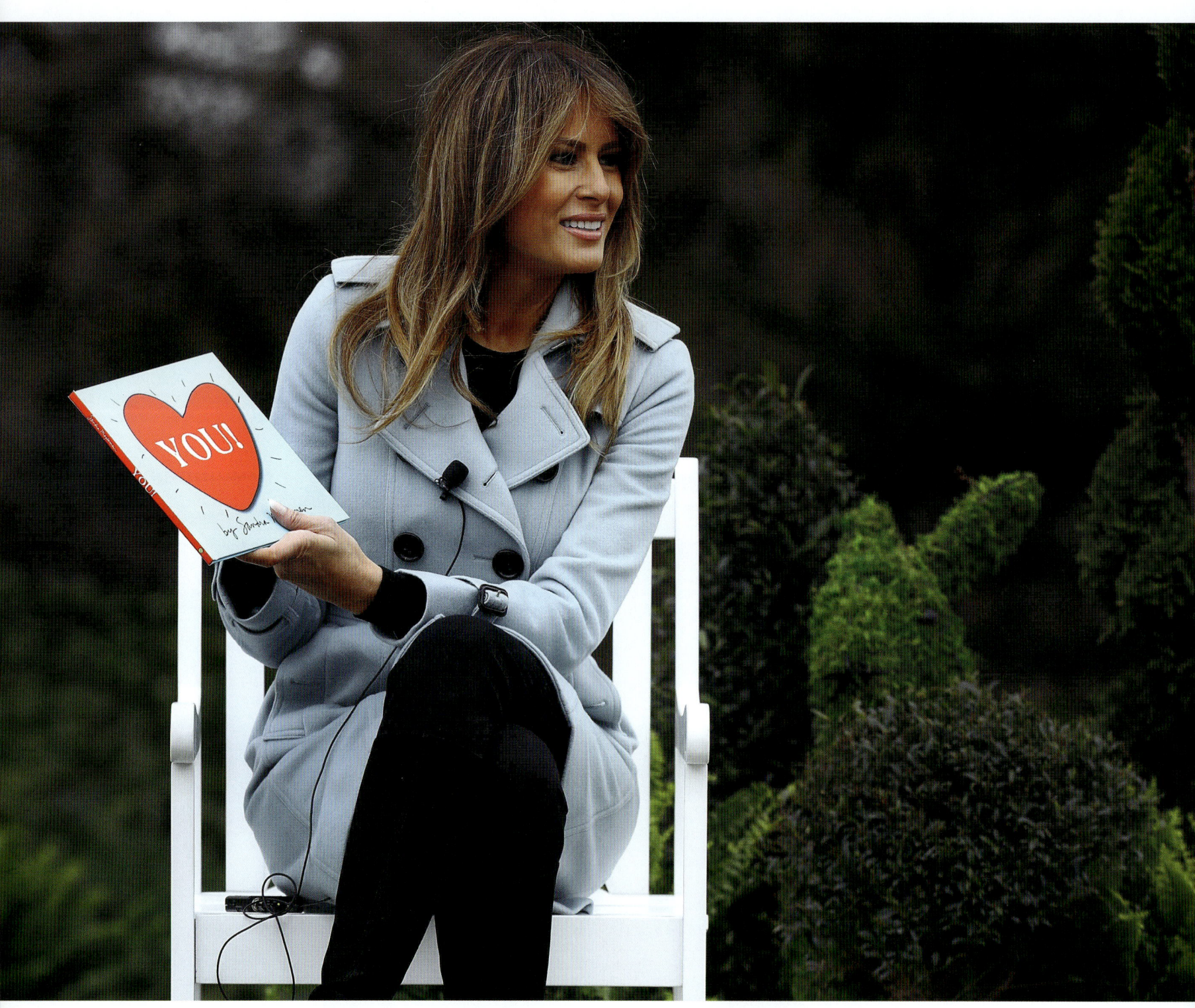

Mrs. Trump reads the book *You!* by Sandra Magsamen during the 140th annual Easter Egg Roll on the South Lawn of the White House, April 2, 2018, in Washington, DC. The tradition was begun in 1878 by President Rutherford B. Hayes.[19]

Heading to the Rose Garden at the White House to unveil her new BE BEST program. BE BEST focuses on three main pillars: well-being, online safety, and avoiding opioid abuse. Children are encouraged to BE BEST in their individual paths, while teaching them the importance of social, emotional, and physical health. This is Melania's signature program as First Lady.[13]

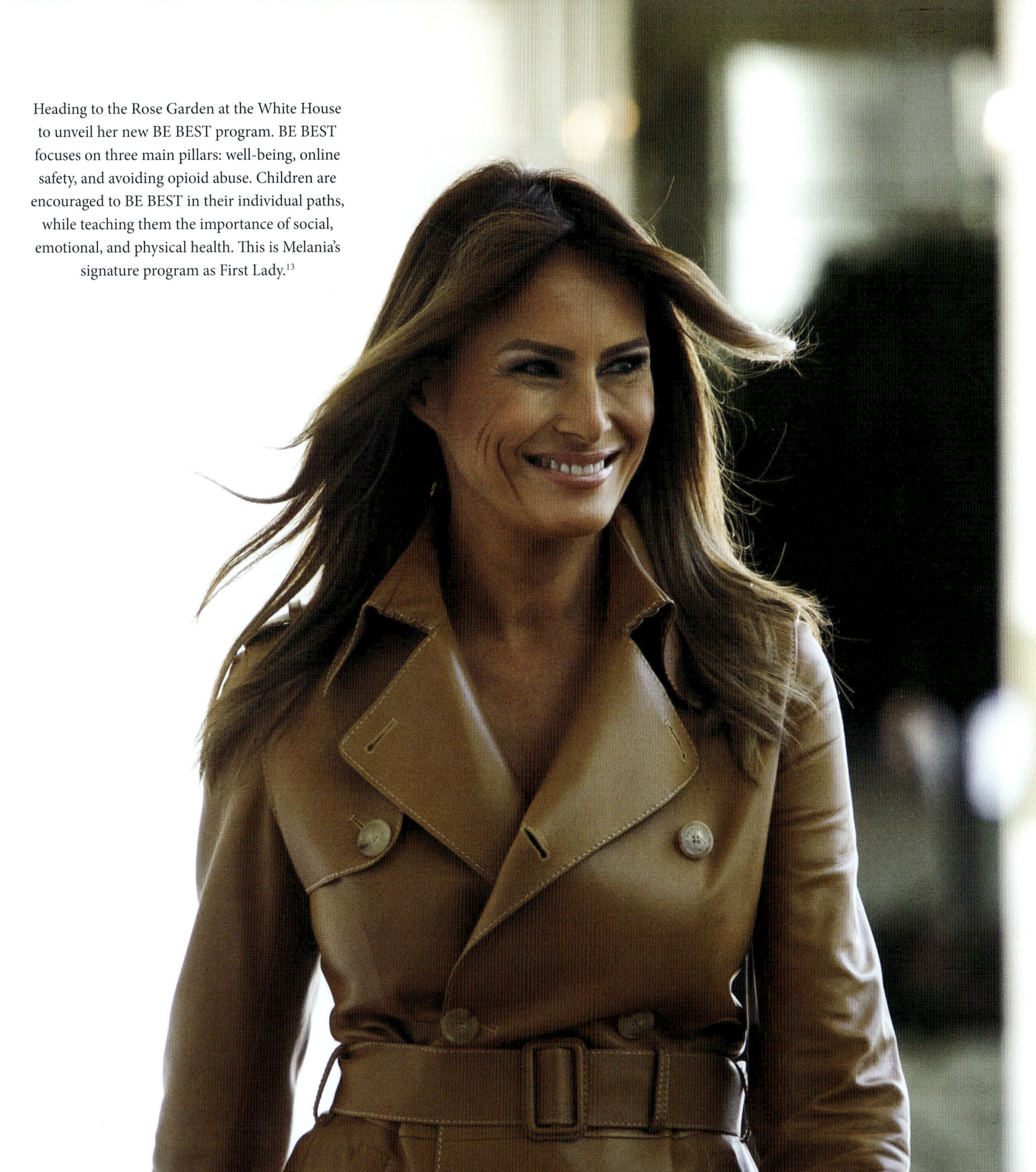

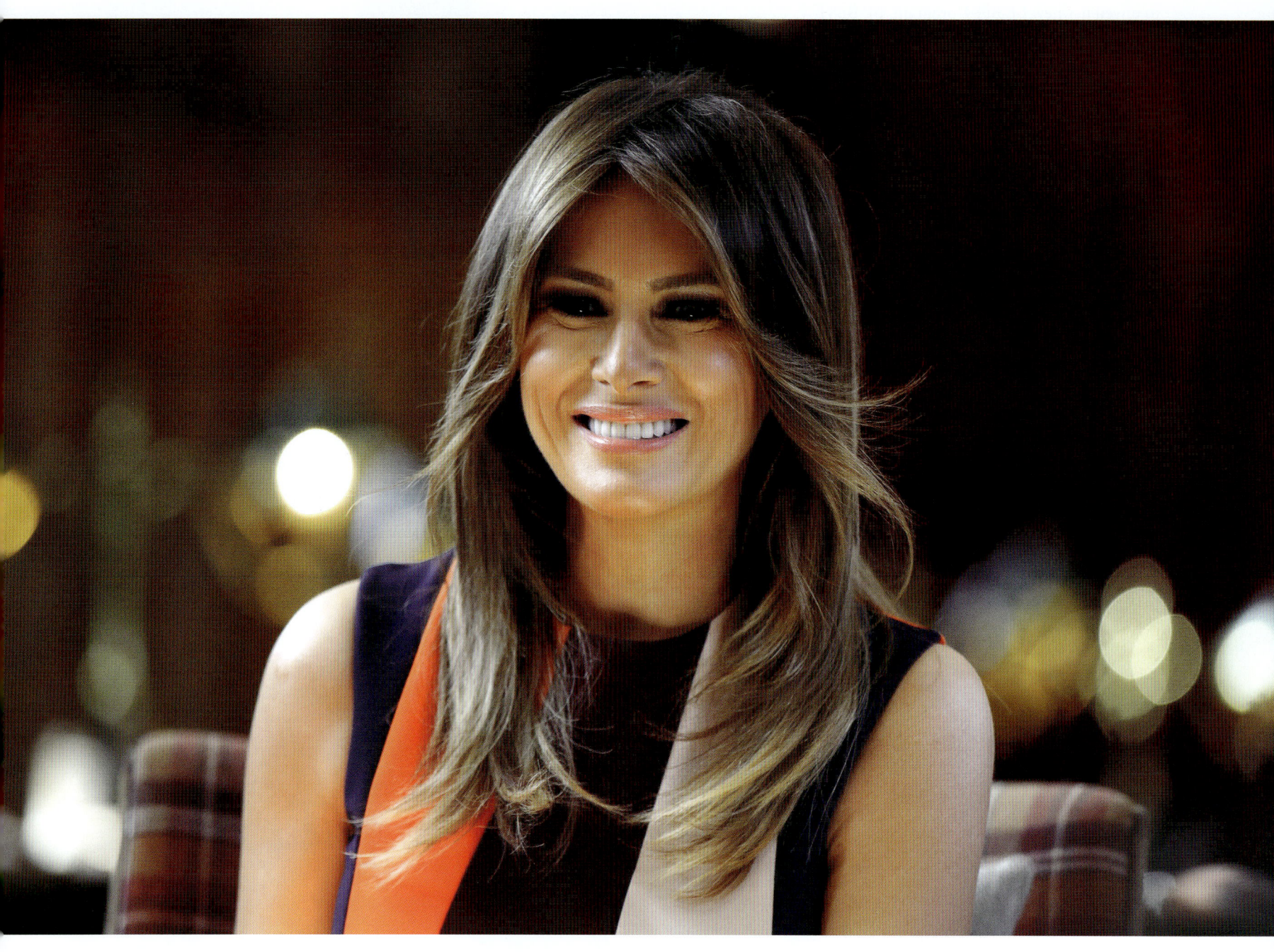

Visiting the Chelsea Pensioners, British Army Personnel who are retired and taken care of at the Royal Hospital in London.[21]

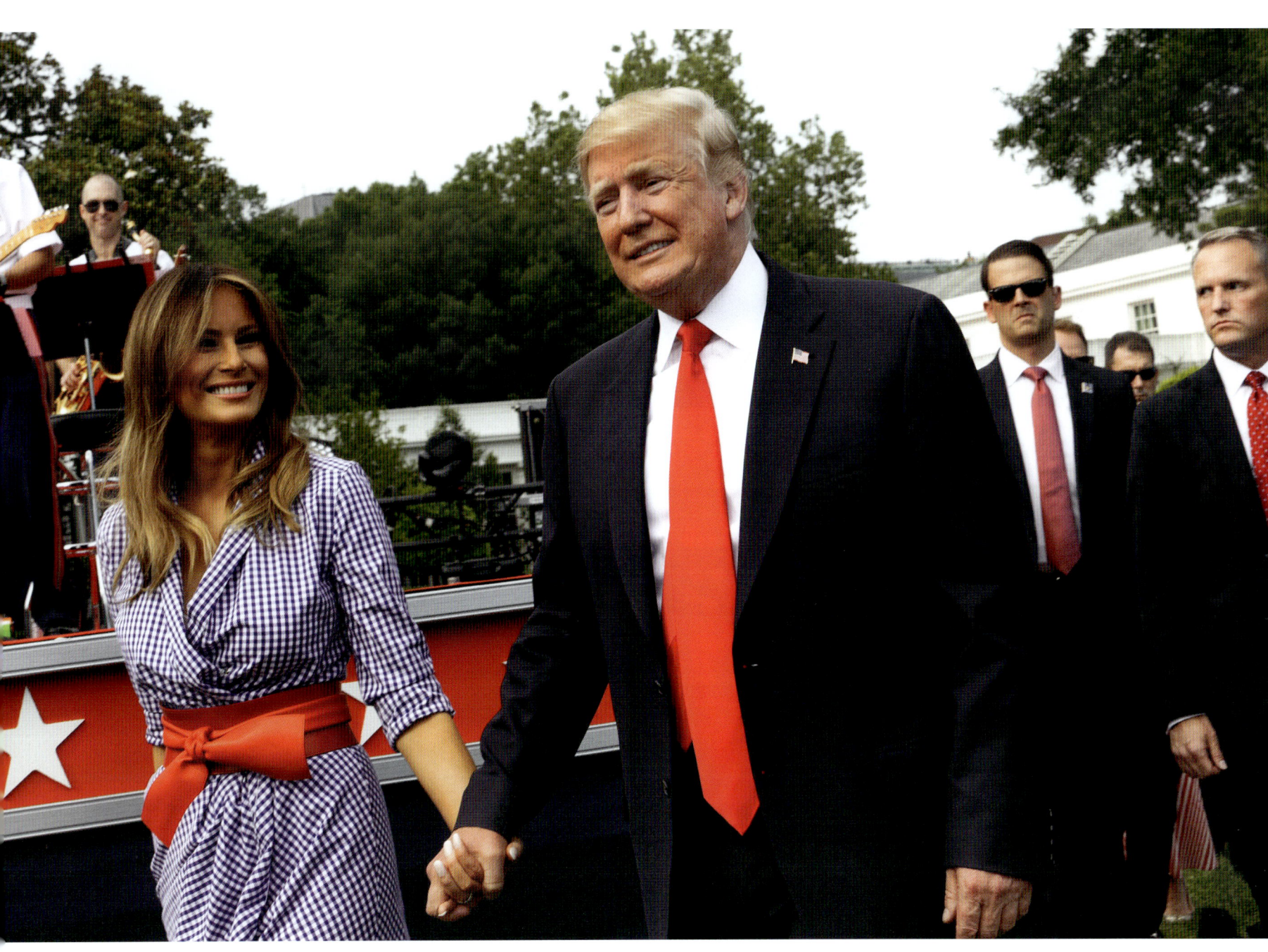

President Donald J. Trump and First Lady Melania Trump participate
in a Fourth of July picnic with military families at the White House, July 4, 2018.[6]

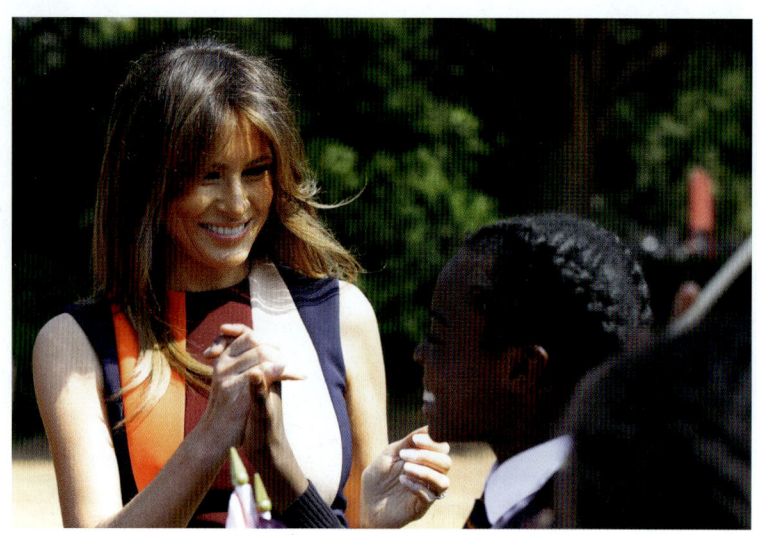

Smiles all around at the Royal Hospital London.[6]

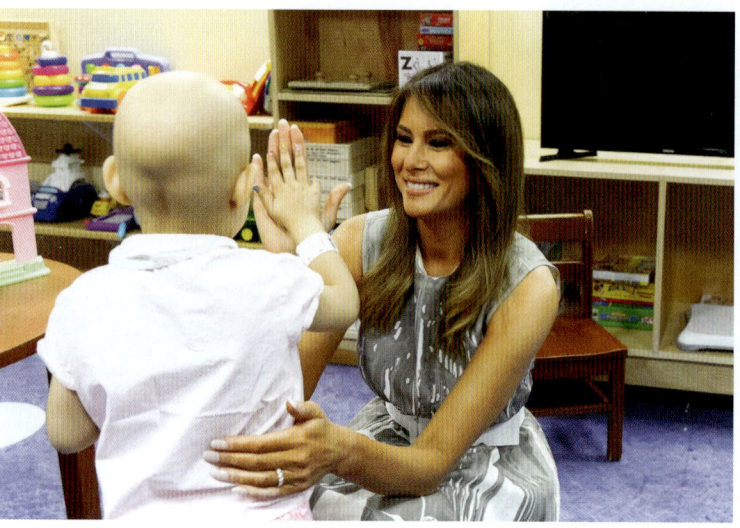

Four-year-old Essence Overton and the First Lady share a high five at the Monroe Carell Jr. Children's Hospital in Nashville, Tennessee.[6]

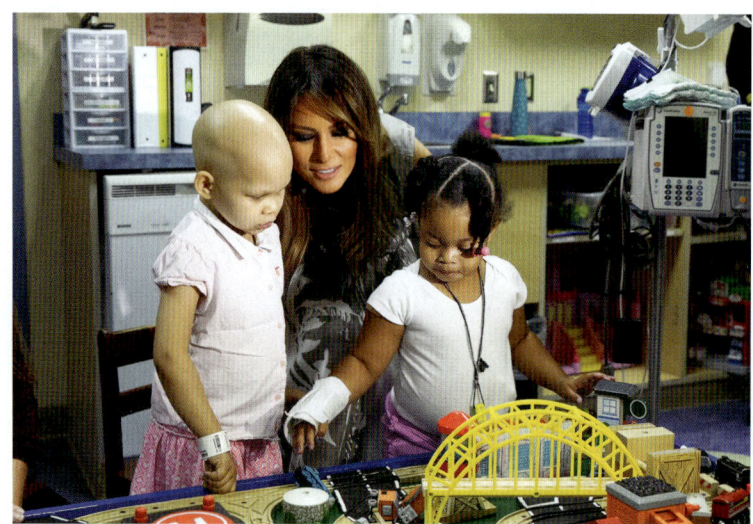

Essence and Natalayah Fields get some quality time with Mrs. Trump at an activities table.[6]

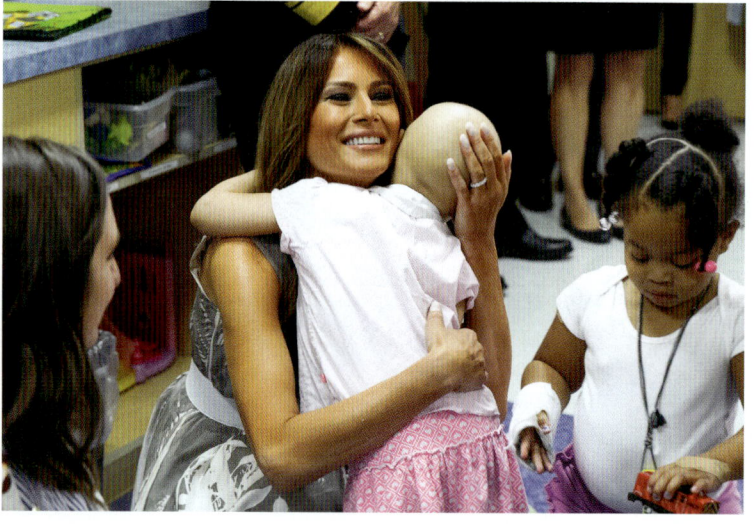

Hugs![6]

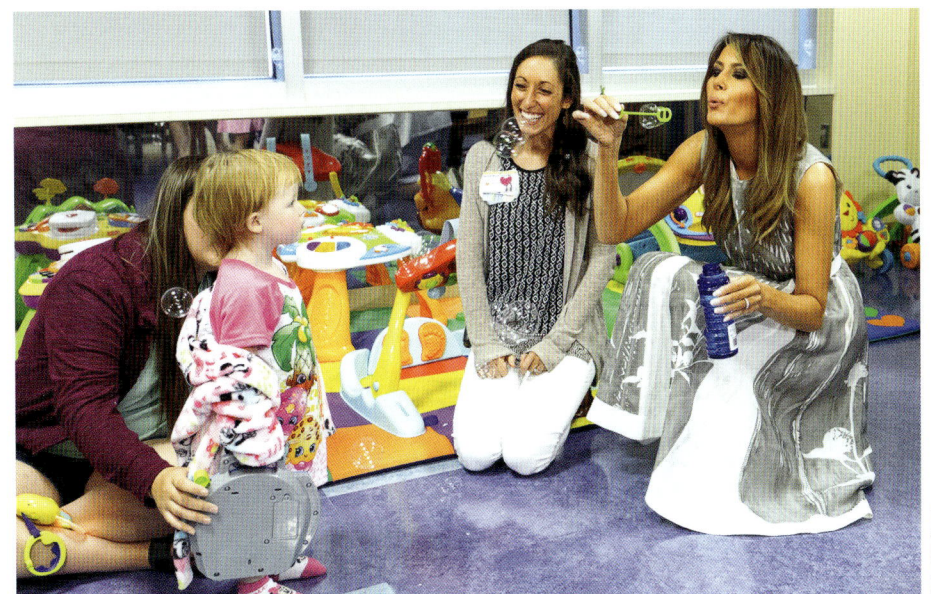

Double bubbles with Elliegh Rasmussen.[6]

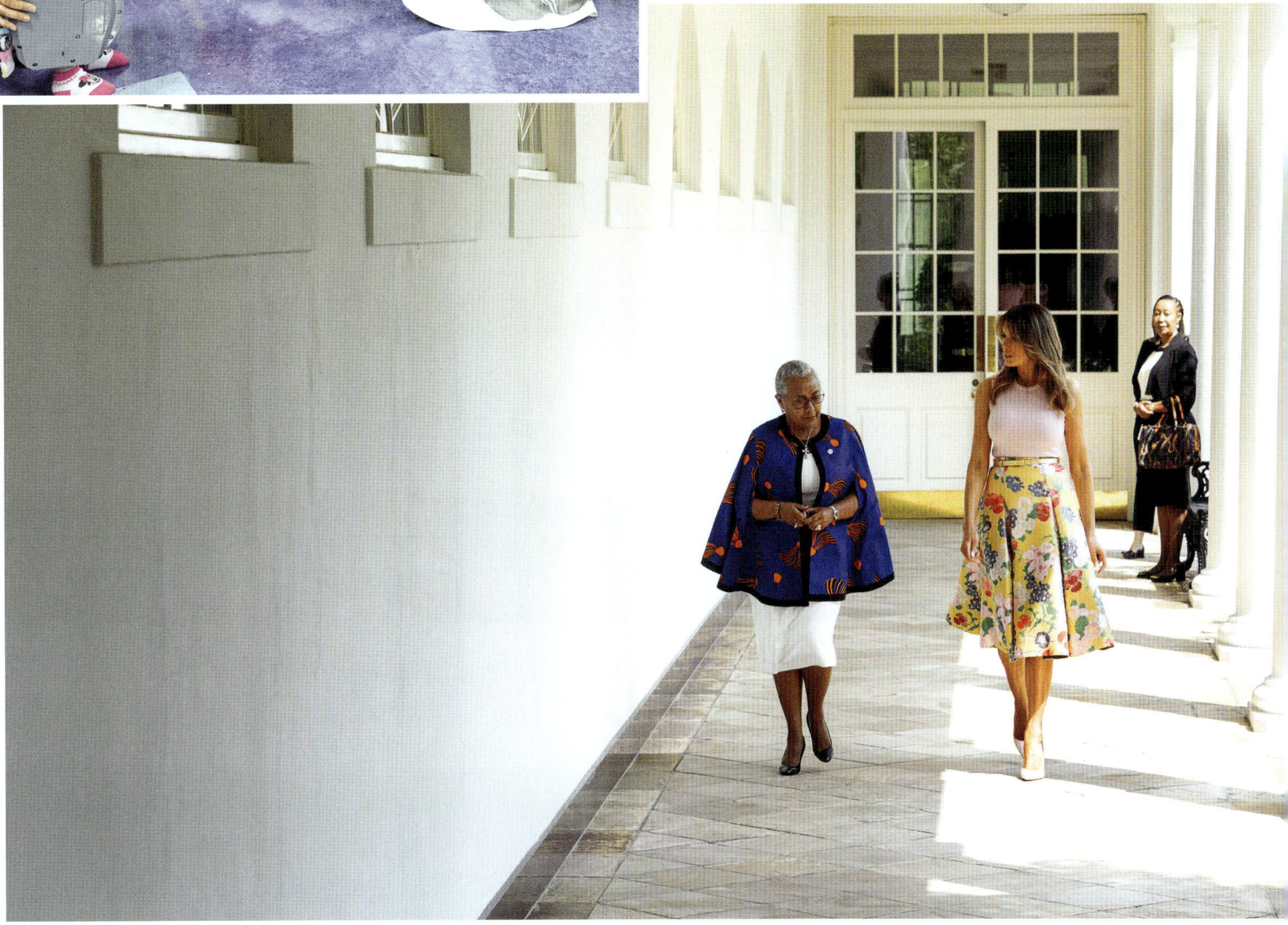

First Lady Melania Trump and Mrs. Kenyatta of the Republic of Kenya.[6]

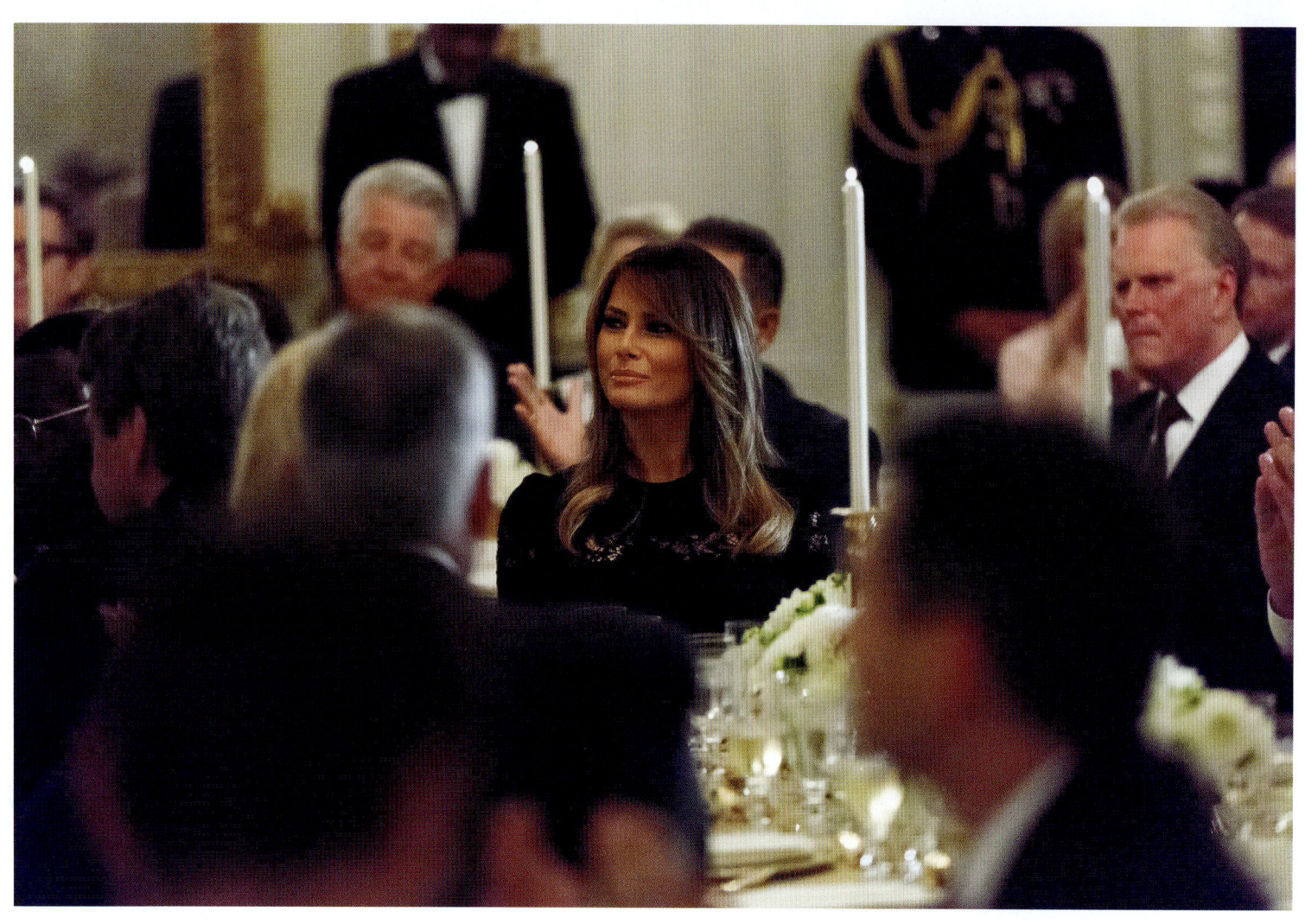

Elegance and Evangelicals.[6]

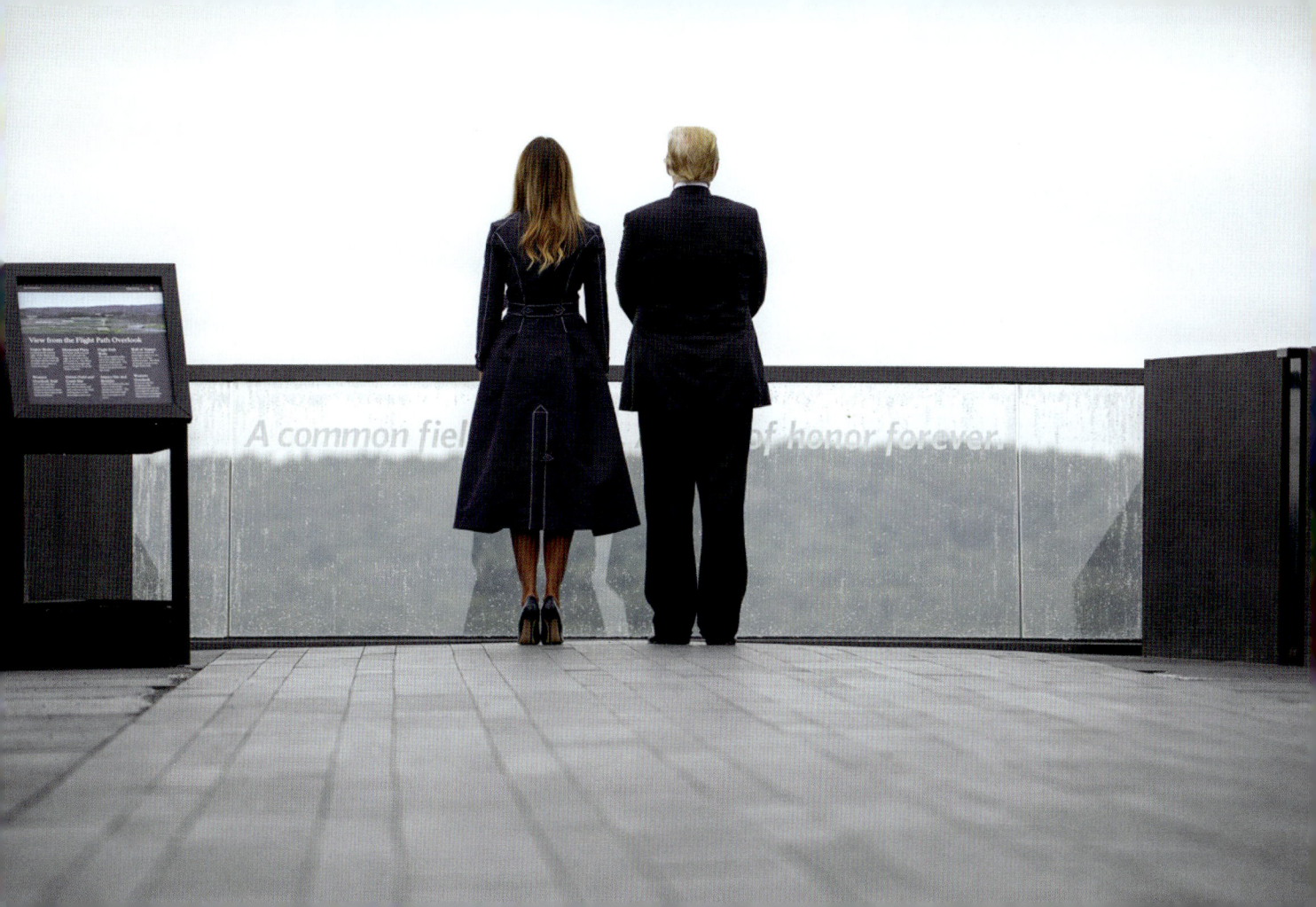

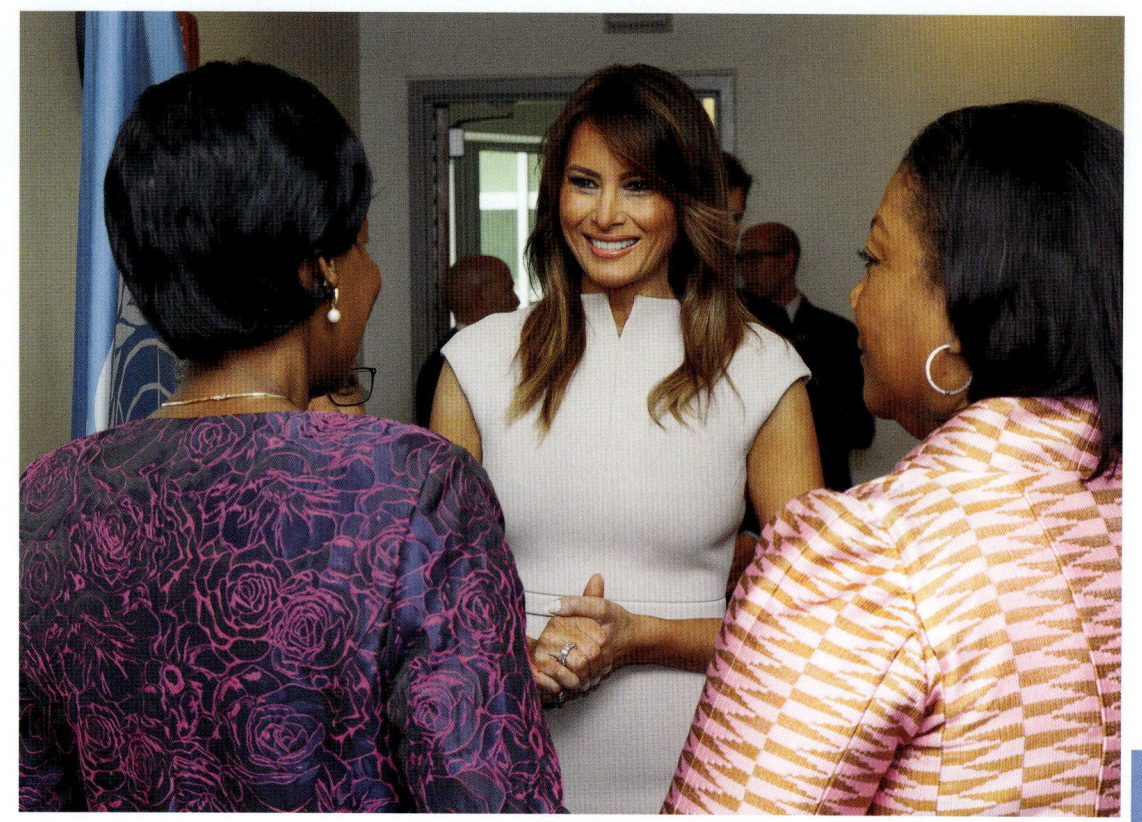

The First Lady speaks with Gertrude Mutharika, the First Lady of Malawi, Rebecca Akufo-Addo, the First Lady of the Republic of Ghana, and Margaret Kenyatta, the First Lady of Kenya while hosting a United Nations reception.[6]

Elegance in Motion as the First Lady gives a presentation at a United Nations reception she hosted.[6]

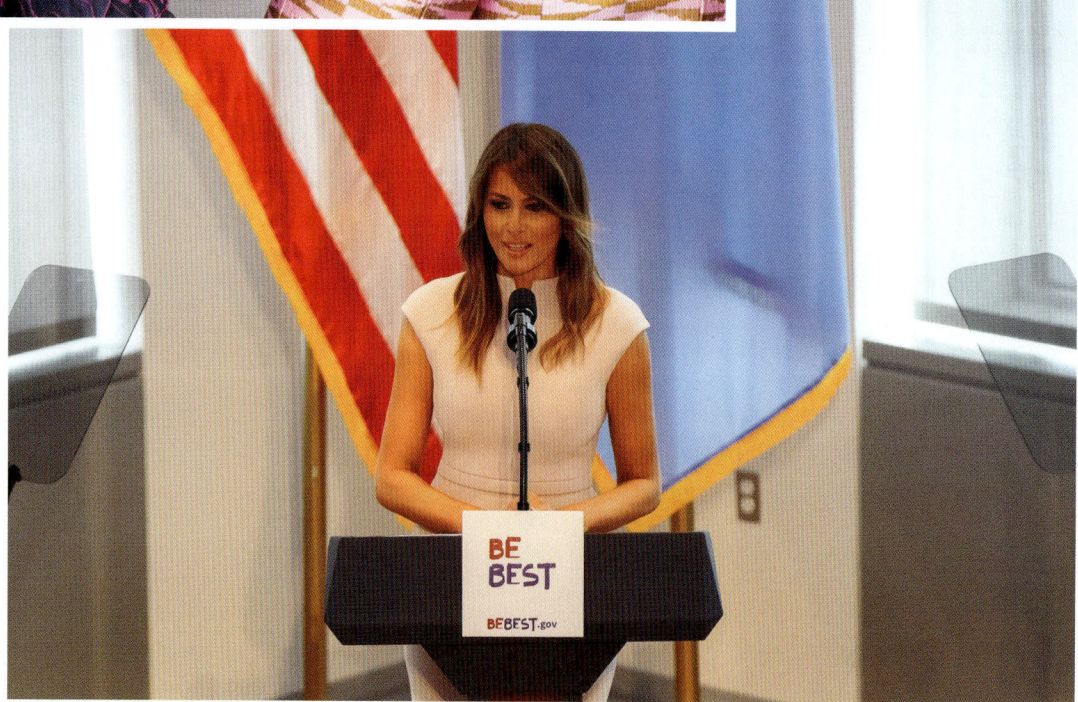

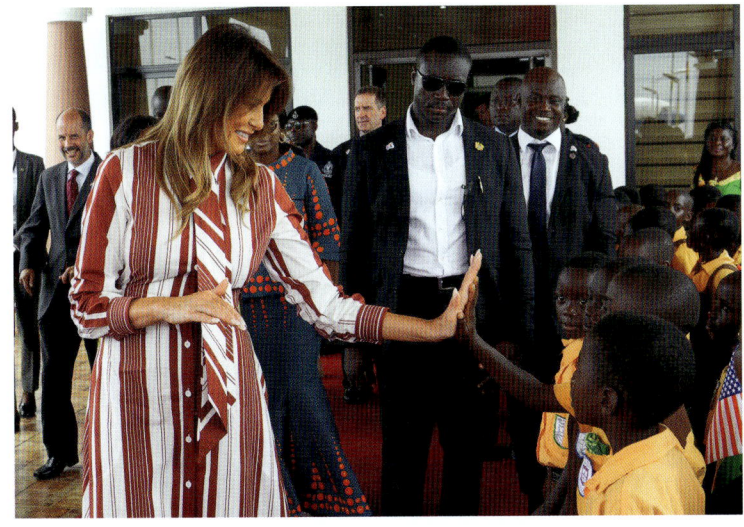

The First Lady is welcomed to Ghana, Africa with a ceremony led by Rebecca Akufo-Addo, the First Lady of the Republic of Ghana, and local schoolchildren at Kotoka International Airport.[6]

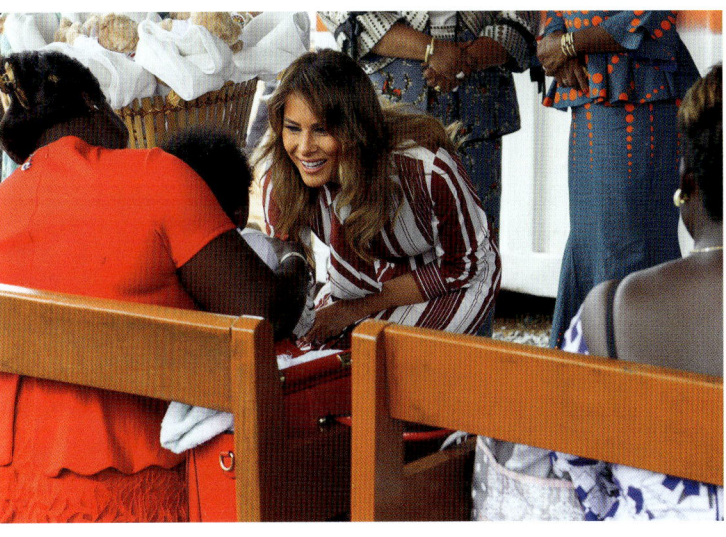

The two First Ladies meet with mothers and children at the Child Welfare Clinic inside the Greater Accra Regional Hospital.[6]

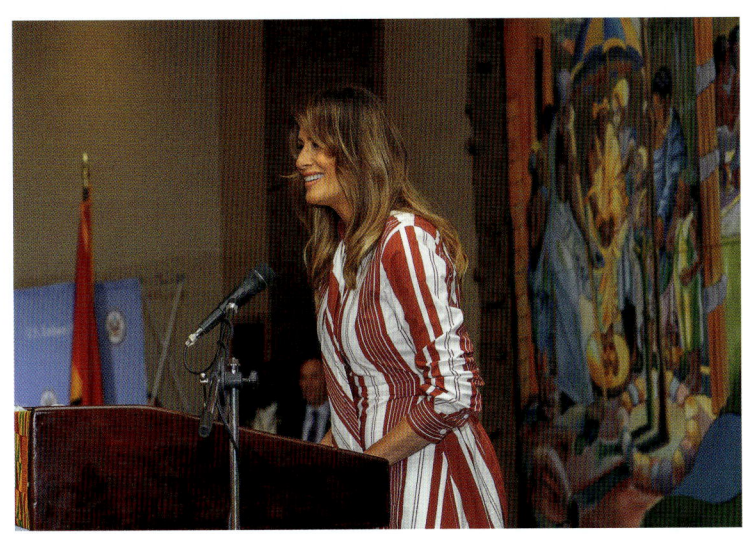

Mrs. Trump speaks to
United States Embassy Ghana staff and families.[6]

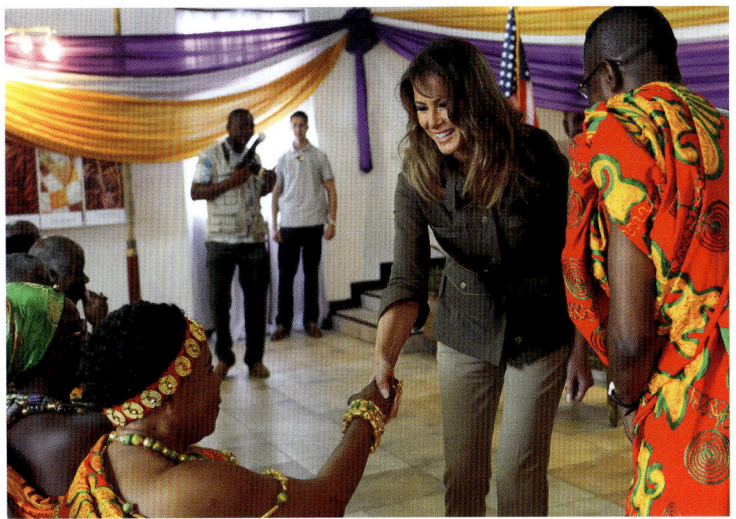

Melania shakes hands with Ghana chieftains at the Emintsimadze Palace in Cape Coast, Ghana.[6]

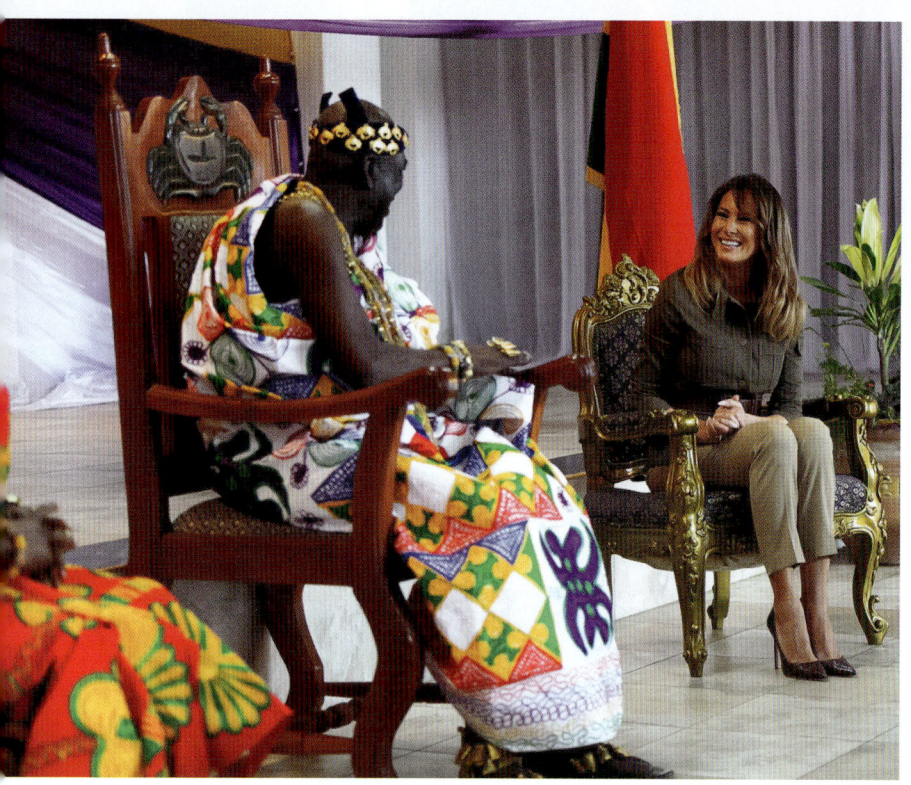

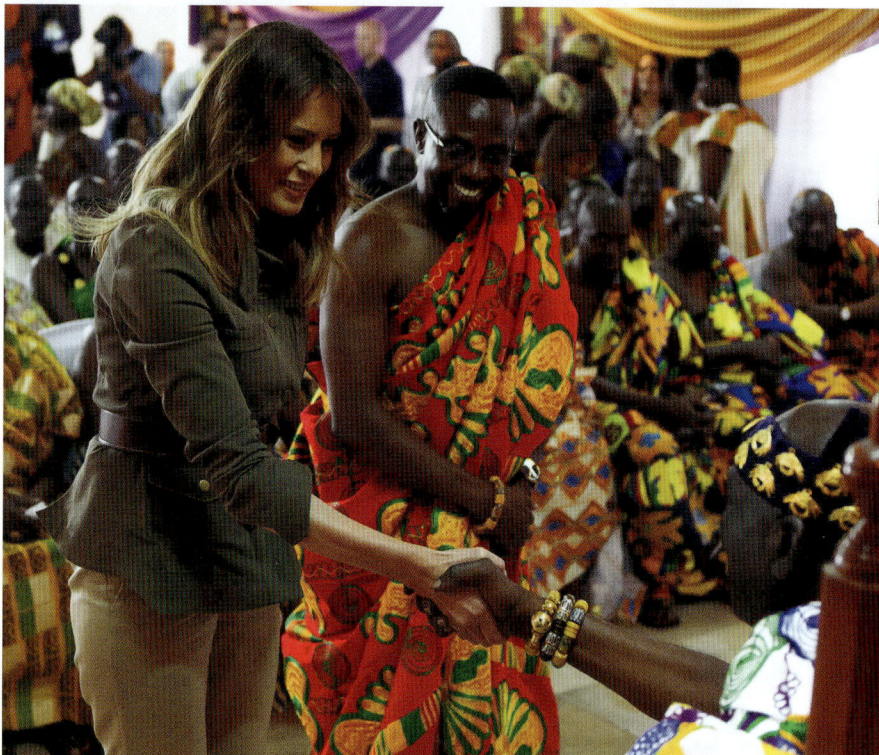

The First Lady Meets Cape Coast's head Chief, Osabarimba Kwesi Atta II for permission to visit the Cape Coast Castle on her African Trip. The Cape Coast Castle was a large slavery trading outpost in Ghana built by European traders. Originally built for trade in goods, it eventually became a major holding area for slaves before the captives were placed on ships.[6]

Shaking hands with the Chief.[6]

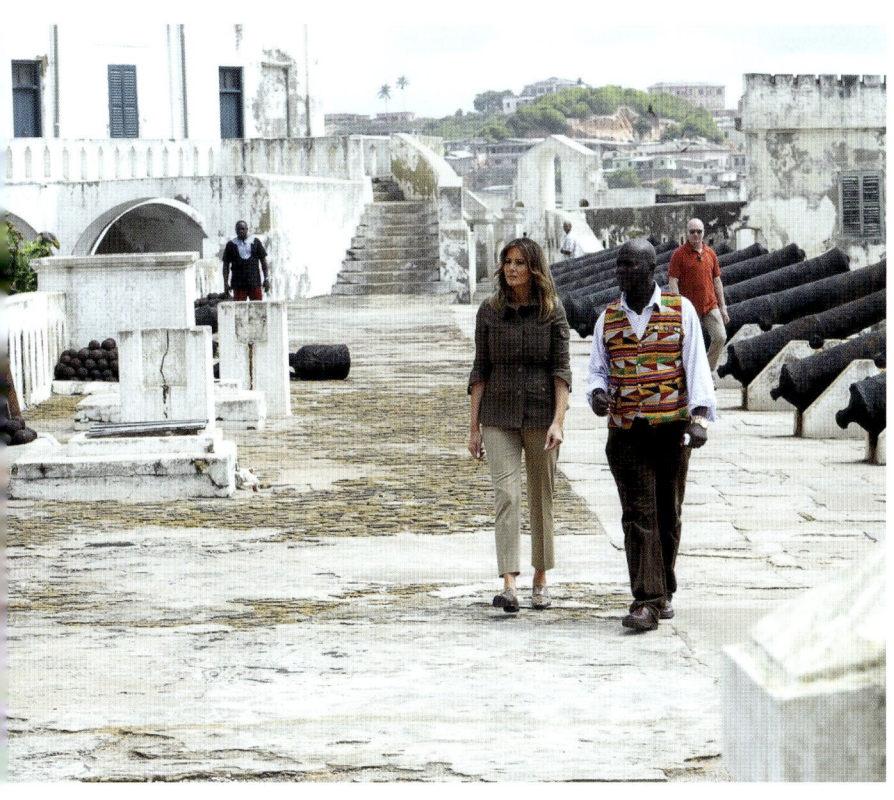

Touring the remnants of Cape Coast Castle.[6]

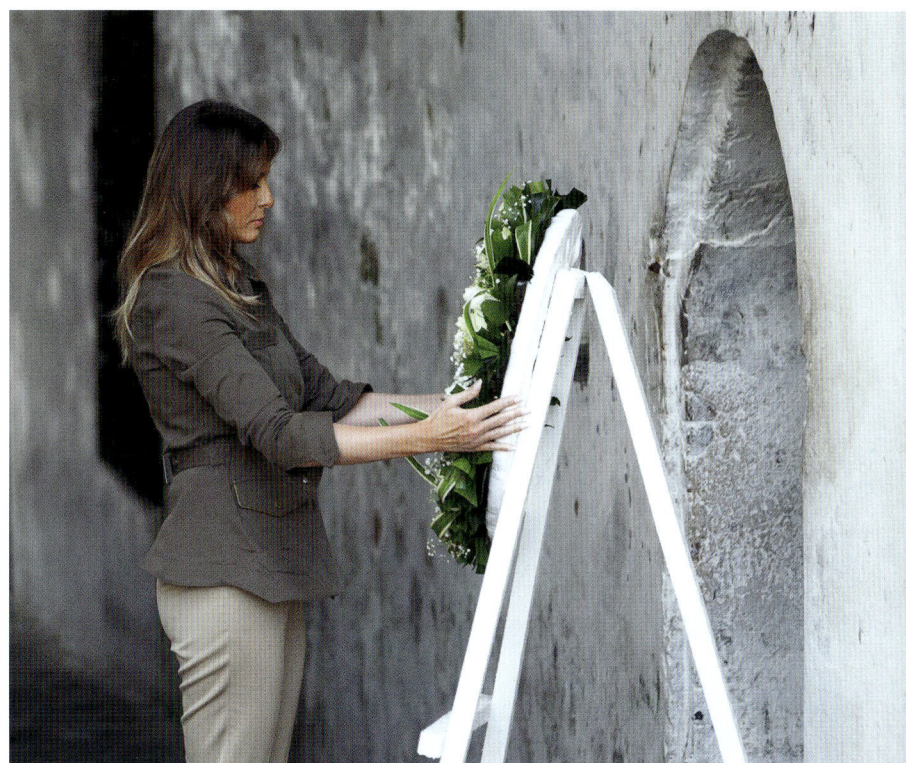

Mrs. Trump places a wreath at the Door of No Return.
After passing through the Door slaves would be lowered into boats
and rowed out to ships, never to return to their homeland again.[6]

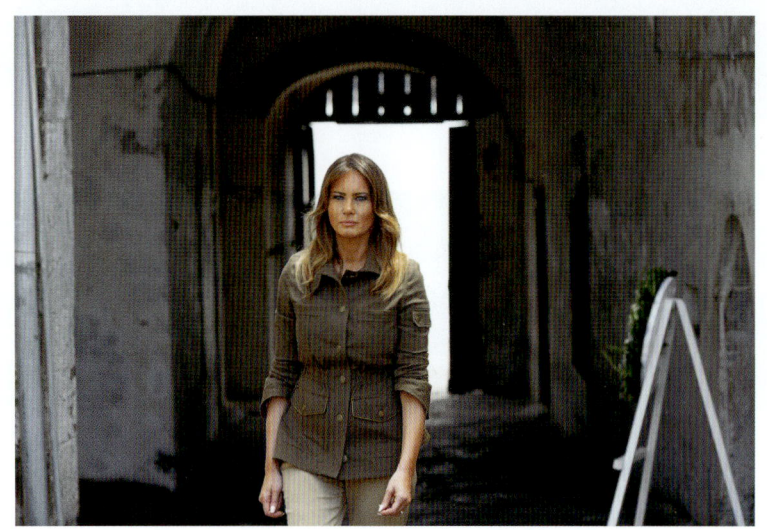

The First Lady walks through the Door of No Return
after placing a wreath there.[6]

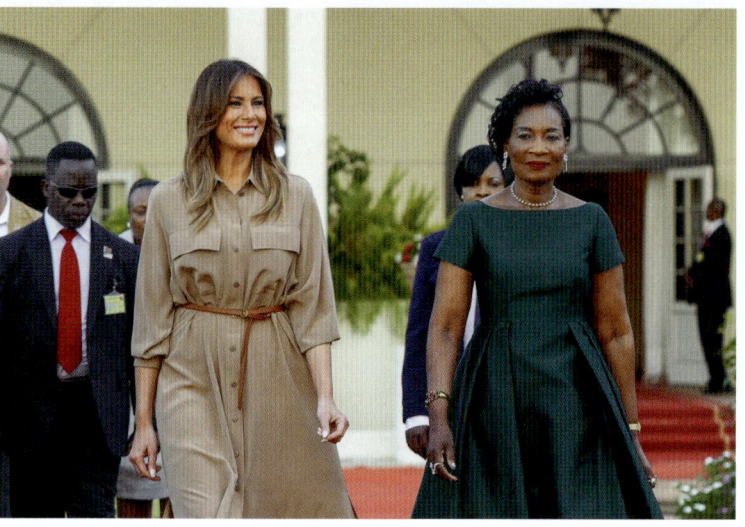

Being met by Gertrude Mutharika, First Lady of Malawi.[6]

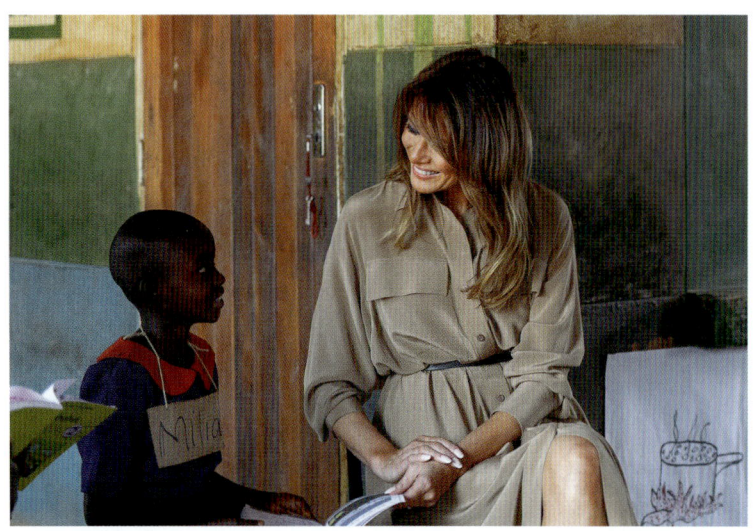

Mrs. Trump makes a new friend at the Chipala Primary School
in Lilongwe, Malawi.[6]

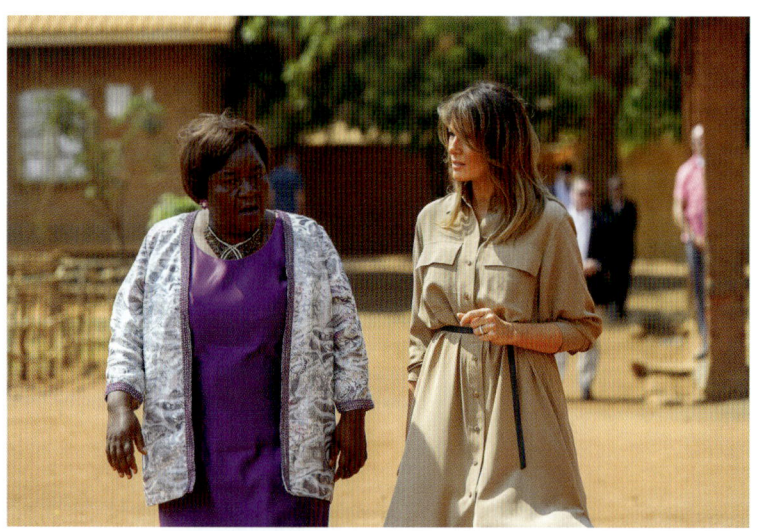

Chatting with Maureen Masi, Head Teacher of Chipala Primary School.[6]

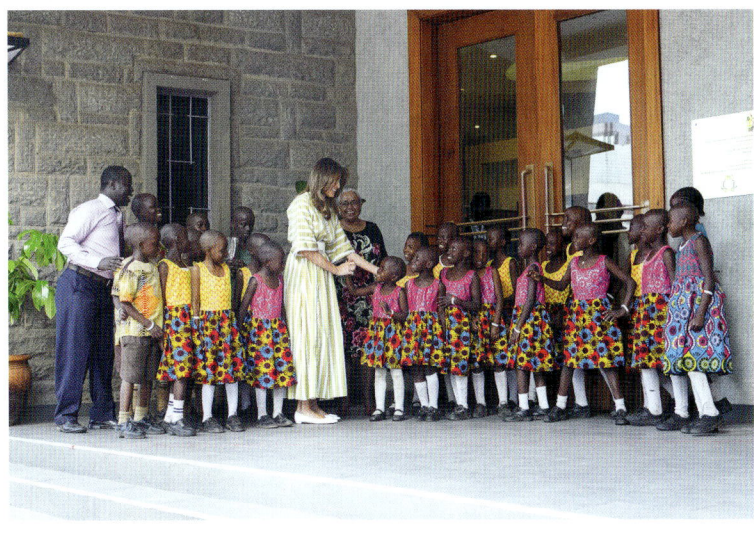

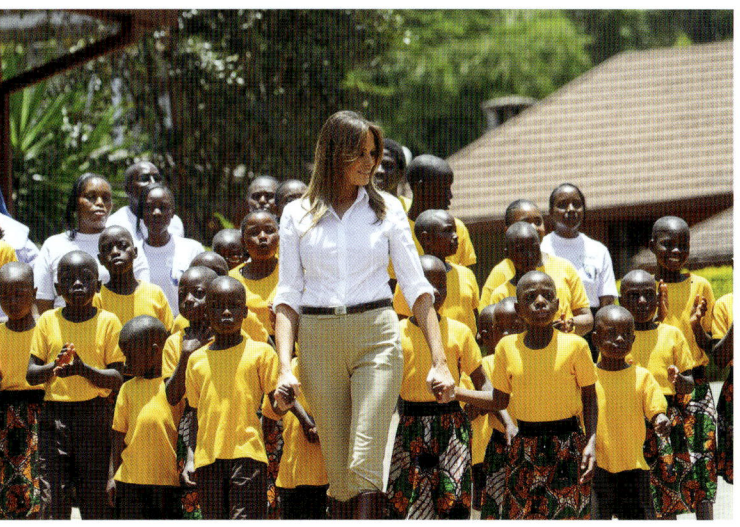

First Lady Melania Trump and Margaret Kenyatta, First Lady of Kenya listen to a welcoming song performed by local children.[6]

Visiting The Nest Children's home in Kenya. The Nest is for children ages two to seventeen whose mothers are imprisoned. Some were abandoned as babies. Most stay until they are reunited with their mothers or find new places to live. Regardless, each child receives care and an education.[6]

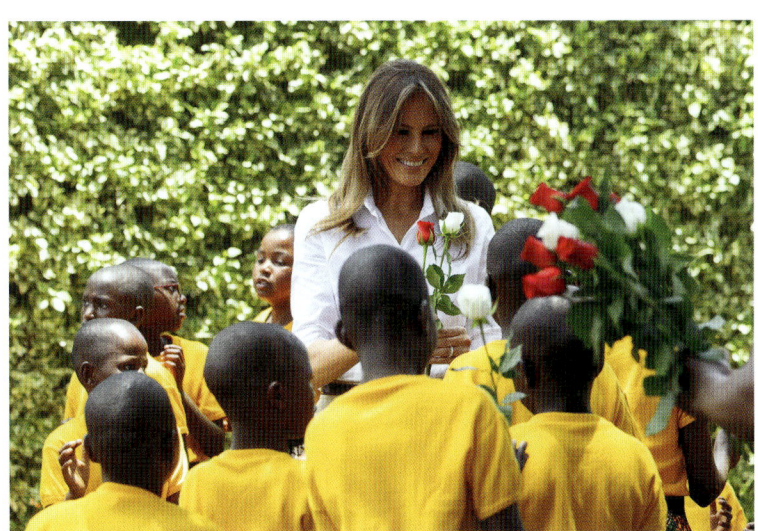

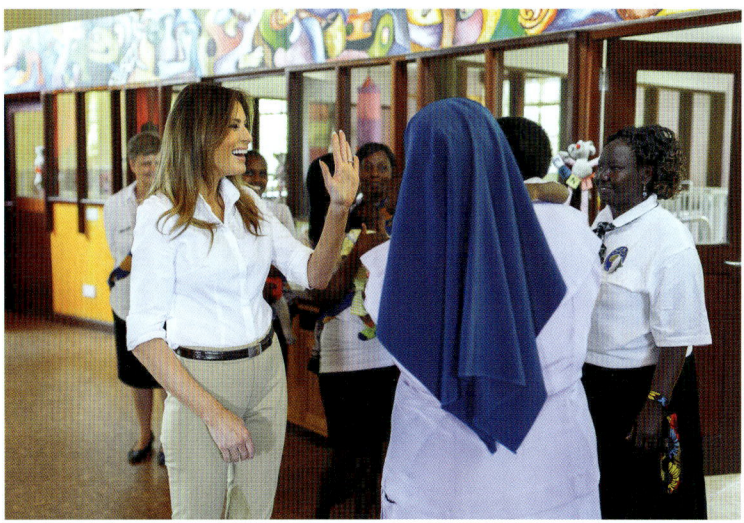

Elegance and roses in Africa.[6]

Meeting teachers at The Nest School.[6]

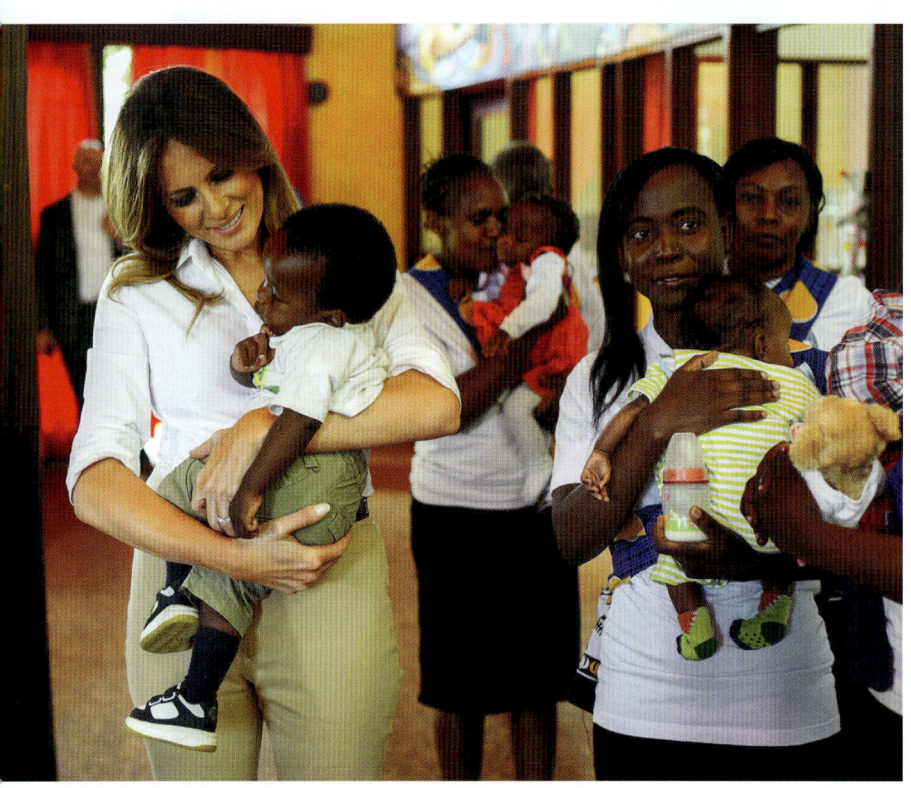

A moment shared.[6]

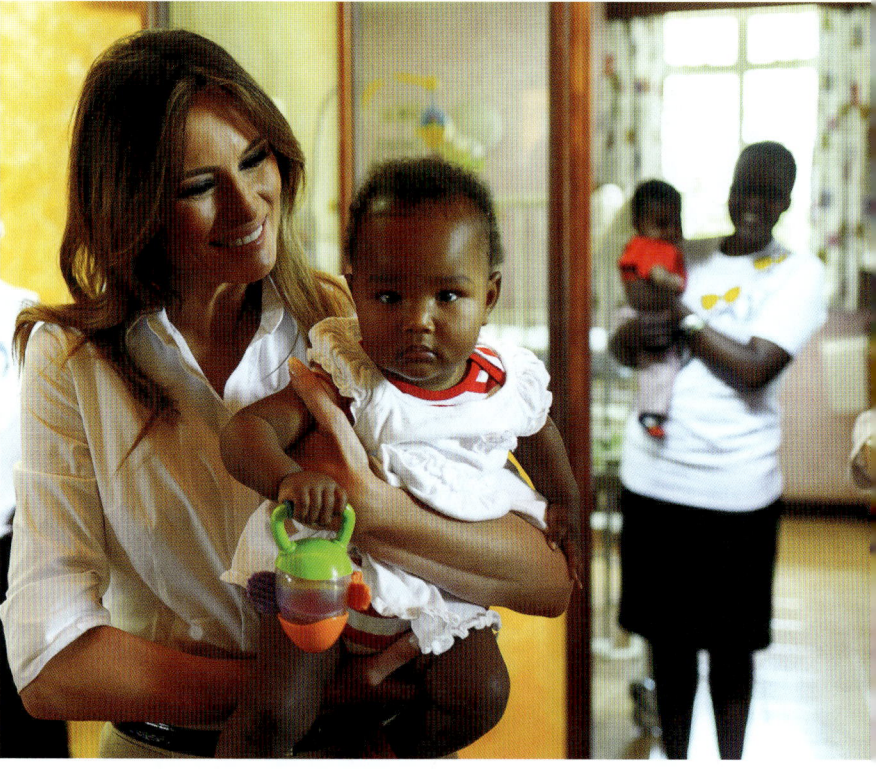

The First Lady is a mother as well as a representative of the United States. You can see the care in her eyes as she interacts with children.[6]

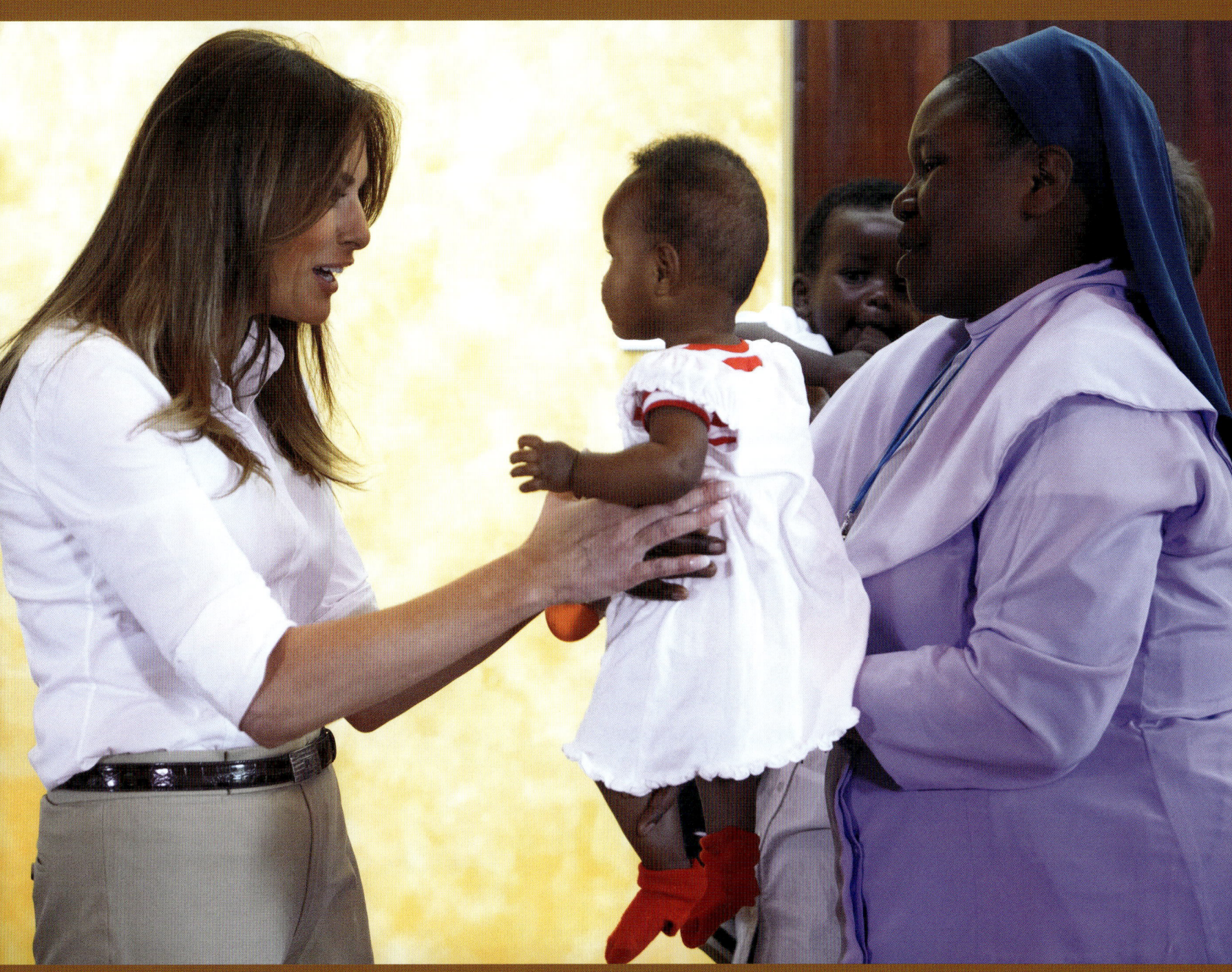

New friends, new smiles.[6]

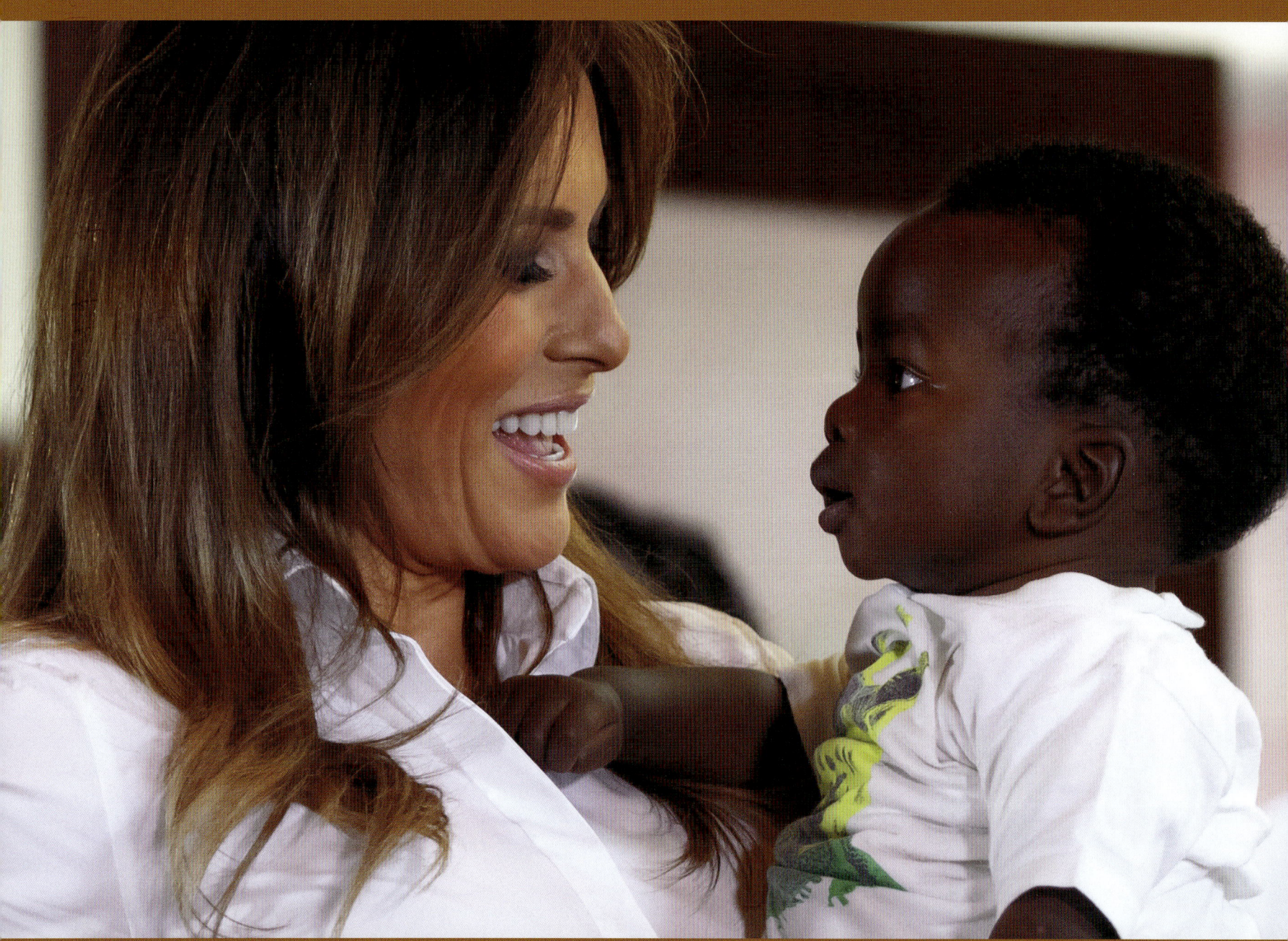

Elegance and Innocence.[18]

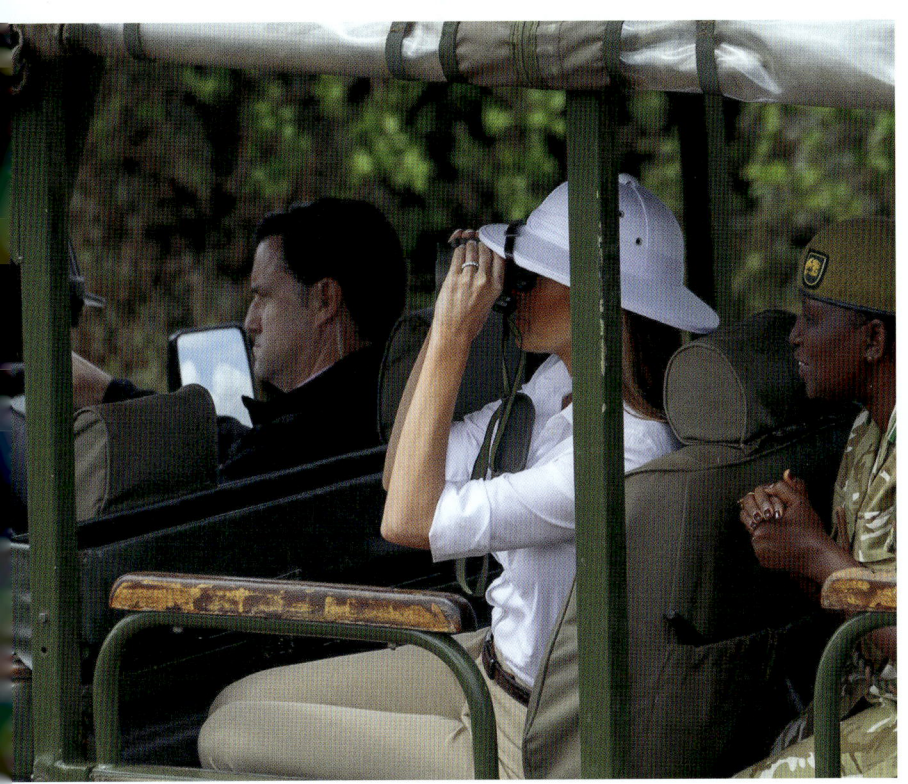

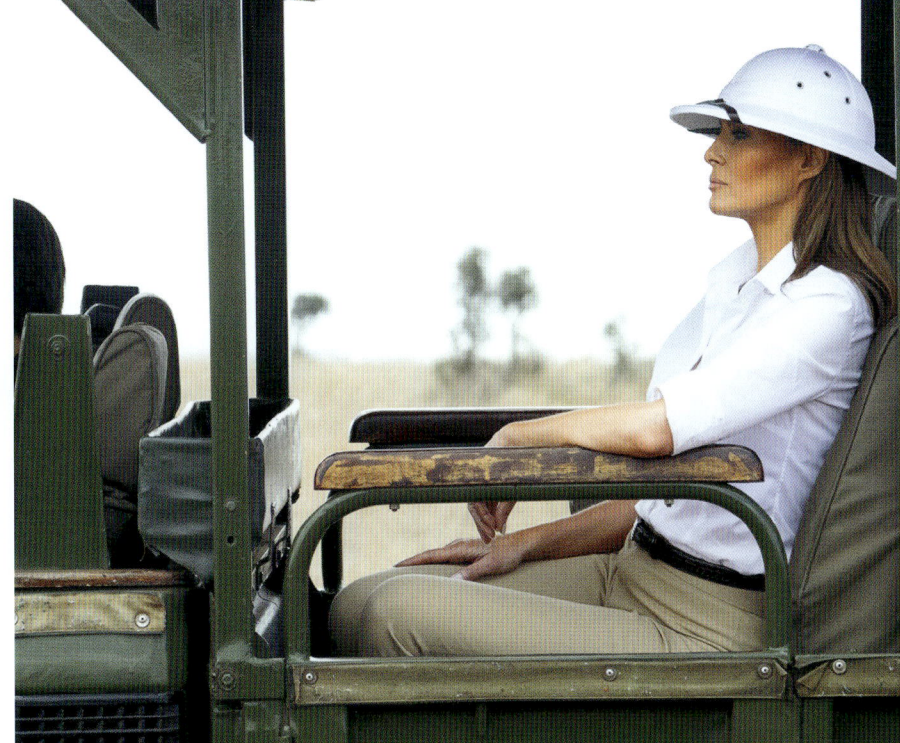

On Safari in Nairobi National Park with Nelly Palmeris,
the Game Warden.[6]

Elegance on safari.[6]

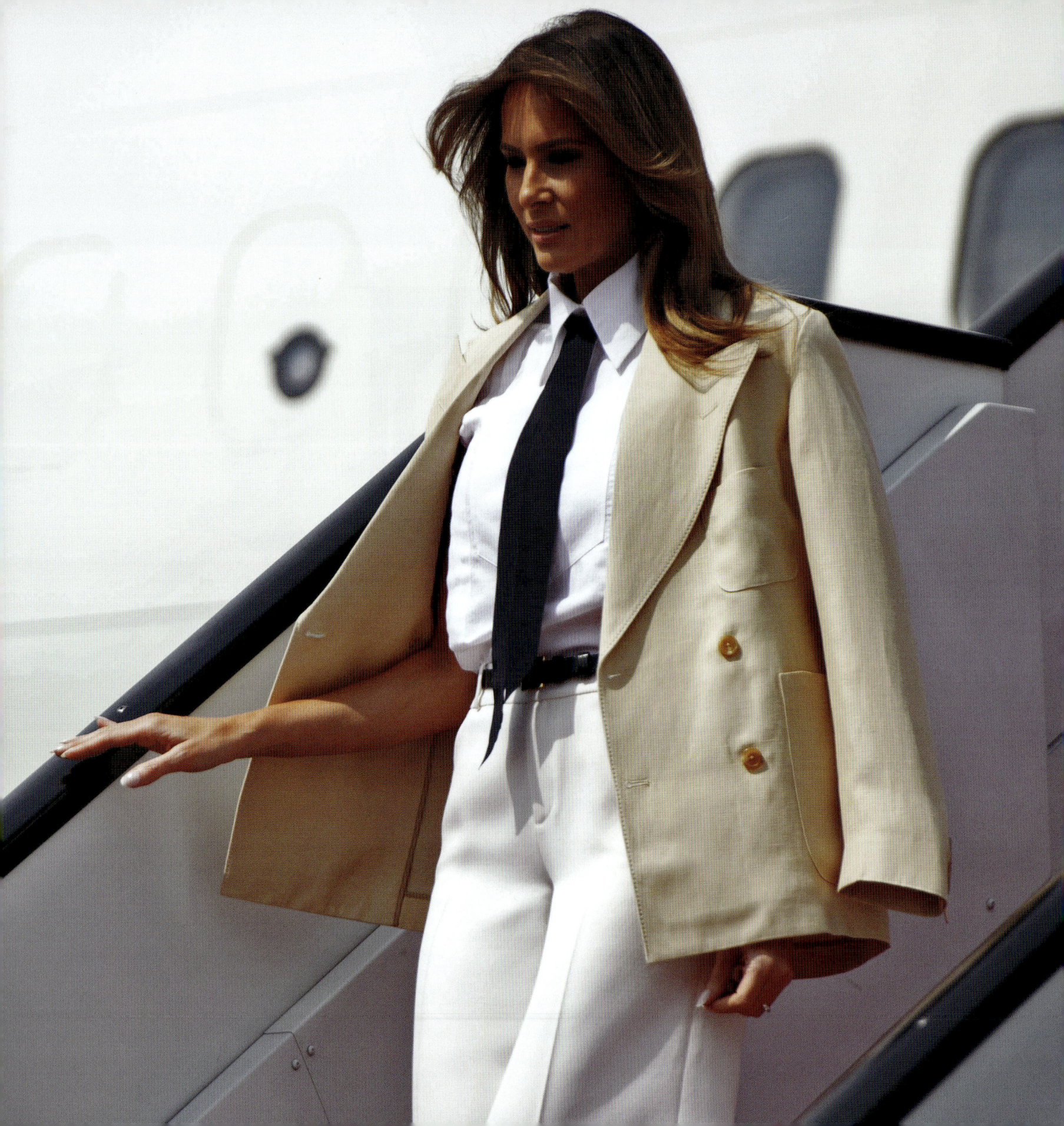

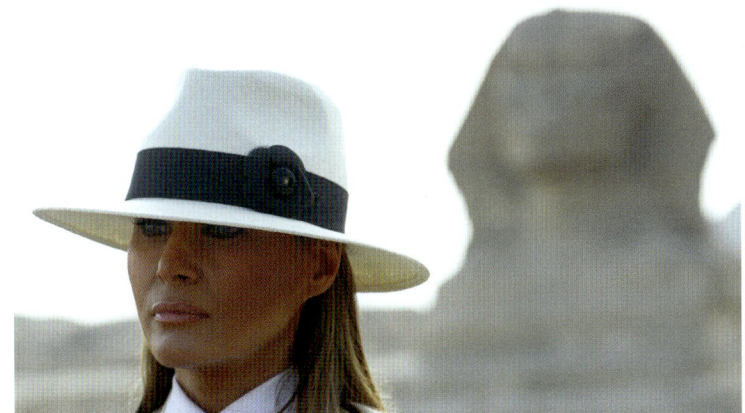

Two elegant enigmas.[6]

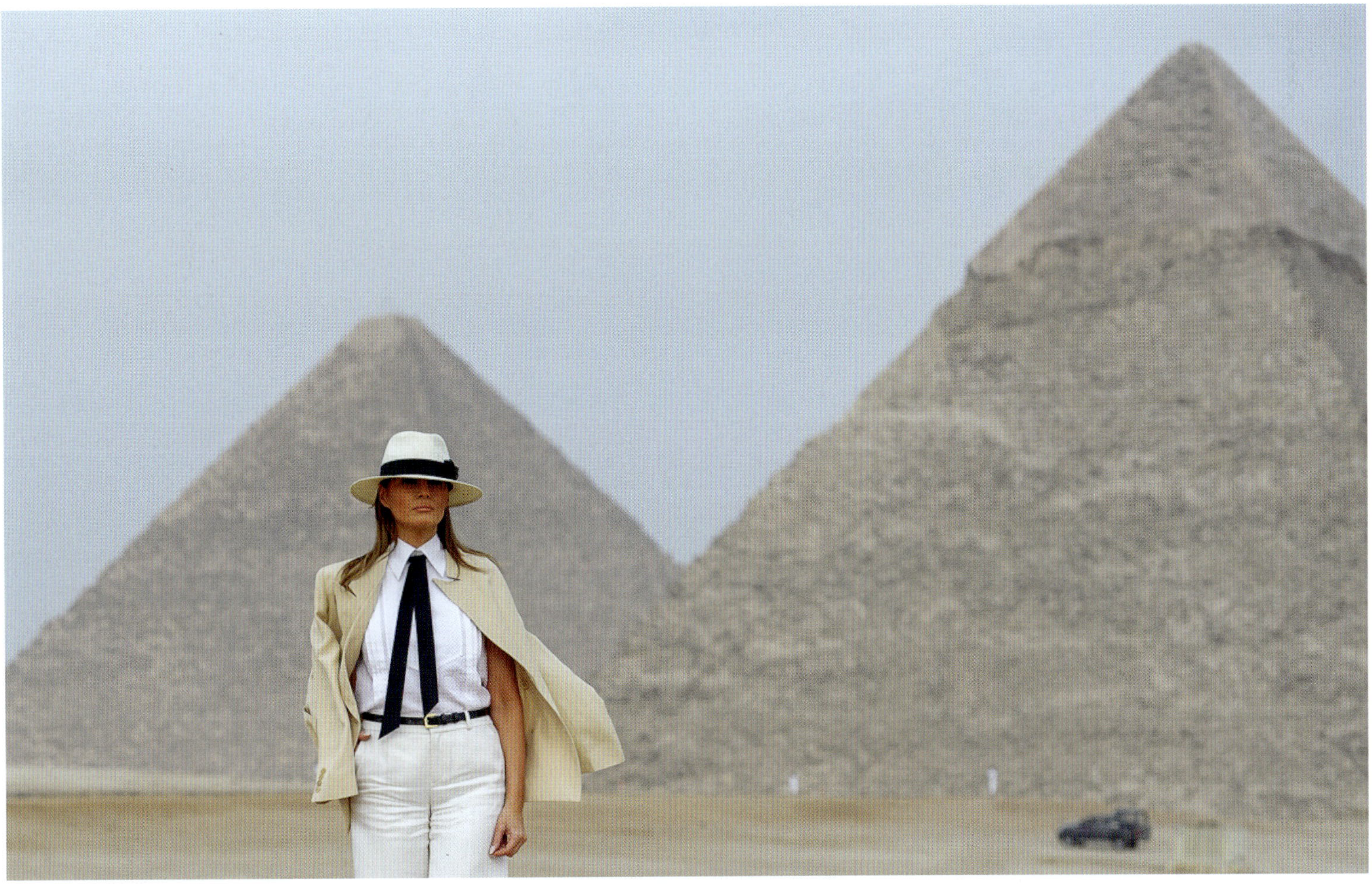

Pyramids at Giza, October 6, 2018, in Cairo.[6]

Left: The First Lady arriving in Cairo.[18]

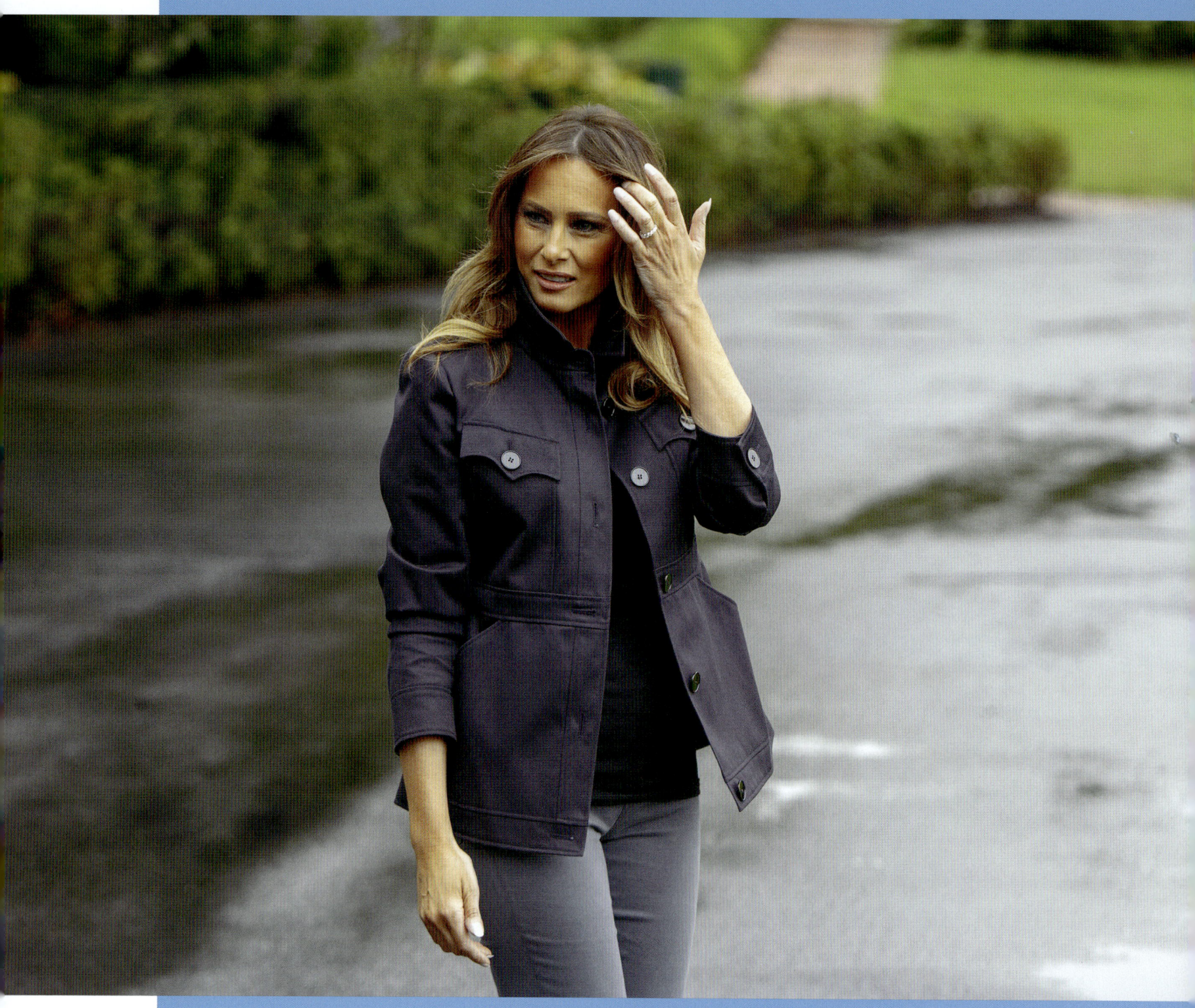

Getting ready to leave for Florida to view damage from Hurricane Michael.[22]

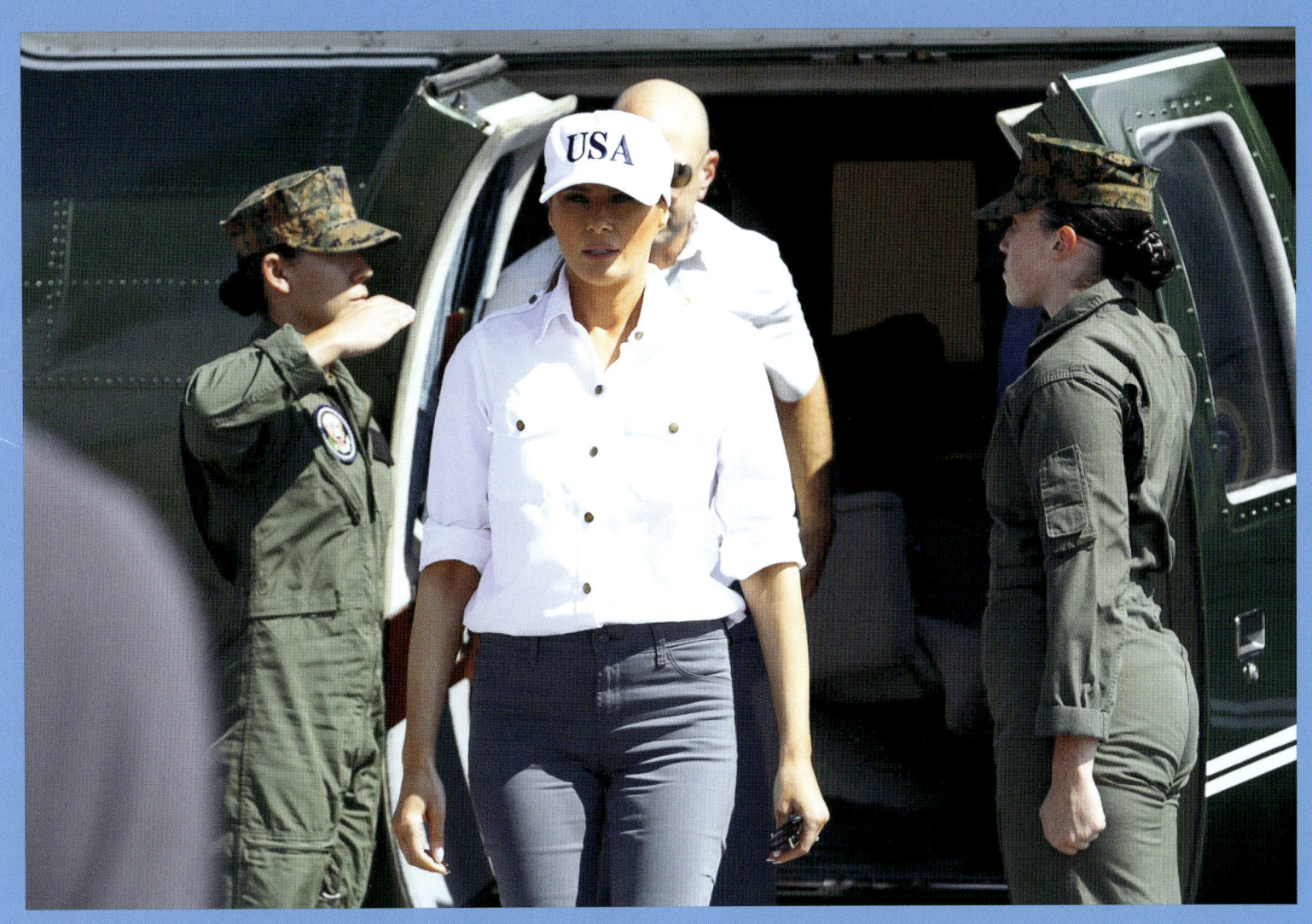

Deplaning from Marine One in Florida.[6]

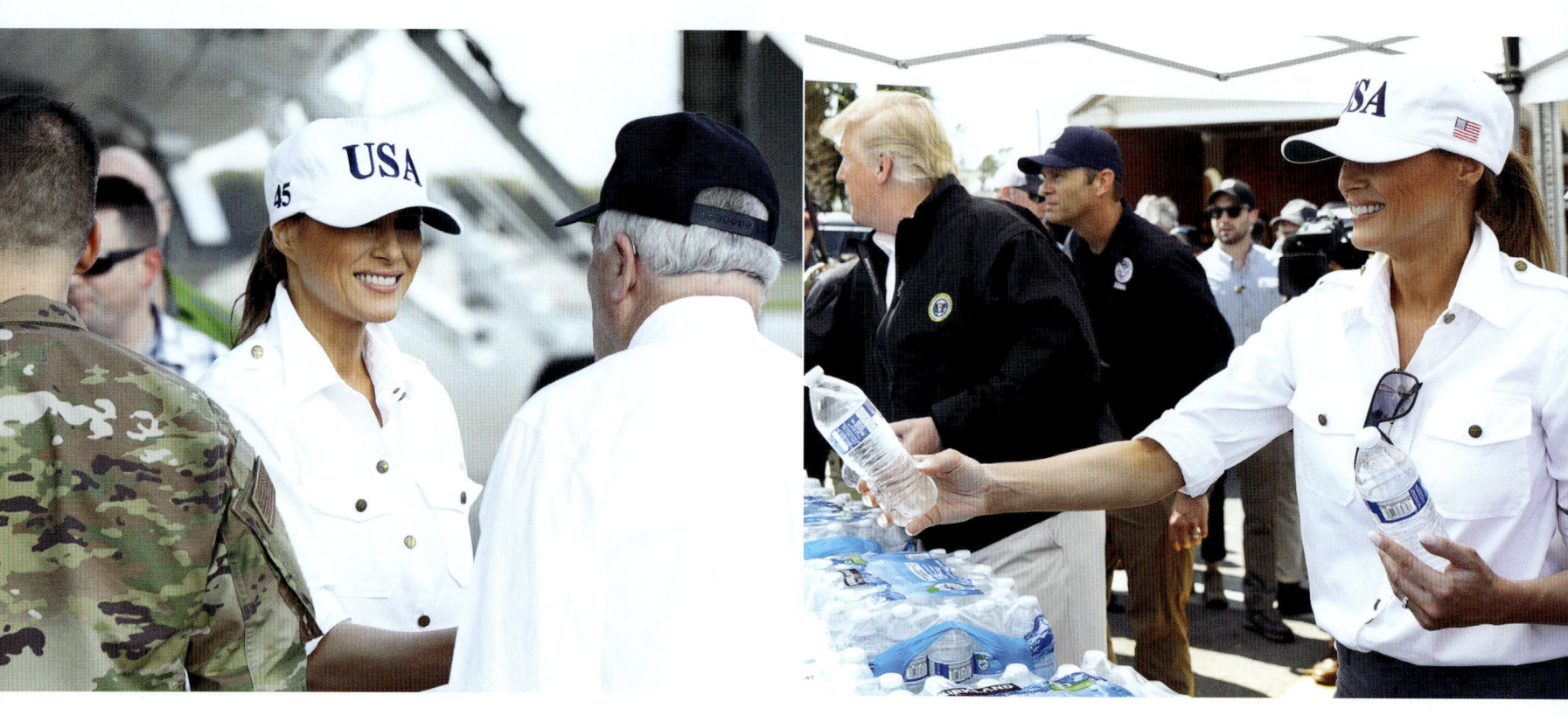

Meeting Georgia Governor Nathan Deal.[6]

Passing out water bottles and aid to victims of the hurricane, in Lynn Haven, Florida.[6]

Right: Melania Trump Speaks at a Neonatal Abstinence Syndrome roundtable discussion. NAS is a group of conditions caused when a baby withdraws from certain drugs they are exposed to in the womb. In most cases the drugs are opioids. Relief from opioid addiction is one of the cornerstones of the First Lady's BE BEST program.[23]

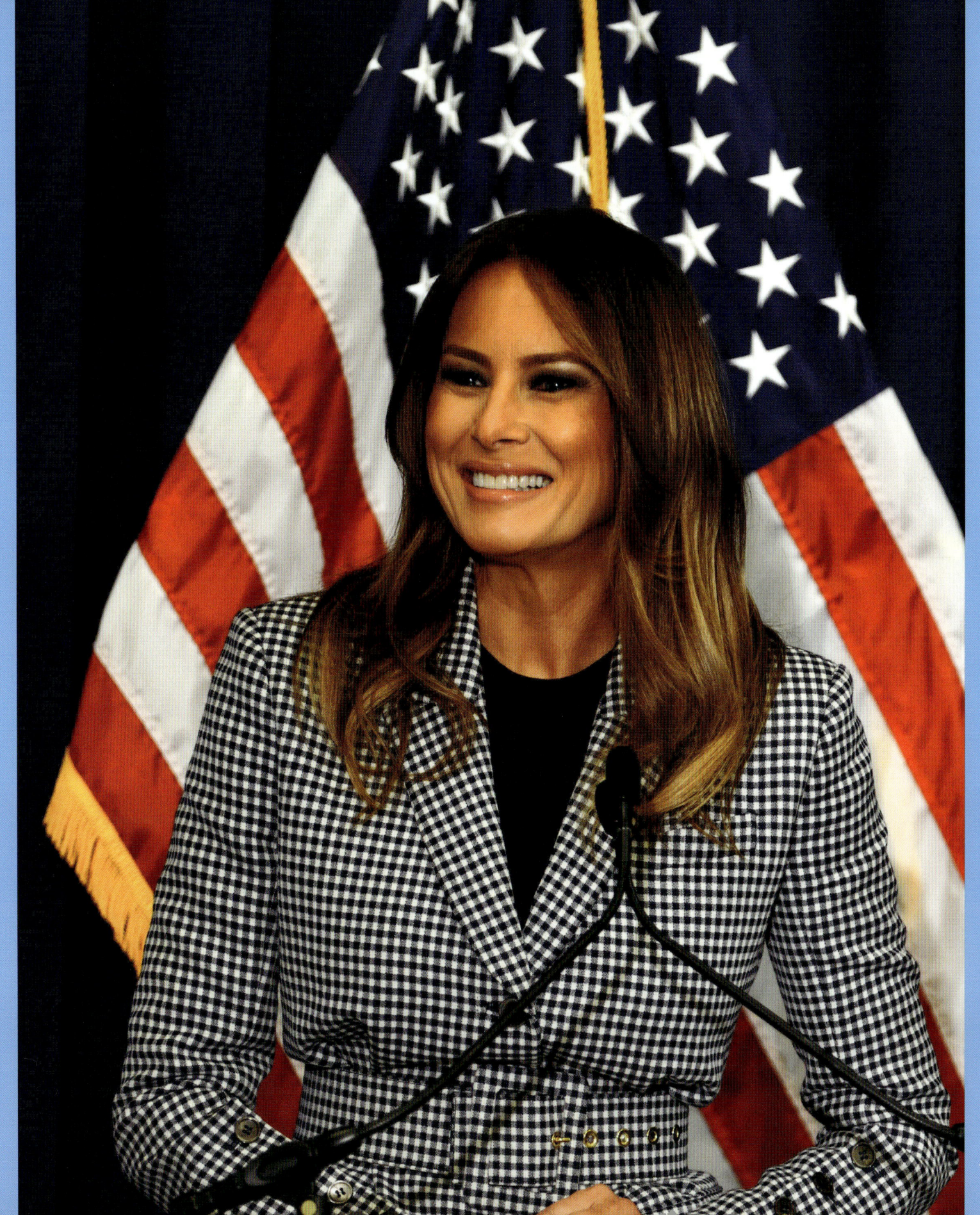

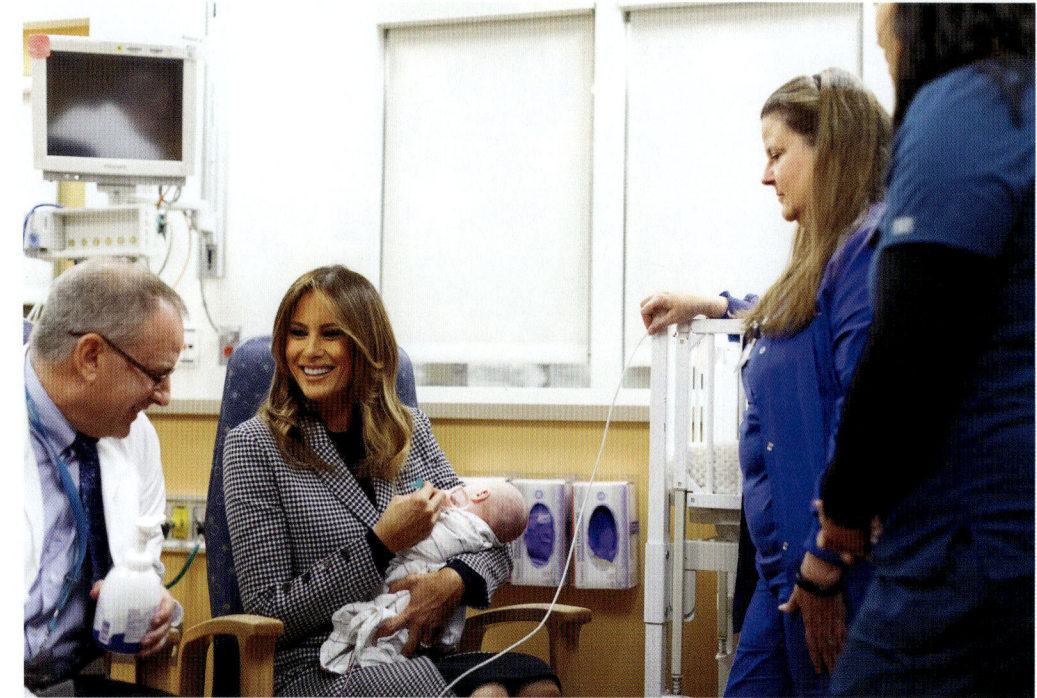

Babies and smiles at Thomas Jefferson University Hospital.[6]

Mrs. Trump visits babies and chats with doctors about Neonatal Abstinence Syndrome.[6]

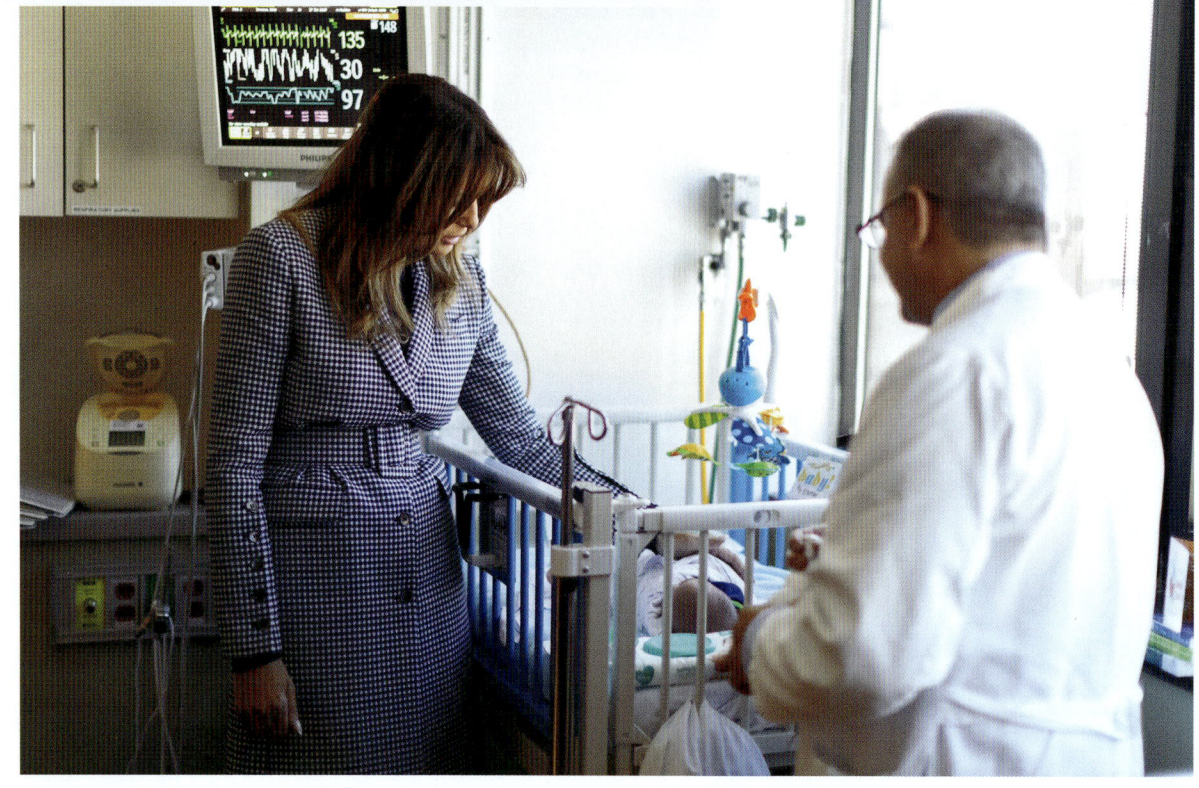

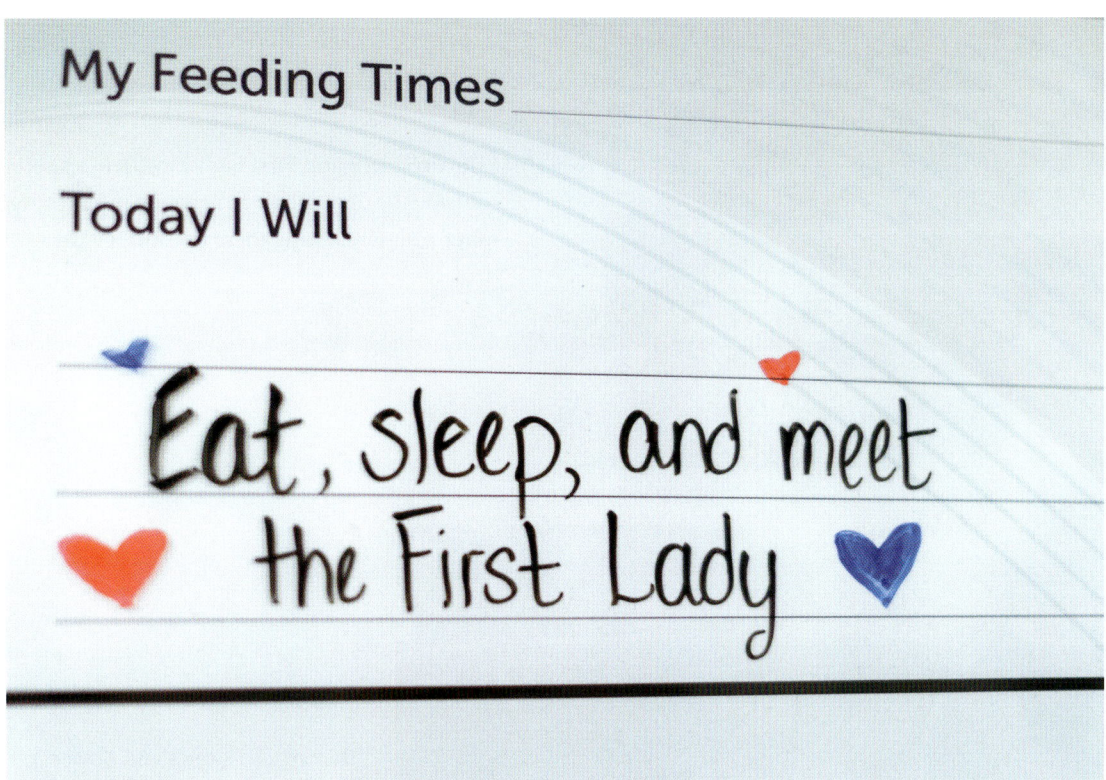

A message for the First Lady.[6]

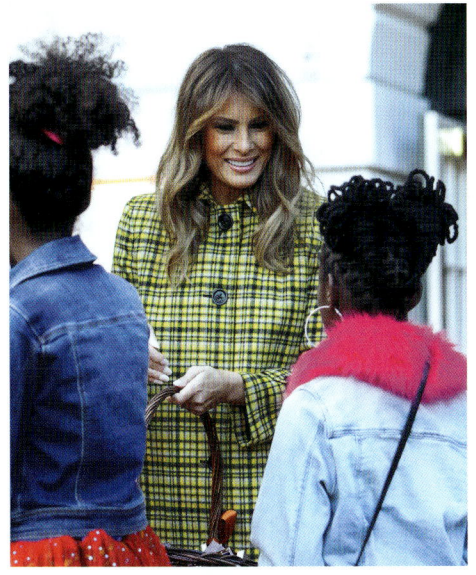

Trick or Treat at the White House.
Handing out candy.[6]

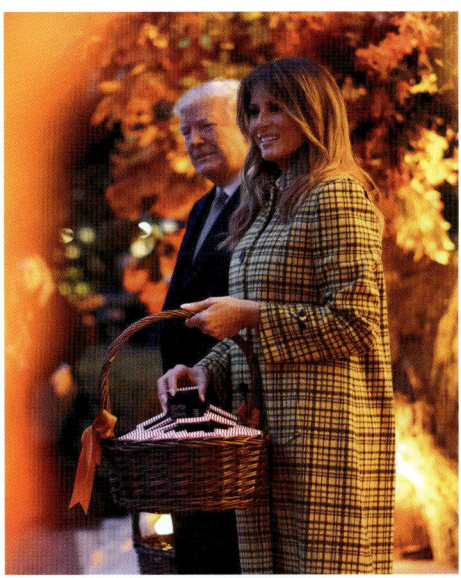

The presidential couple with
their candy baskets.[6]

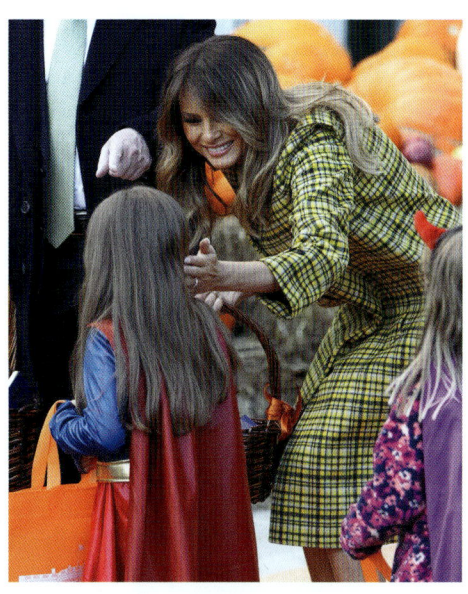

Supergirl gets a treat![6]

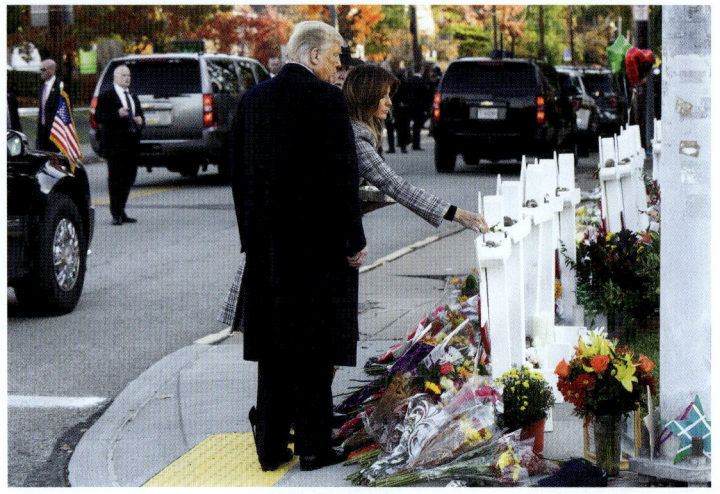

The President and First Lady pay their respects outside the Tree of Life Synagogue in Pittsburg after a mass shooting there in October 2018.[6]

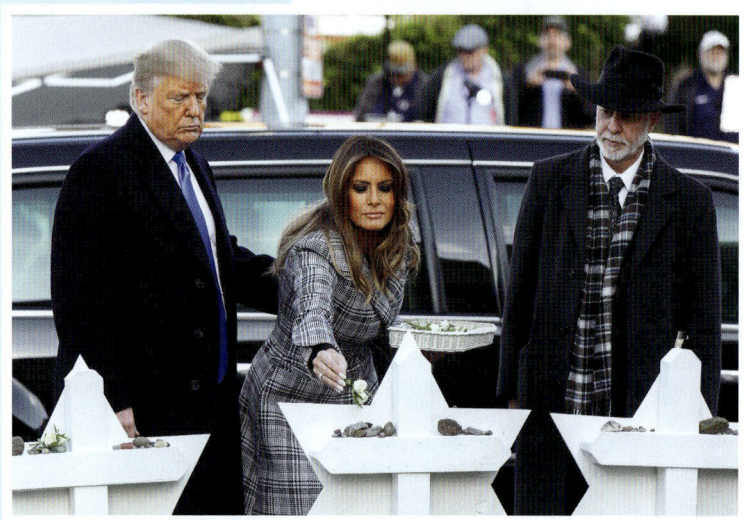

They placed stones and flowers on the memorial of the shooting.[6]

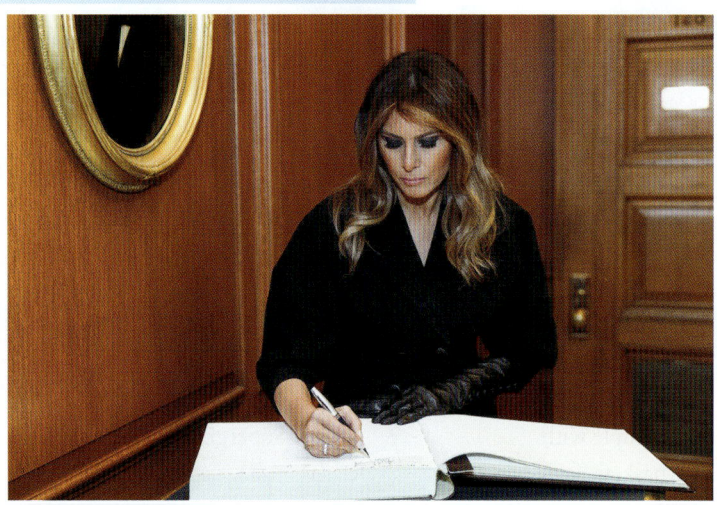

Elegance visits the Supreme Court.[5]

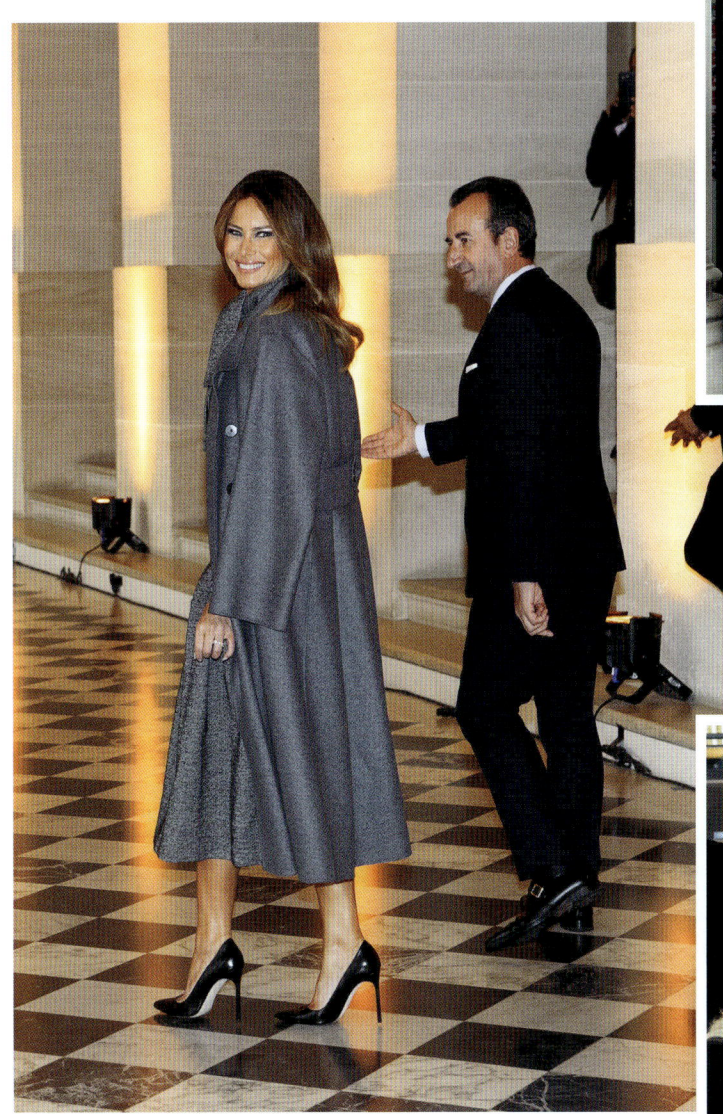

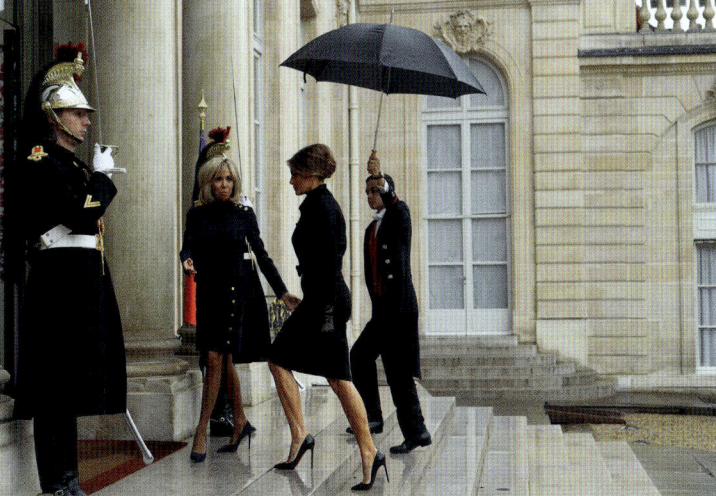

First Lady Melania Trump arrives at the Élysée Palace in Paris, Saturday, Nov. 10, 2018, and is greeted by Mrs. Brigitte Macron wife of French President Emmanuel Macron.[6]

Arrival at the Palace of Versailles.[6]

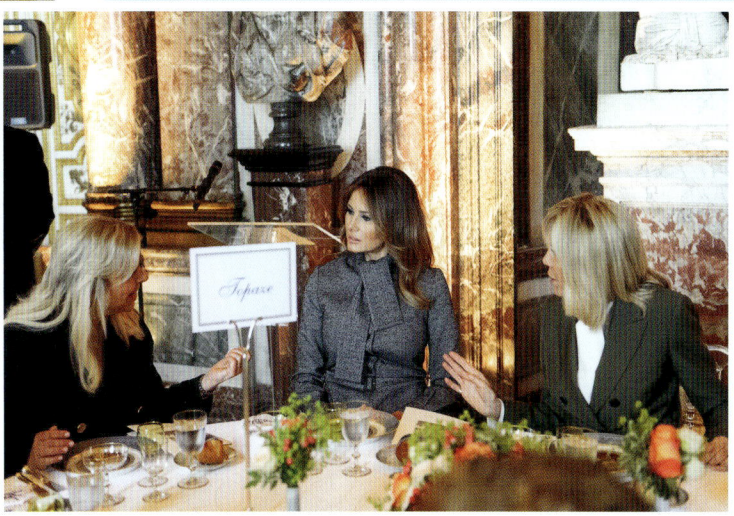

At luncheon with Sara Netanyahu and Brigitte Macron at the Salon de Vénus in the Palace of Versailles in France.[6]

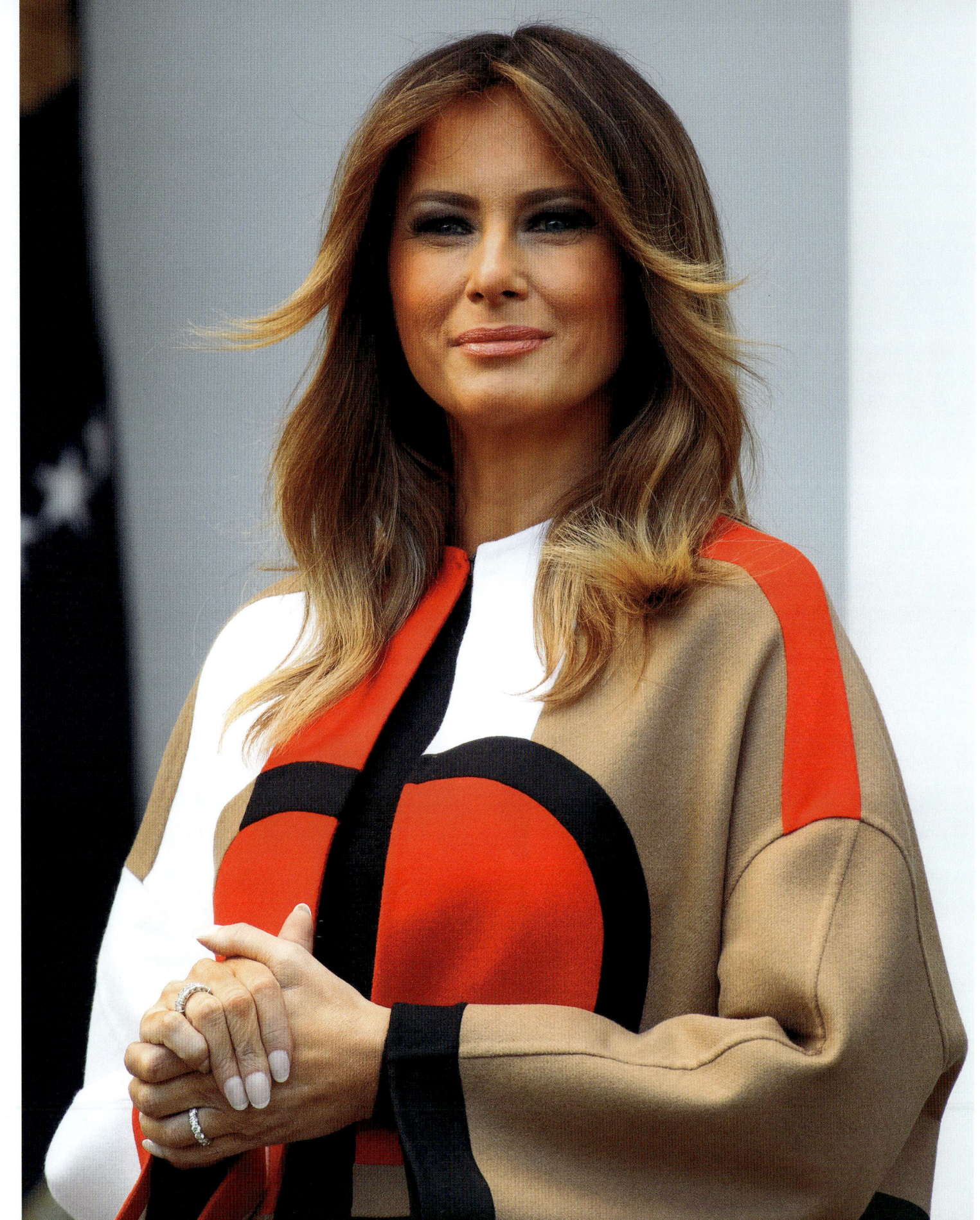

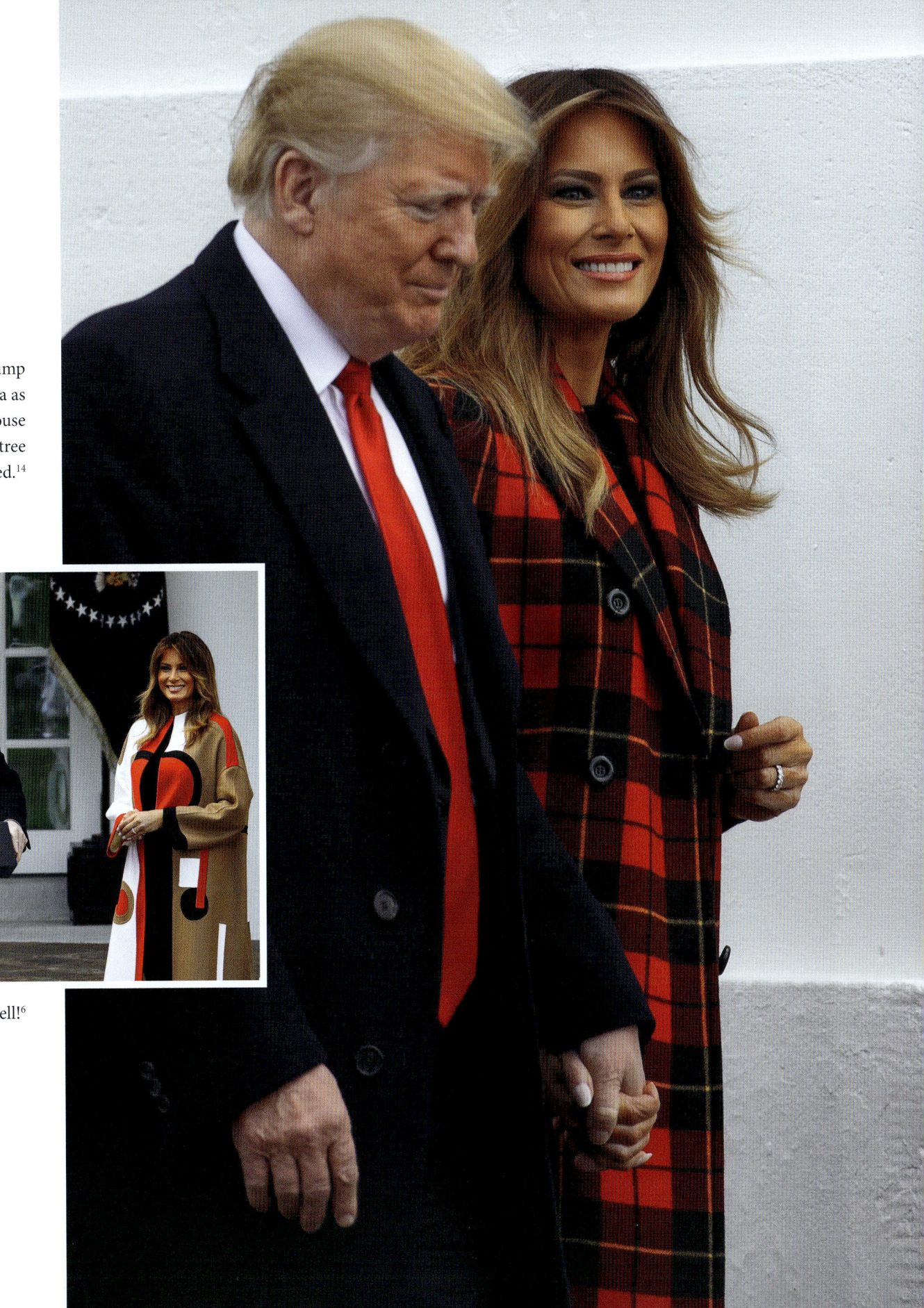

President Trump watches with Melania as the official White House Christmas tree is delivered.[14]

Carrots the turkey gets his pardon as well![6]

Left: The First Lady listens in on Peas the turkey's pardon by President Trump for Thanksgiving.[14]

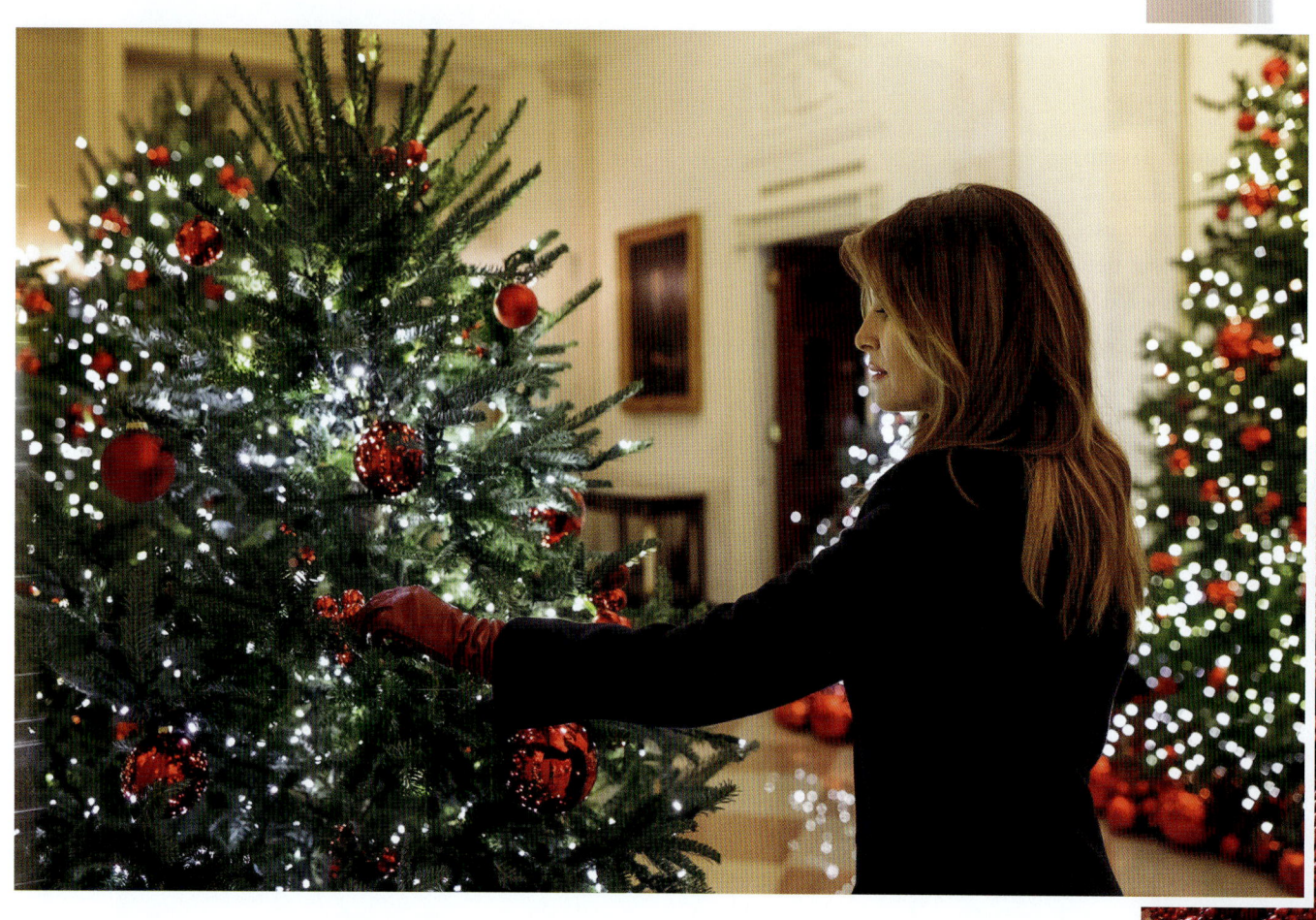

Touching up the White House Christmas decorations.[6]

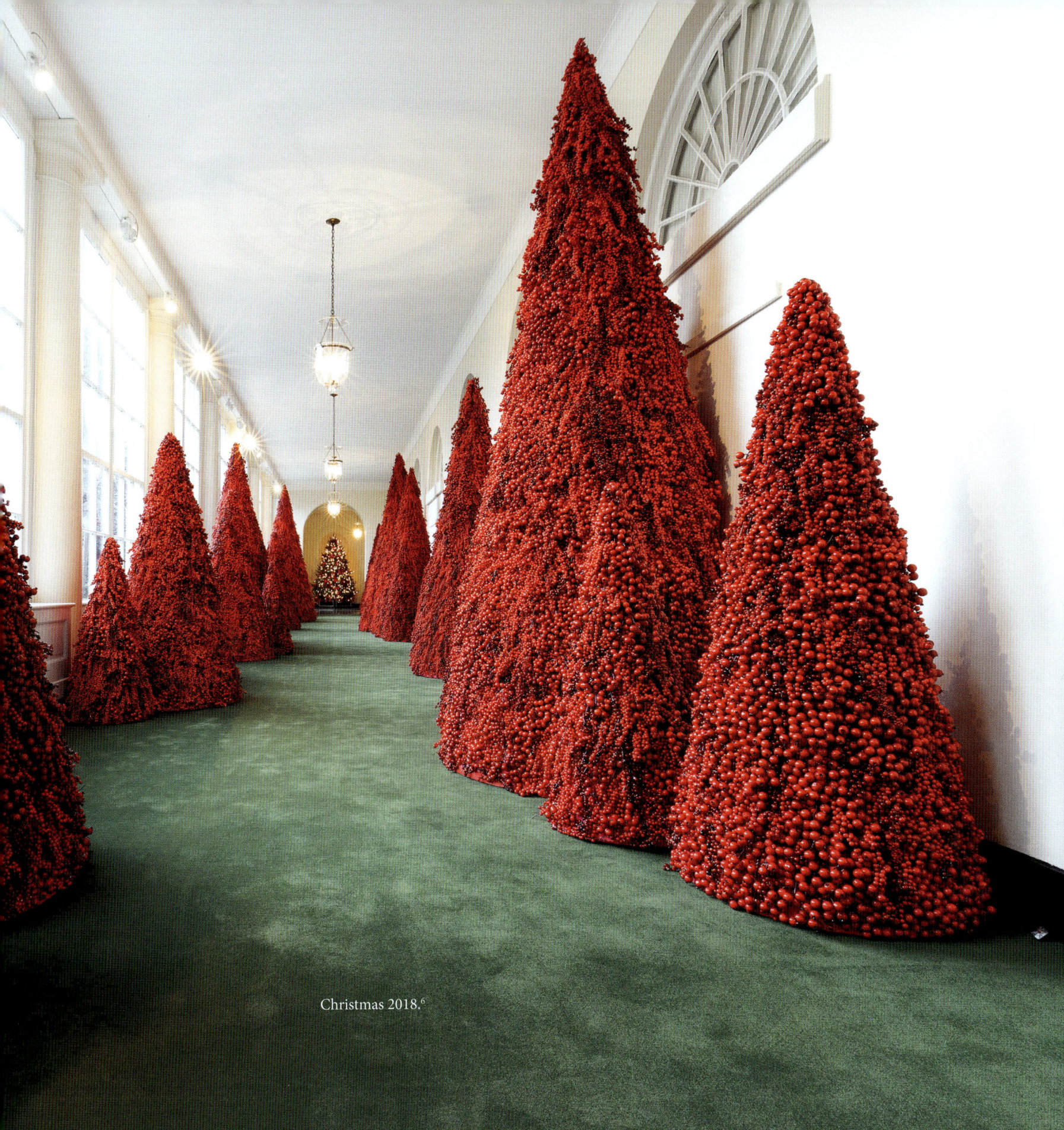

Christmas 2018.[6]

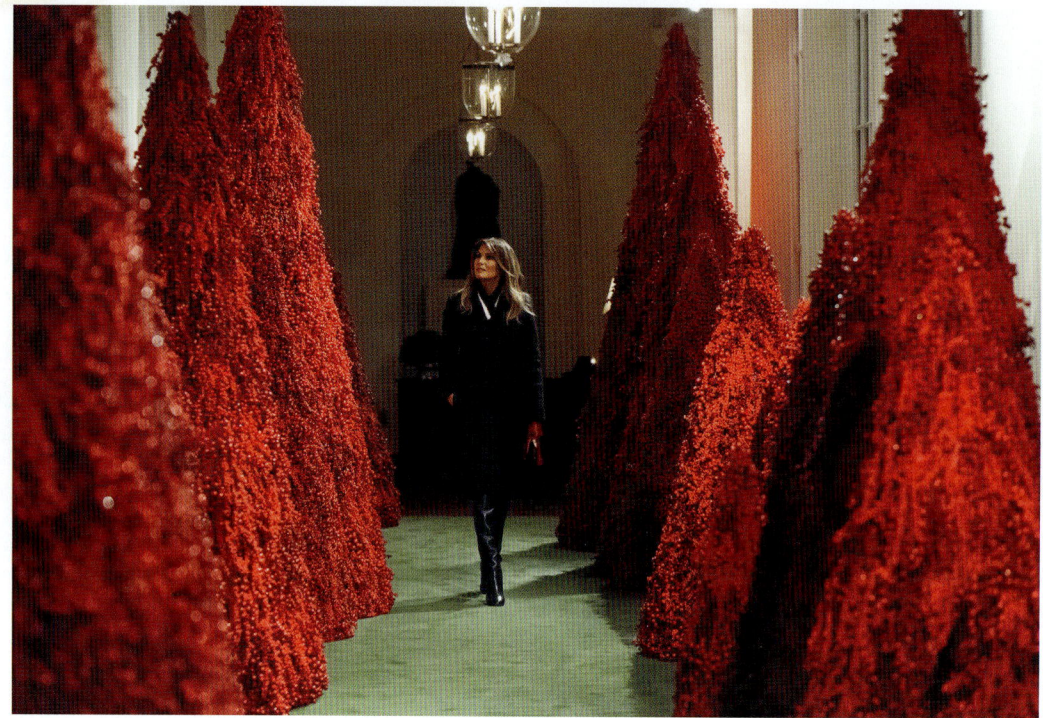

Inspecting the East Colonnade.[6]

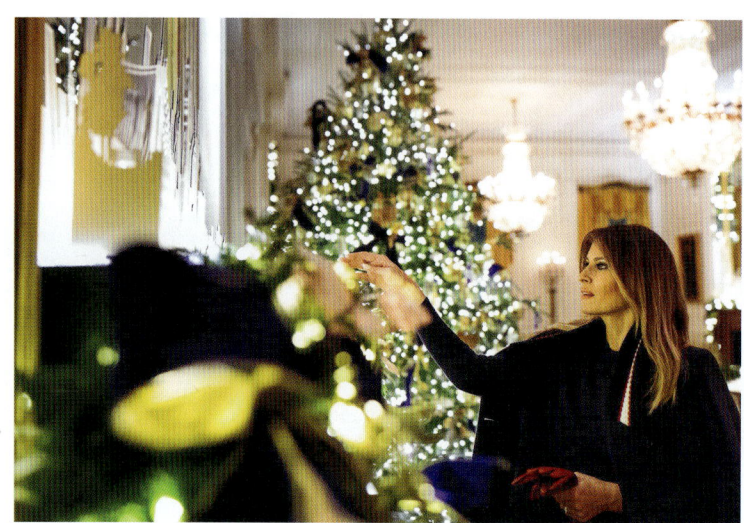

Pure elegance in the lights.[6]

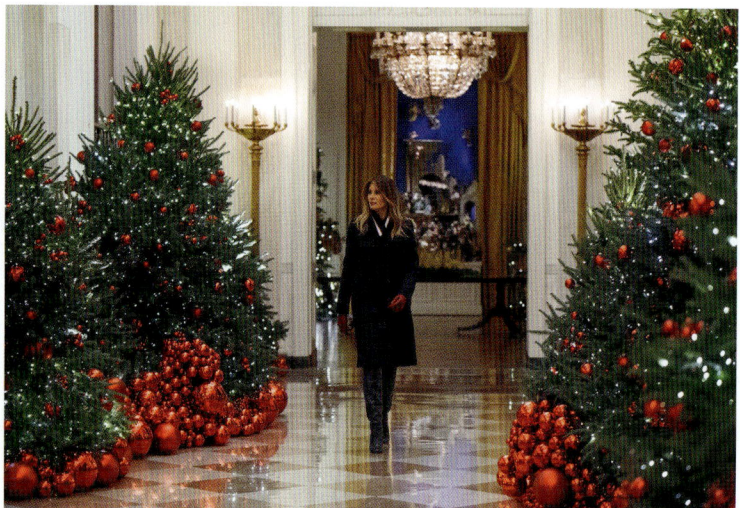

Everything looks fantastic! [6]

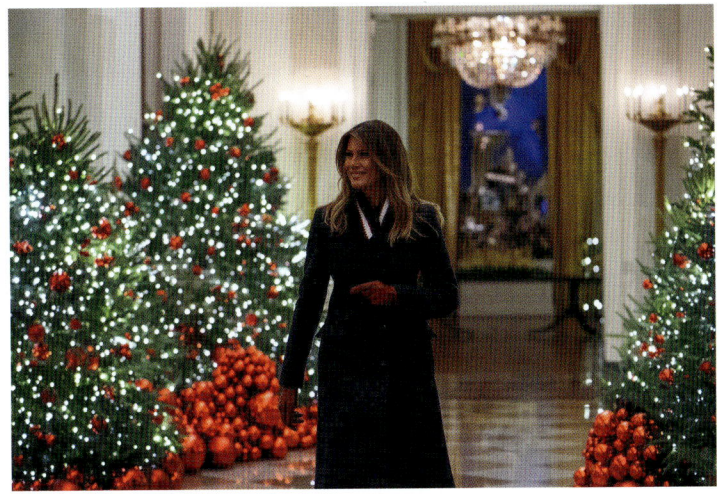

Perfection![6]

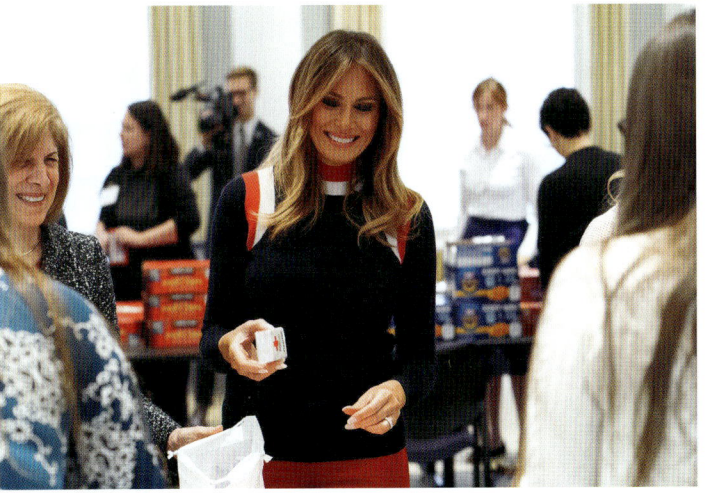

Making Red Cross care packages for overseas military personnel.[6]

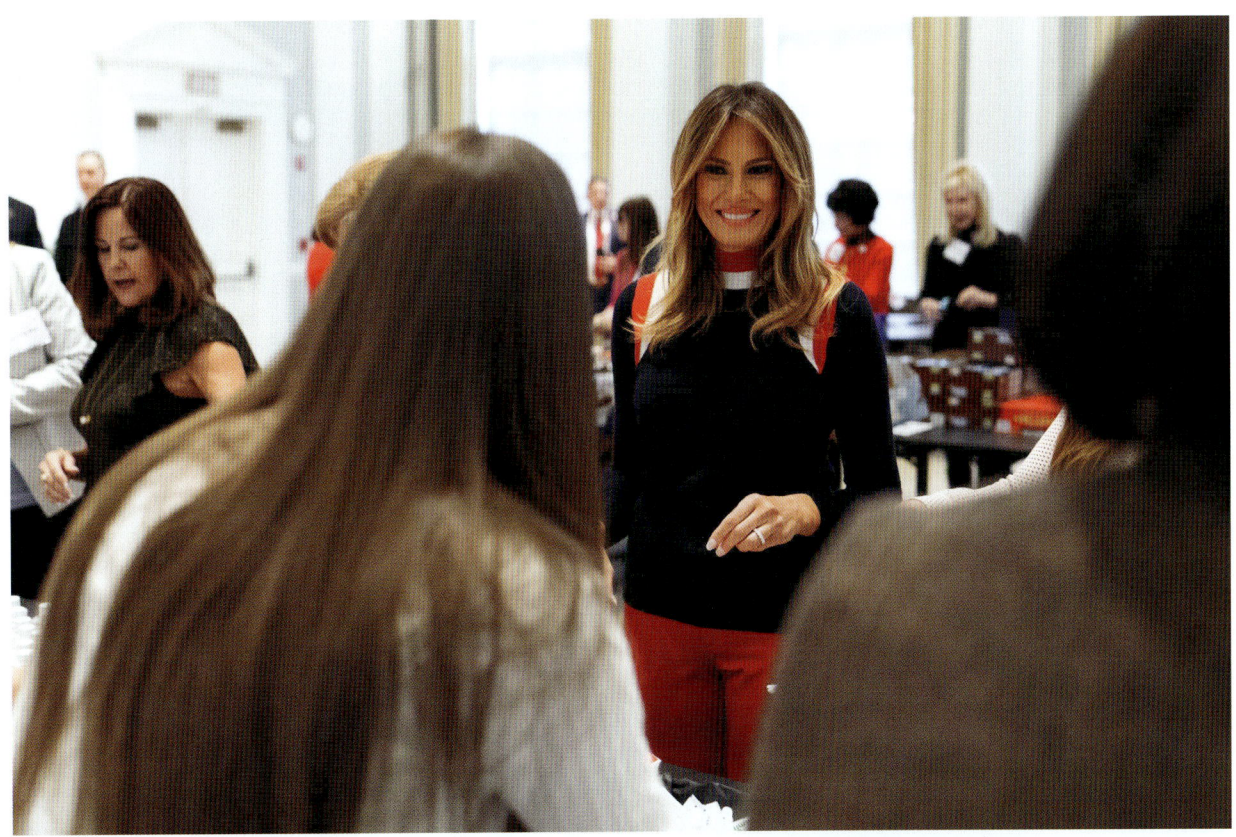

Melania Trump and Mrs. Karen Pence help volunteers assemble military comfort kits for deployed American troops.

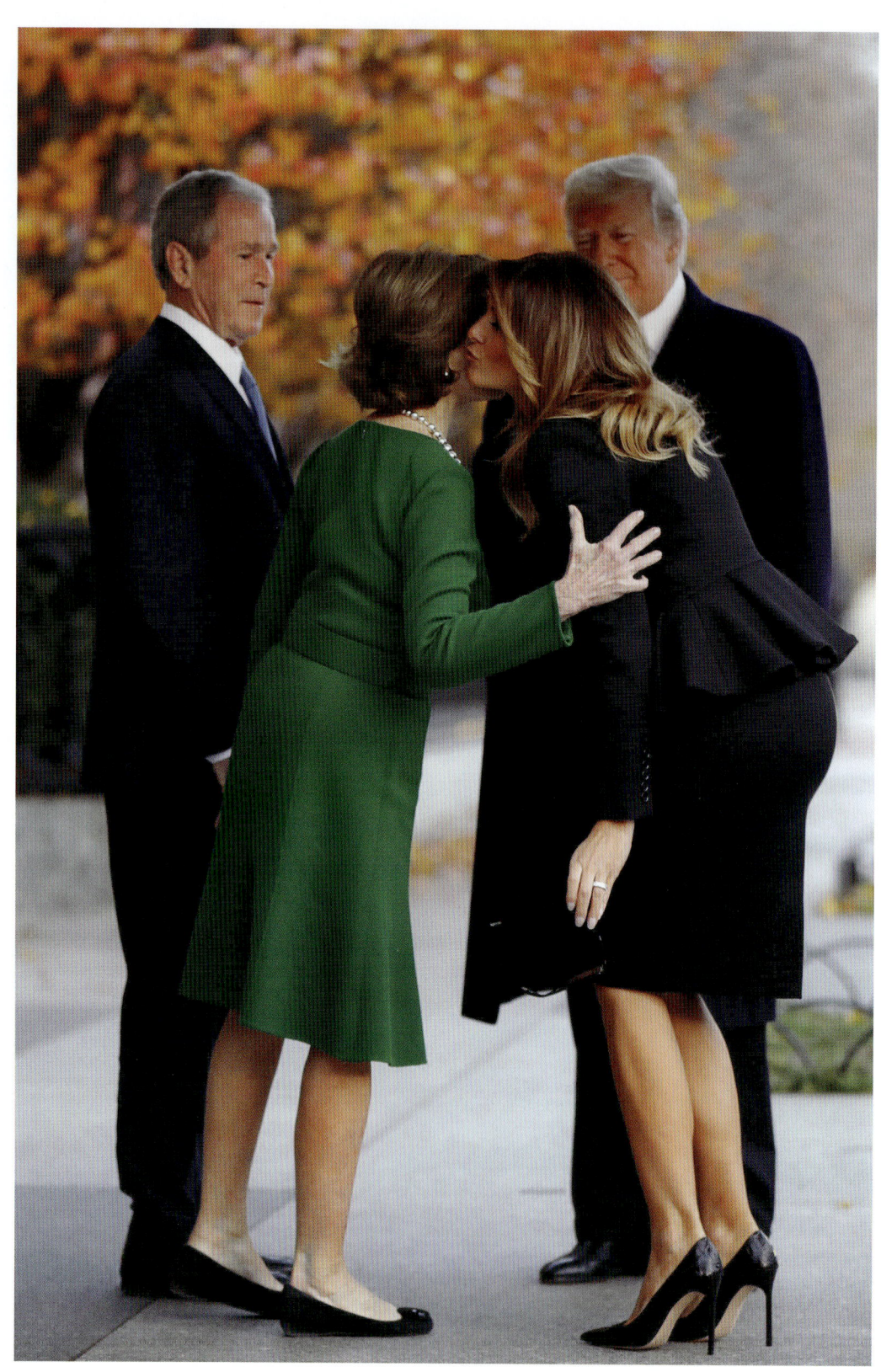

The Trumps pay their condolences to the Bush family prior to George Herbert Walker Bush's funeral.[3]

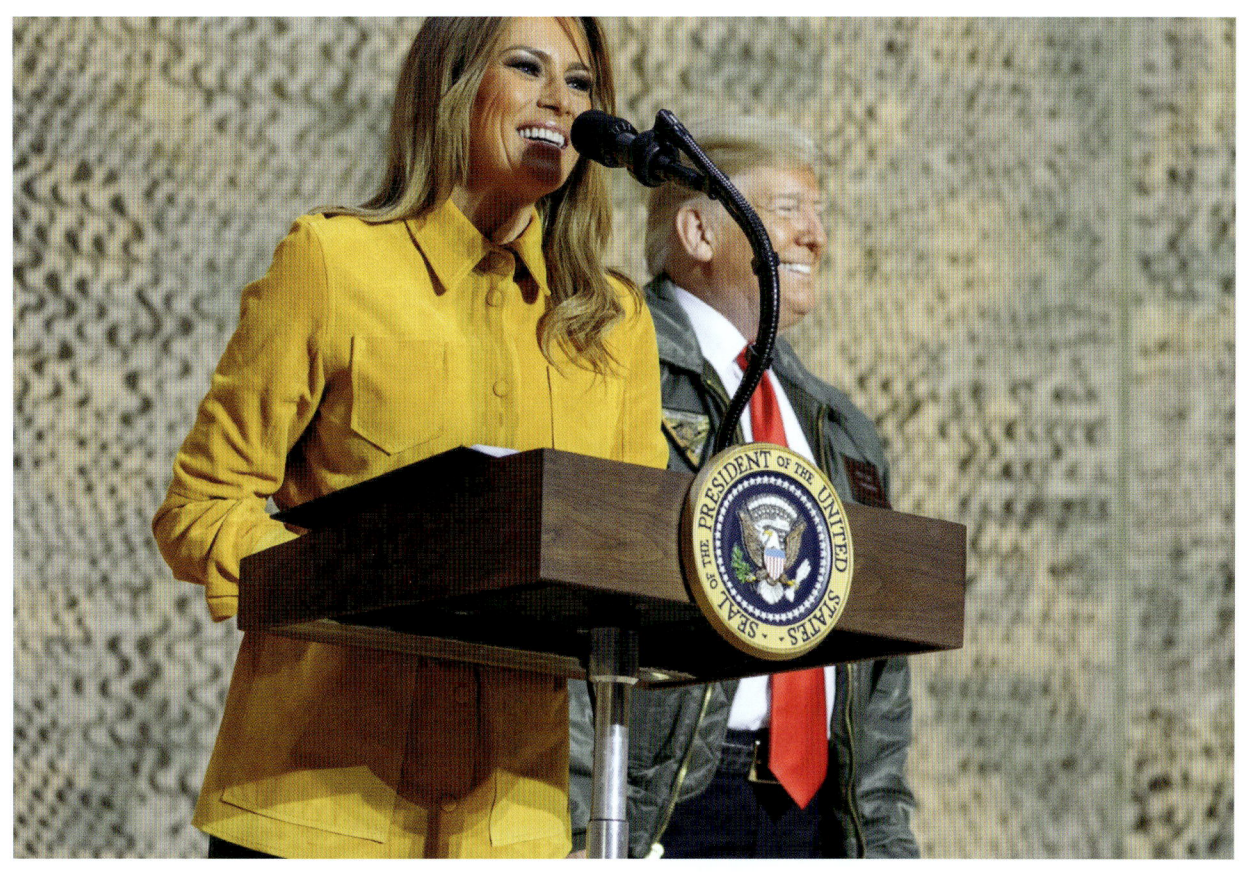

The First Lady speaks to the troops at Al-Asad Airbase in Iraq.[5]

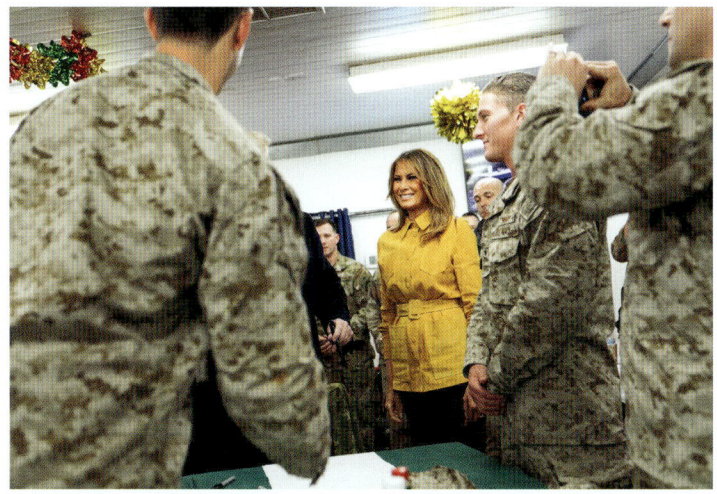

Spending time and shaking hands with military personnel in Iraq.[5]

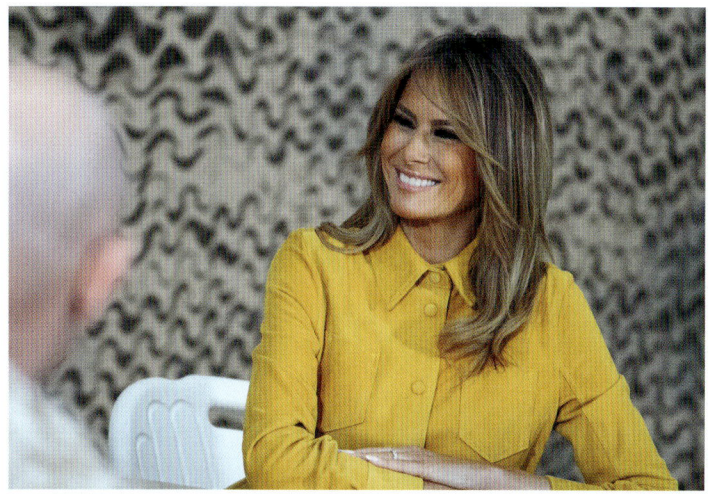

Attending a military briefing with military leaders in Iraq.[5]

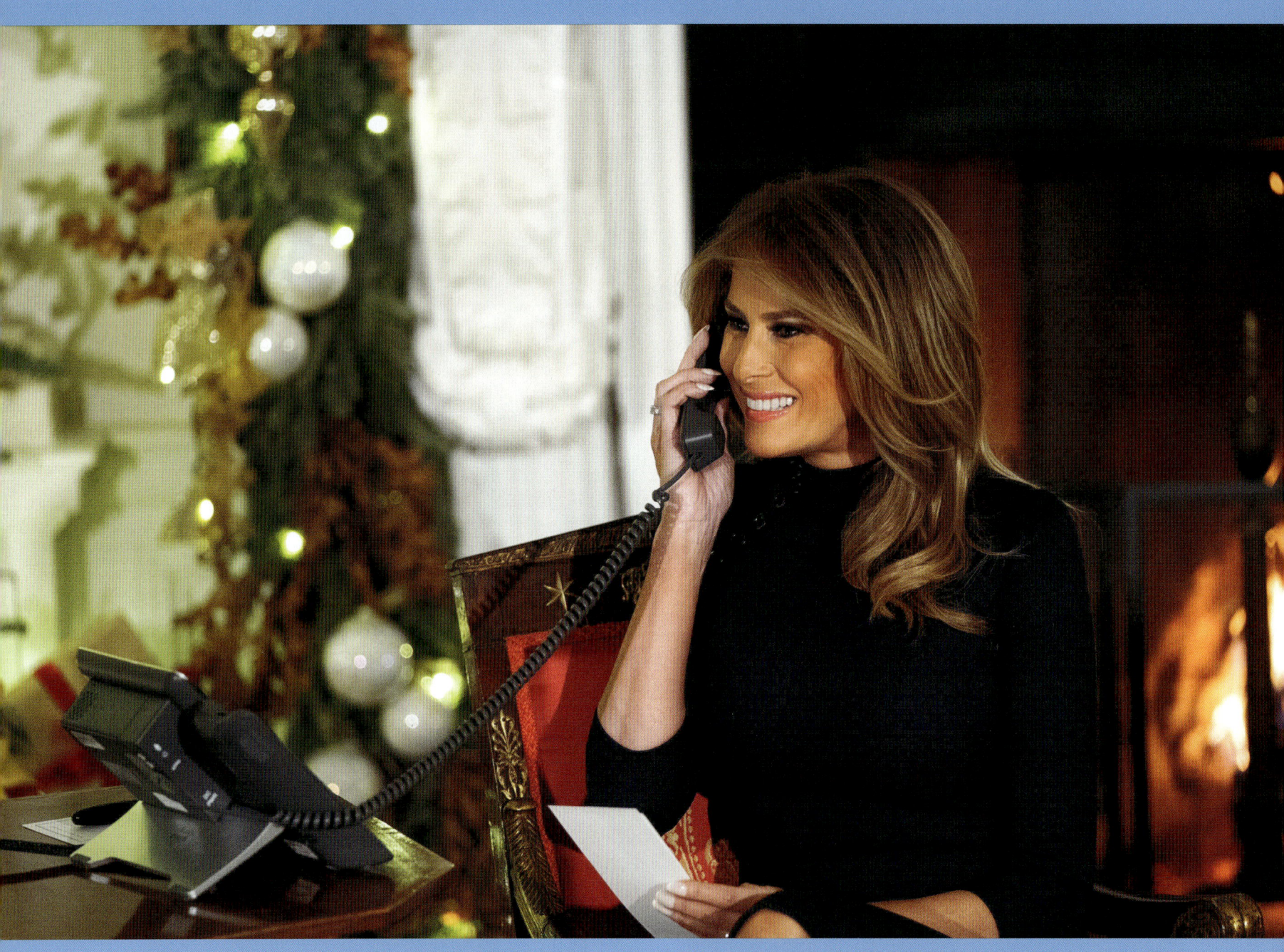

Melania Trump on the phone with NORAD, tracking Santa Claus' location on Christmas Eve. Tracker calls have been a Christmas Eve tradition for sixty years to keep track of Santa's delivery route.[5]

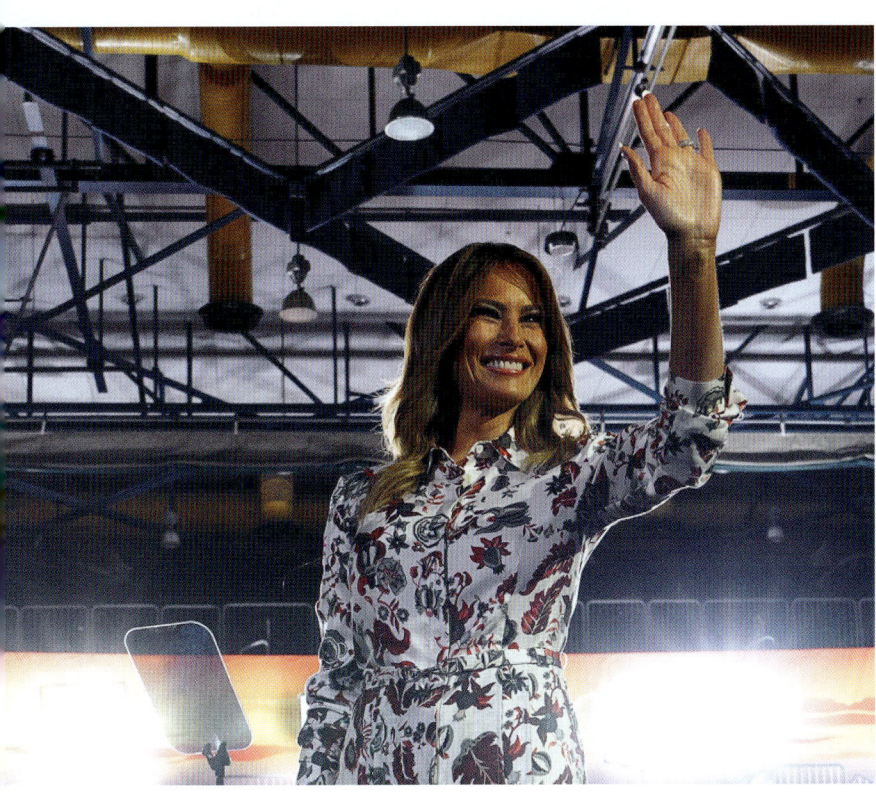

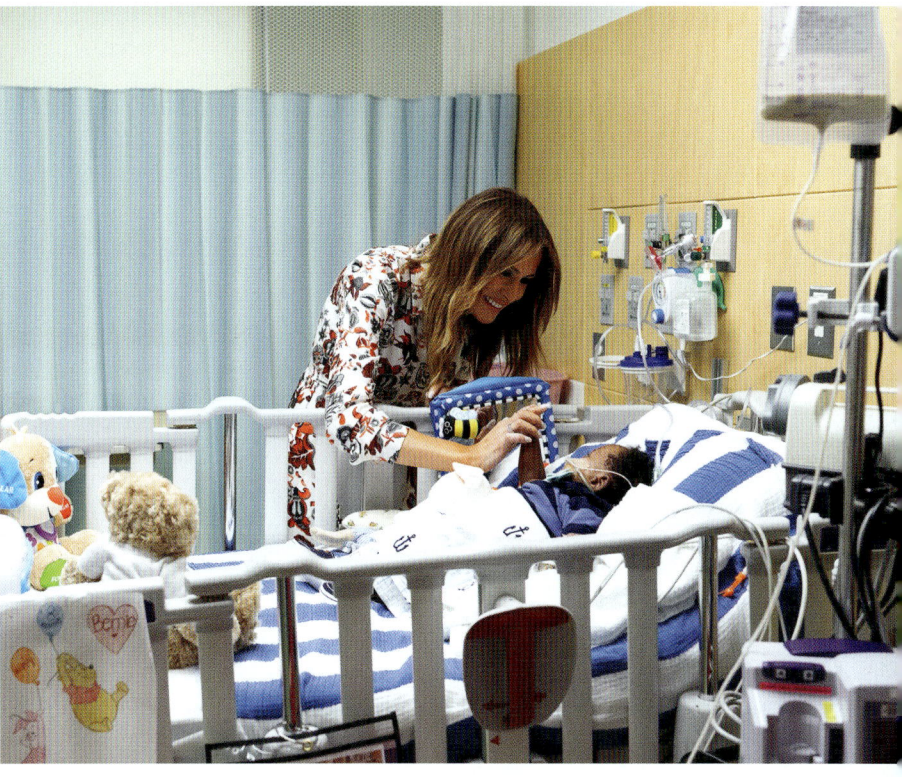

Mrs. Trump waves to members of the US Venezuelan community after remarks by her husband.[6]

The First Lady is all smiles as she meets eight-month-old Bernard McClain at the Nicklaus Children's Hospital in Miami.[6]

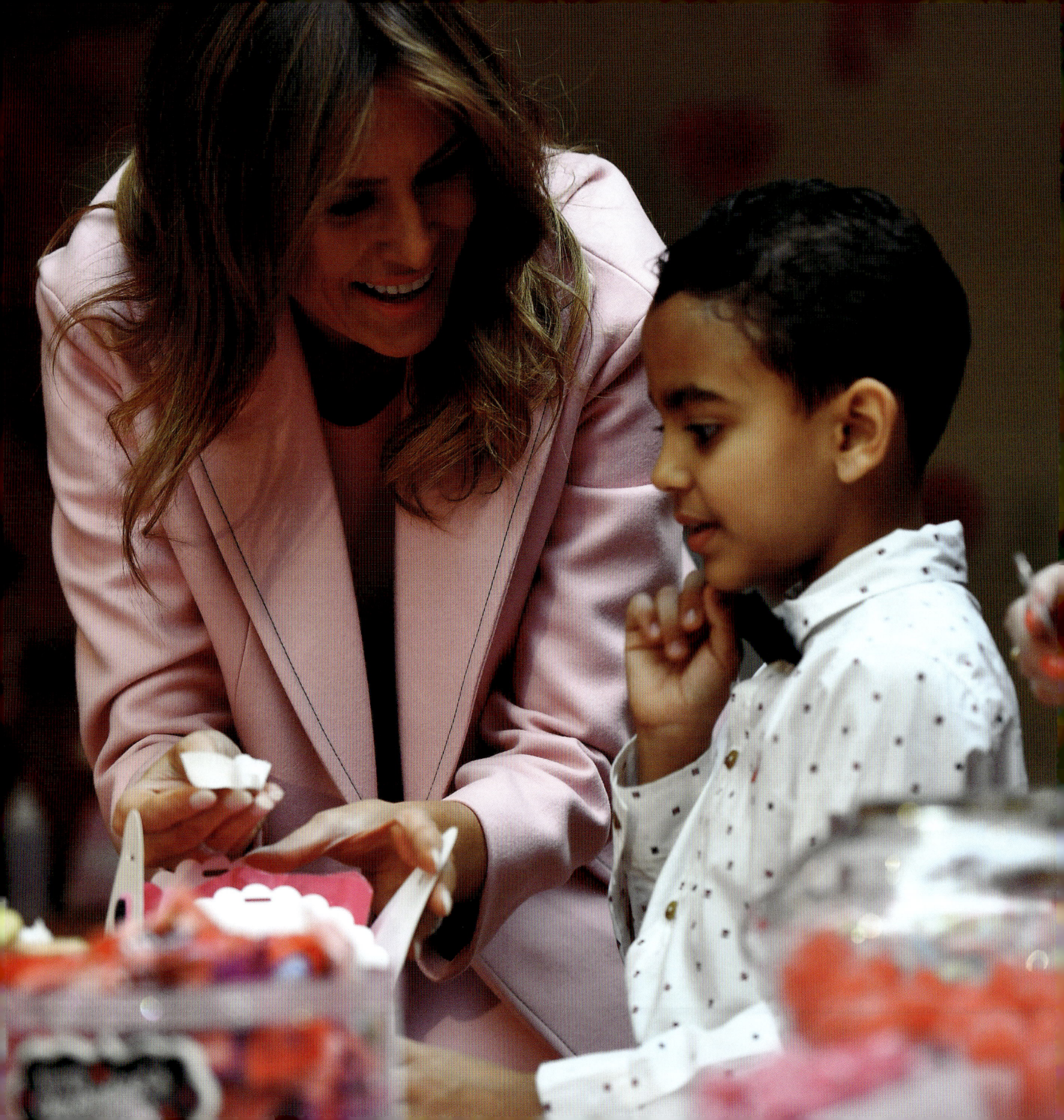

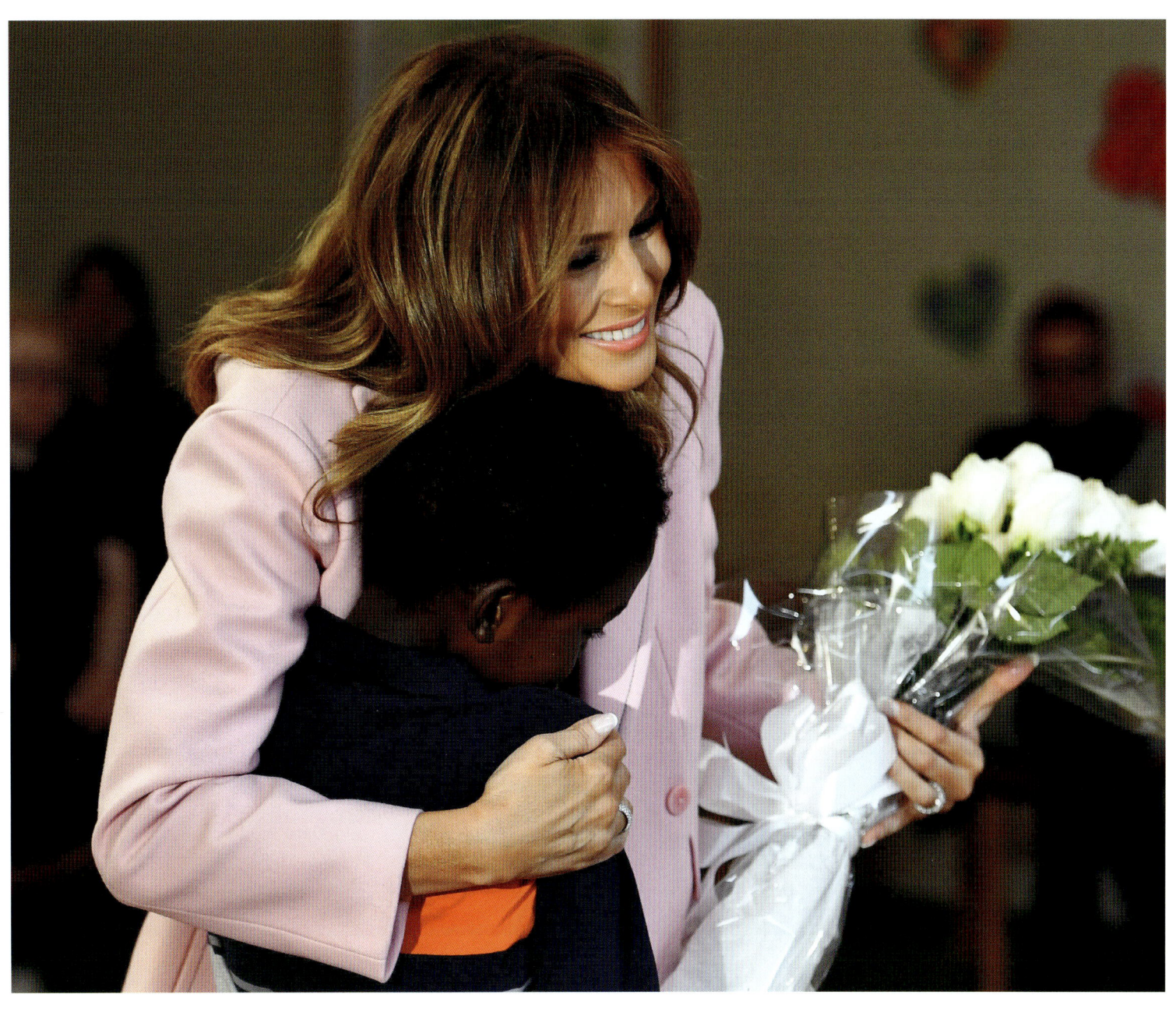

The First Lady gets hugs and flowers from Amani,
a child from Kenya at the Children's Inn at the National Institute of Health in Bethesda, Maryland.[12]

Left: Happy Valentine's Day![12]

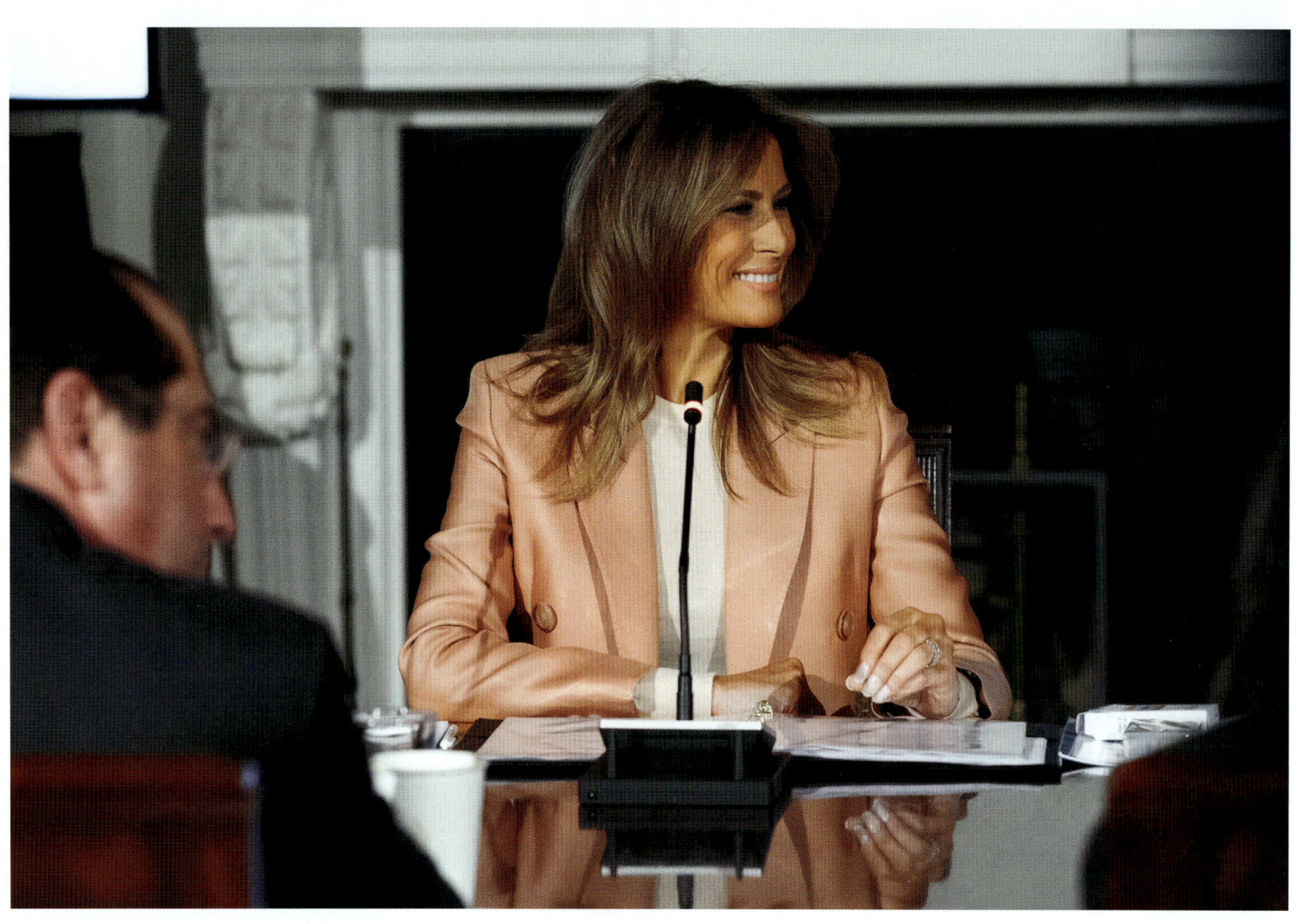

BE BEST interagency meeting focusing on the three pillars of the program: well-being of children, social media safety, and families affected by opioid abuse. Mrs. Trump led the meeting and gave opening remarks.[6]

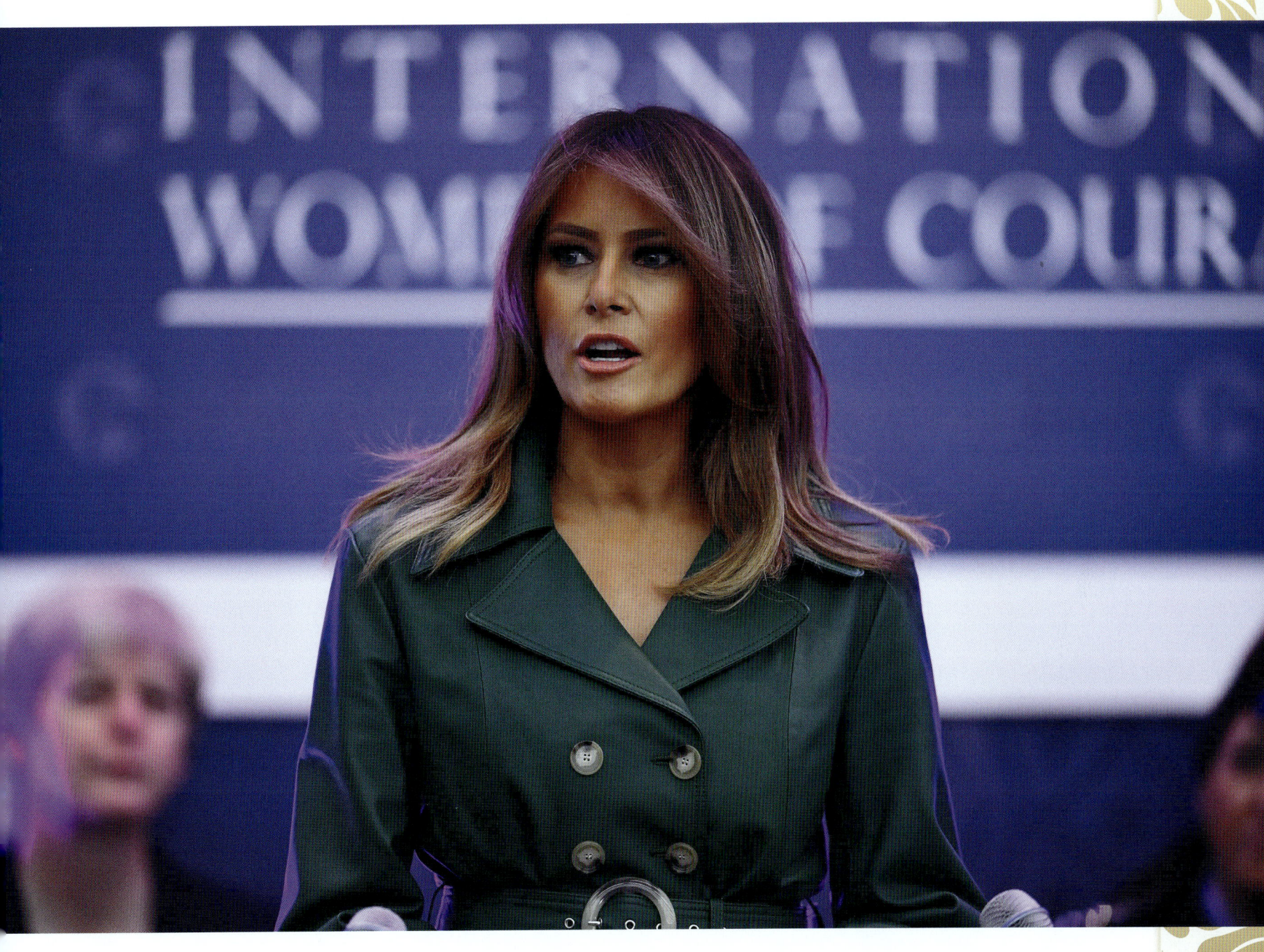

Speaking at the 2019 International Women of Courage awards.[12]

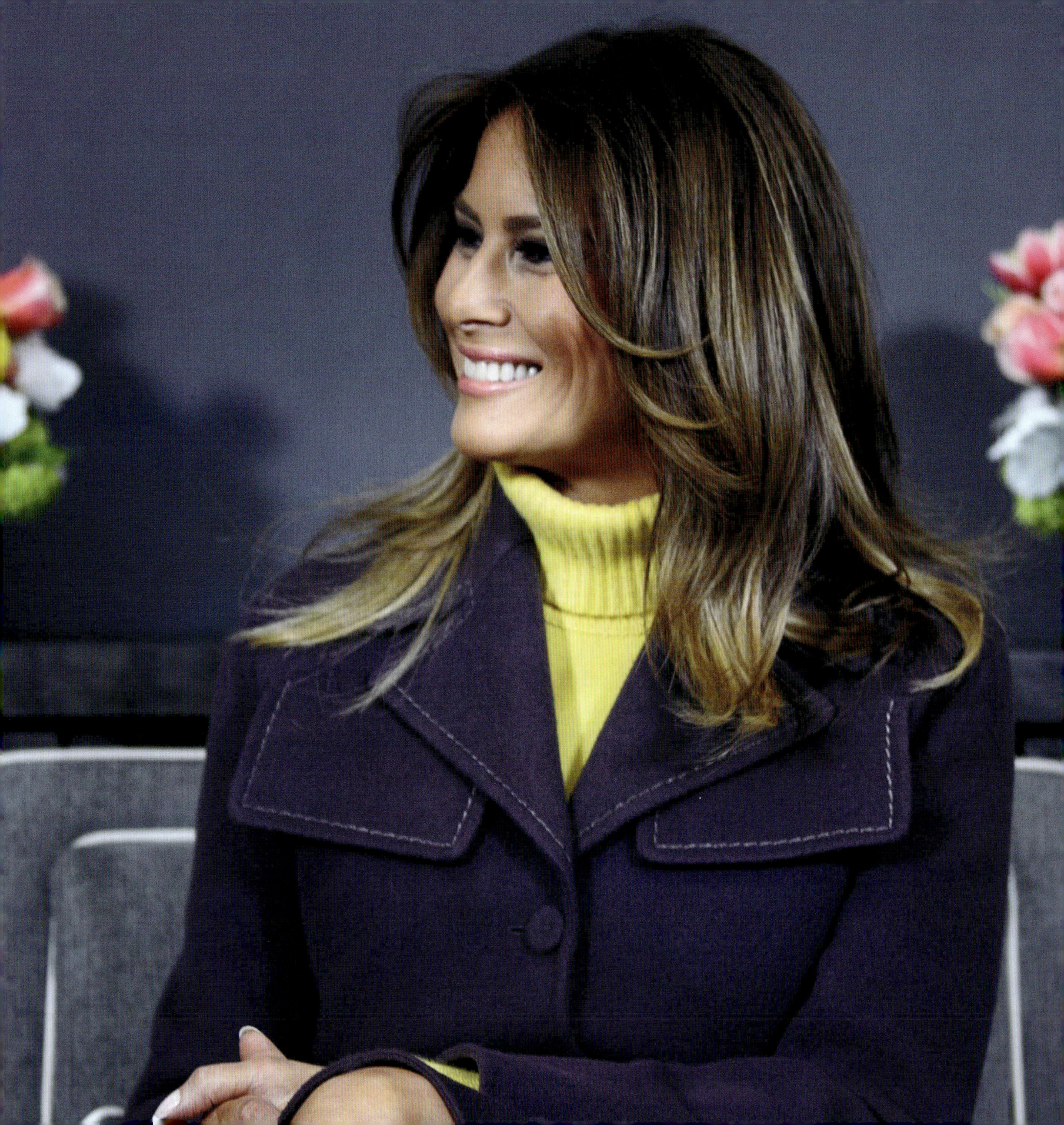

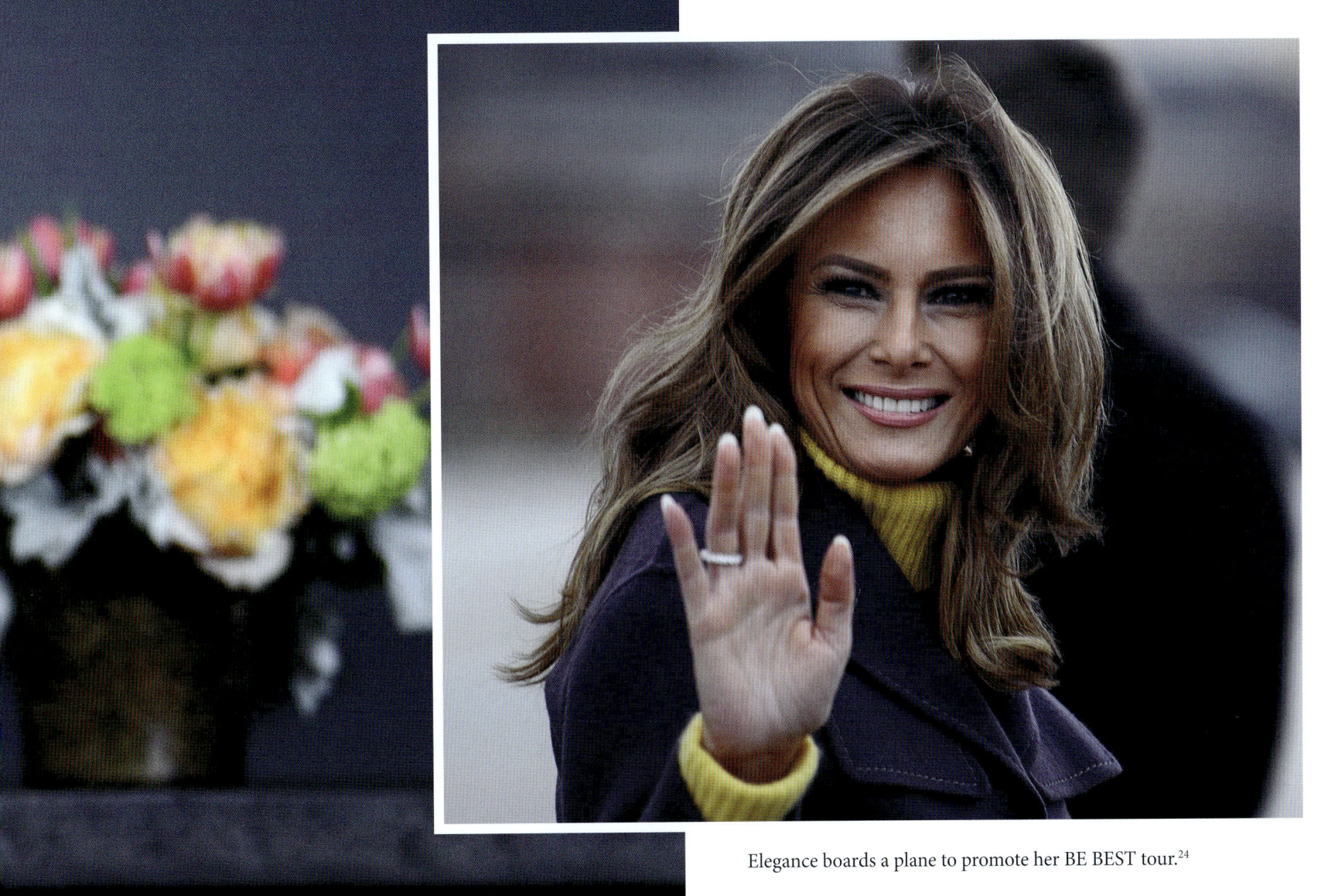

Elegance boards a plane to promote her BE BEST tour.[24]

The First Lady on her BE BEST tour.[24]

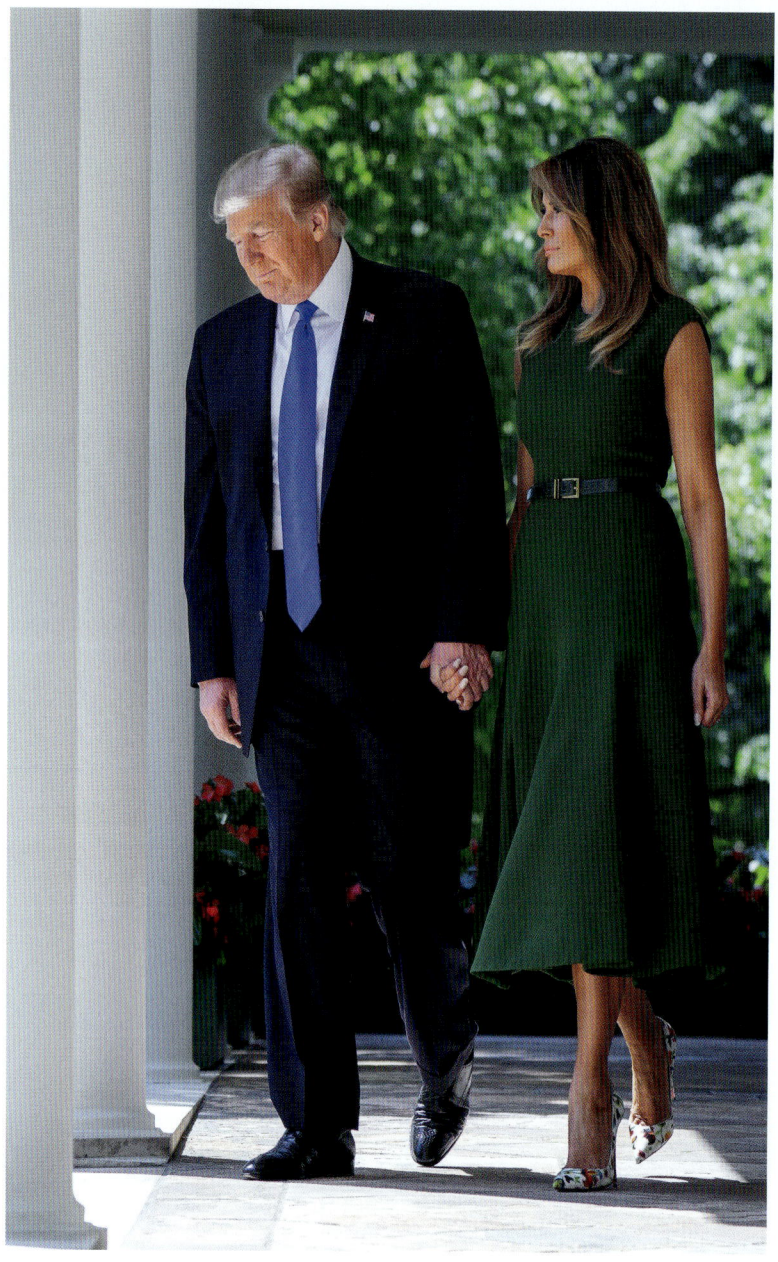

The President and First Lady walk along the Colonnade prior to attending the National Day of Prayer service in the Rose Garden of the White House.[9]

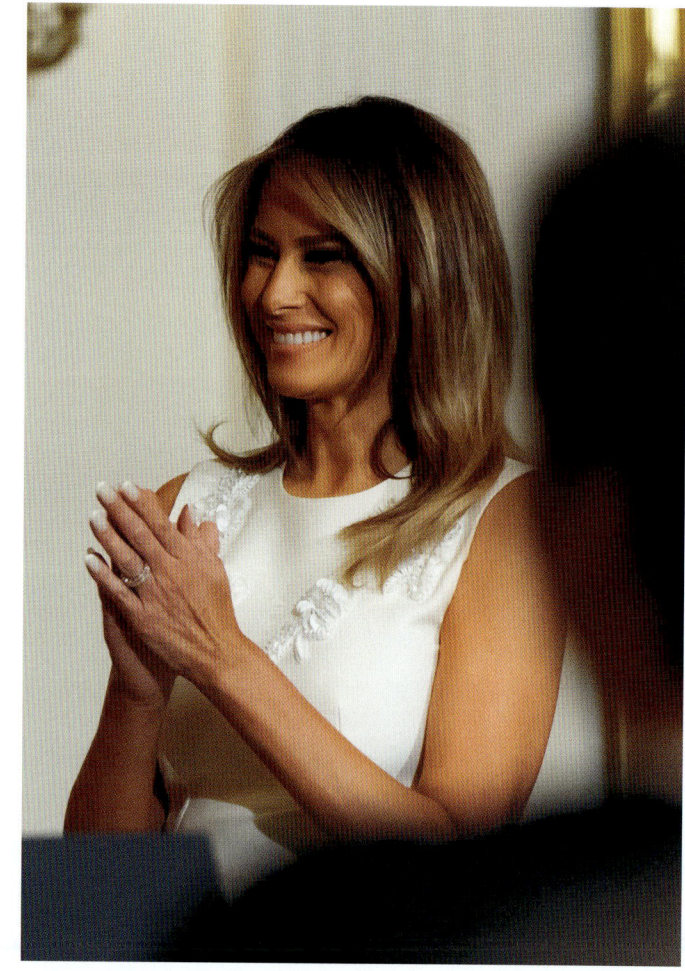

First Lady Melania Trump beams during the Celebration of Military Mothers in the East Room of the White House, May 10, 2019.[6]

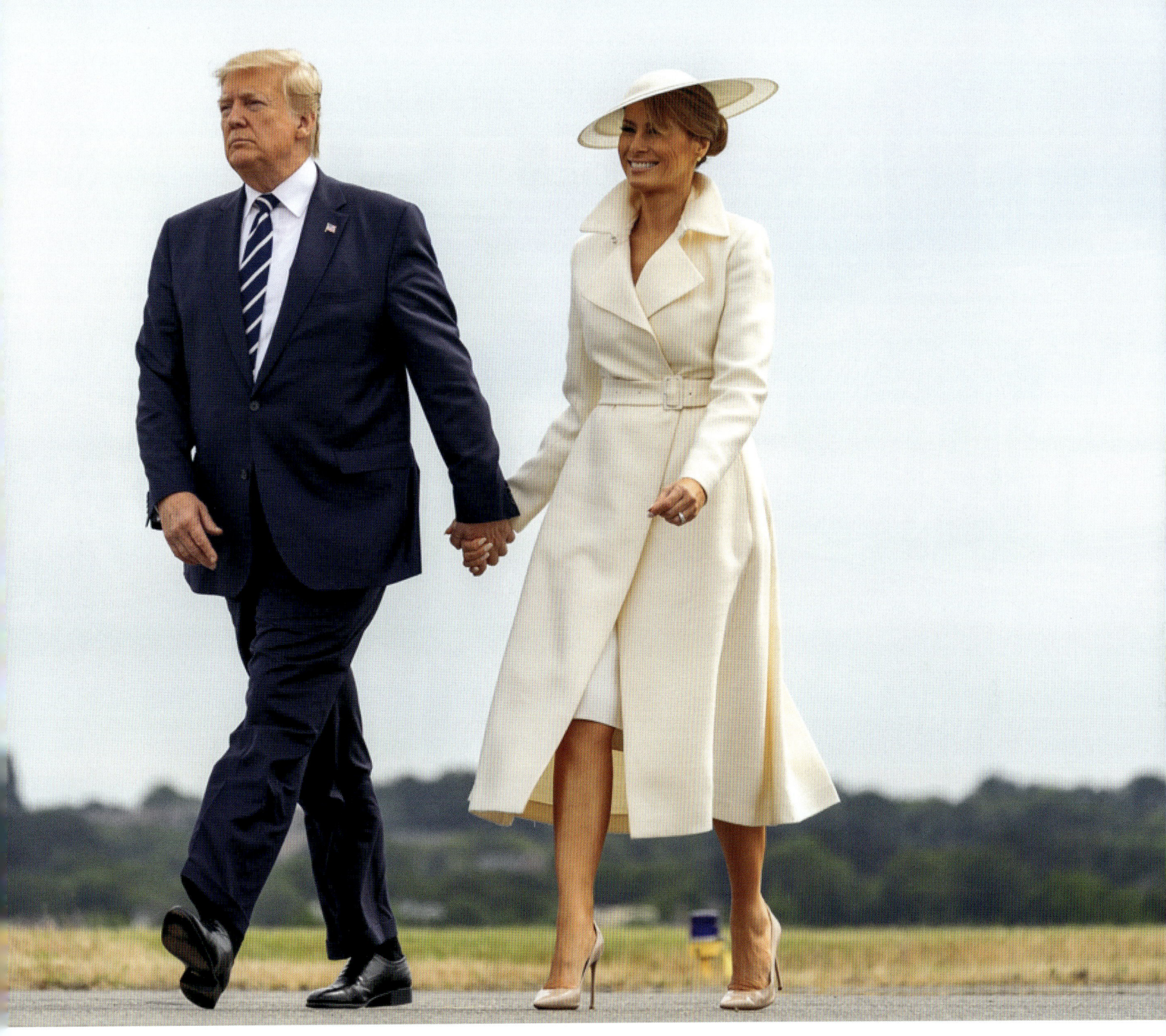

President Donald J. Trump and First Lady Melania Trump walk to Air Force One at Southampton Airport in Southampton, England, Wednesday, June 5, 2019, en route to Shannon Airport in Shannon, Ireland.[5]

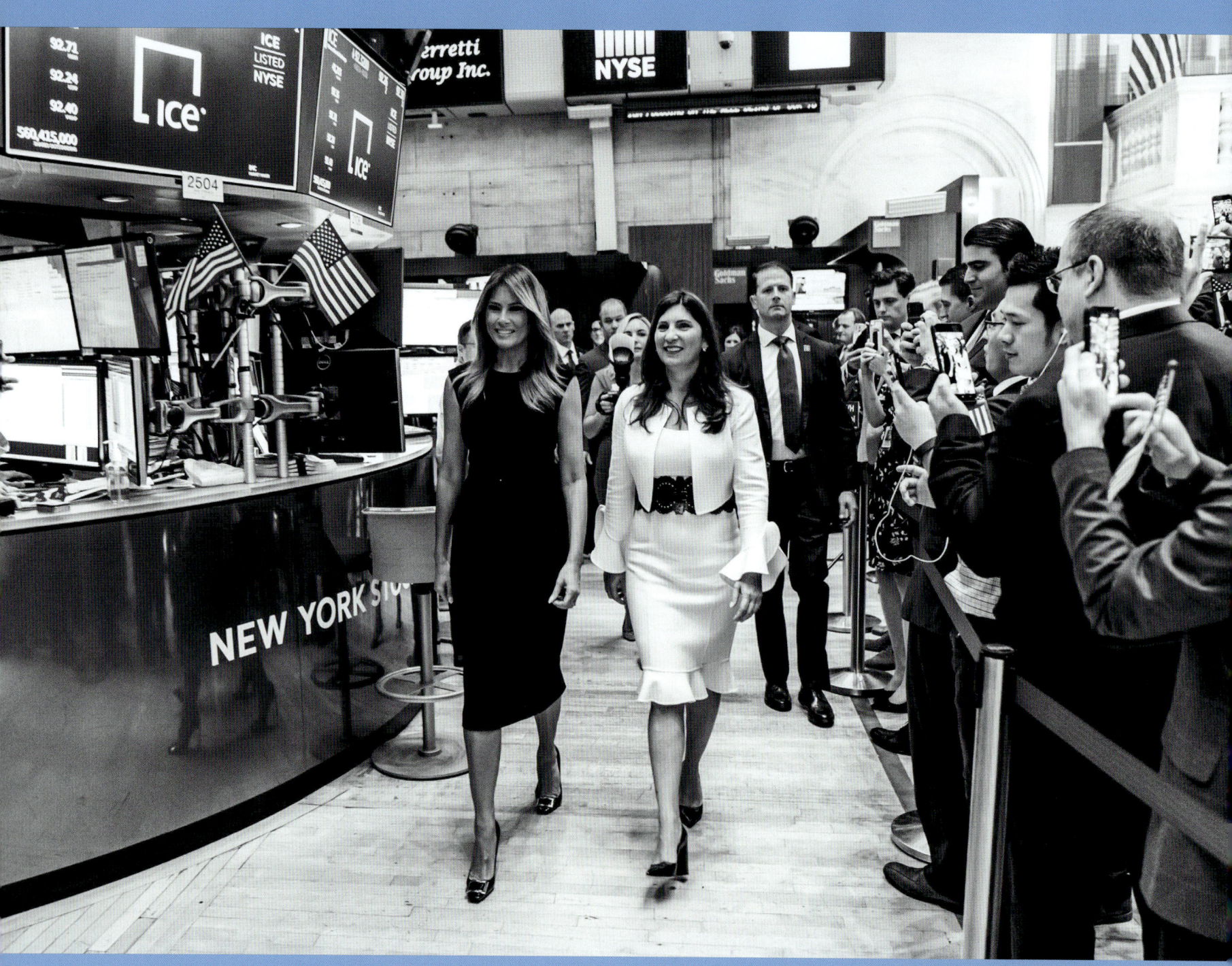

First Lady Melania Trump visits the New York Stock Exchange to participate in the timeless tradition of ringing the Opening Bell in celebration of the well being of children, a pillar of her BE BEST campaign, Monday, September 23, 2019.[6]

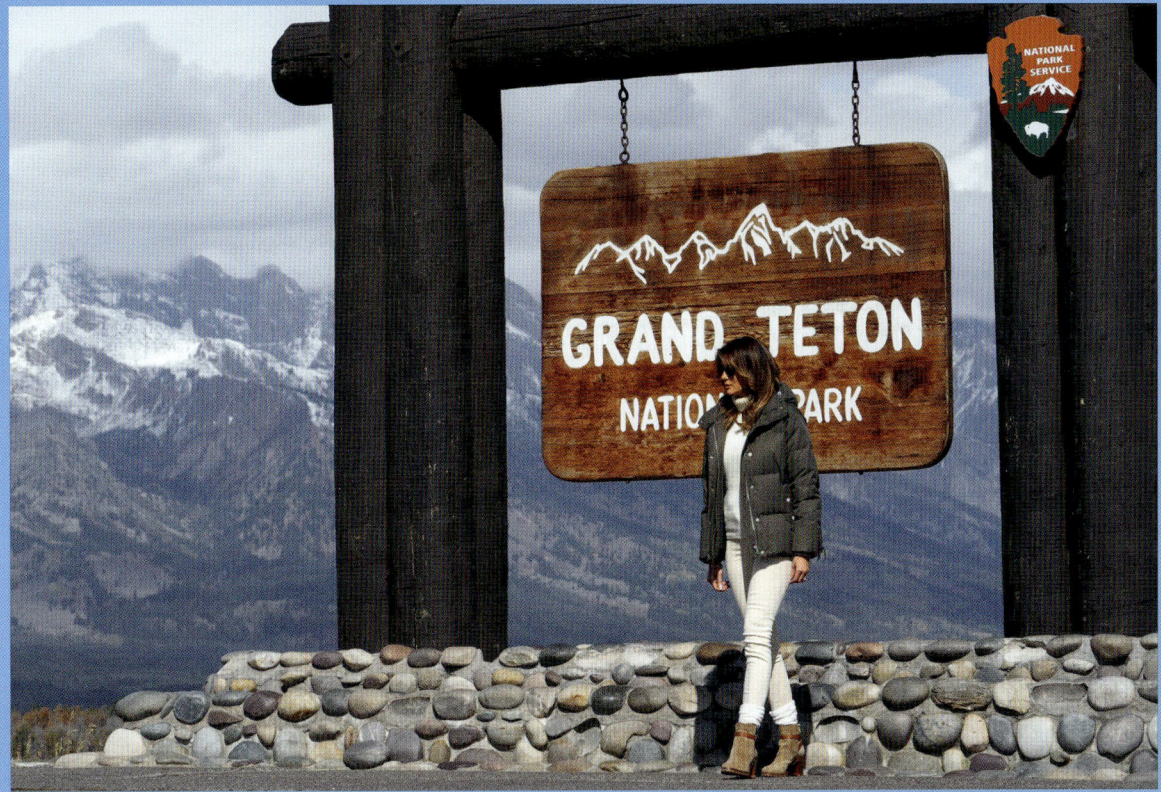

Elegance in Jackson, Wyoming.[6]

The First Lady and Secretary of the Interior Bernhardt participate in a National Park Service Arrowhead Ceremony with elementary school students at the Craig Thomas Discovery Center in Grand Teton National Park, Wyoming.[6]

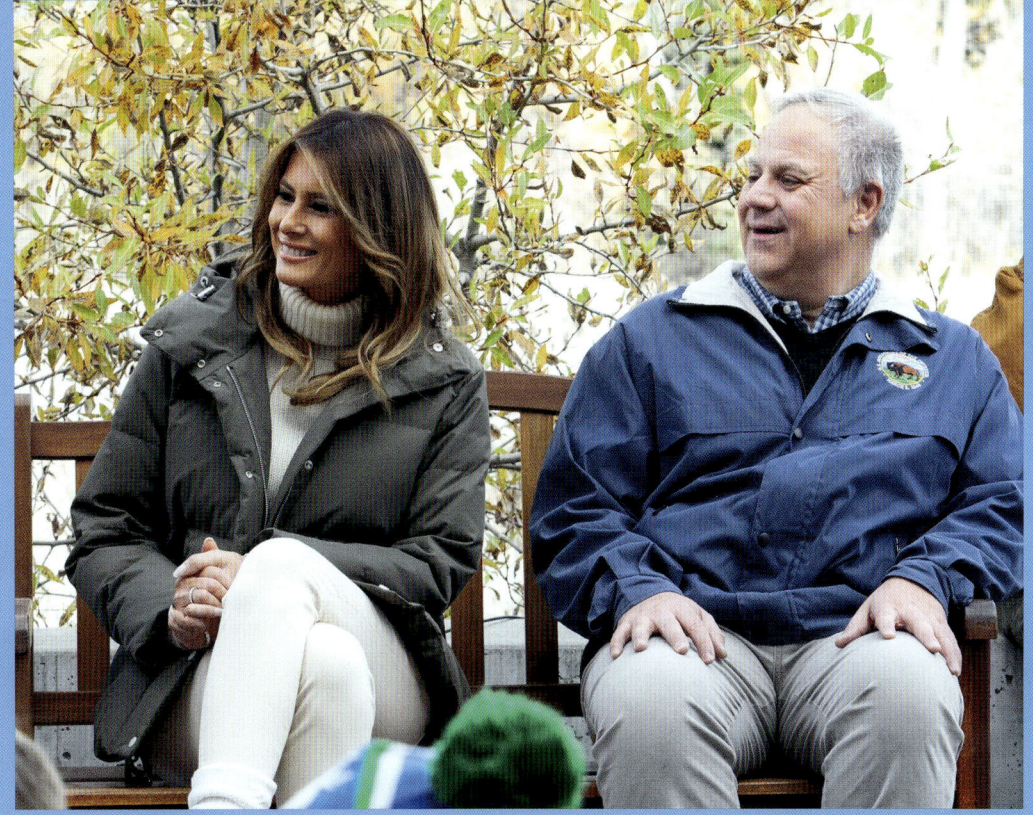

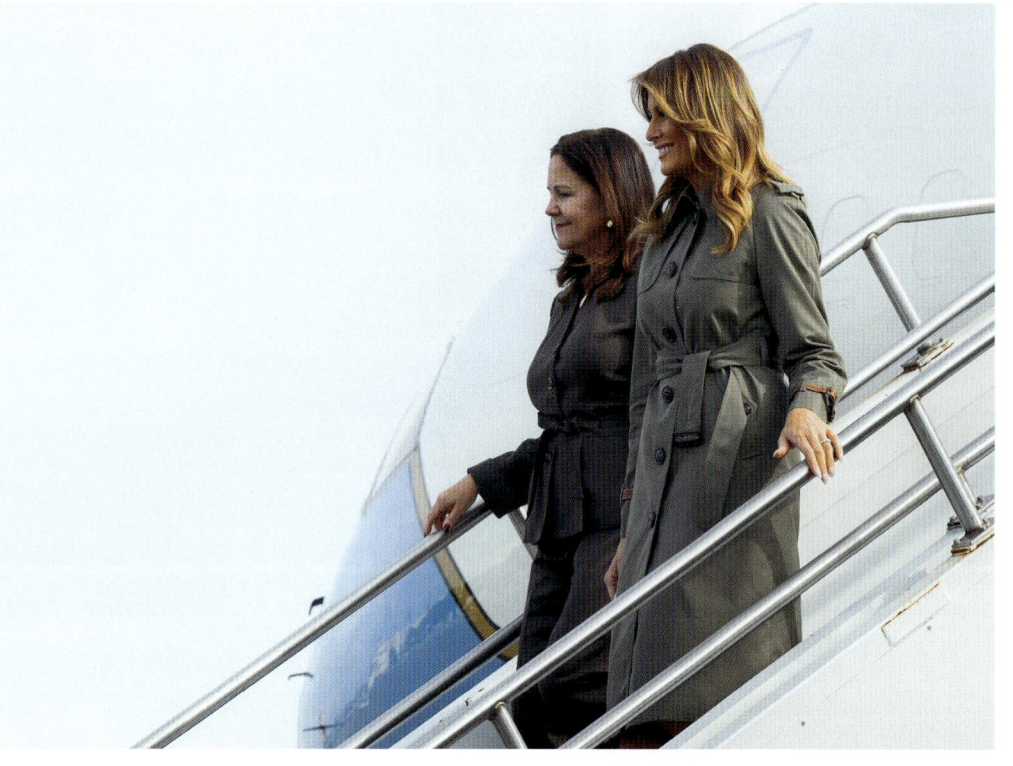

First Lady Melania Trump and Second Lady Karen Pence disembark Bright Star at Charleston Air Force Base.[6]

The First Lady is all smiles while talking with 5th grade students participating in the Red Cross Pillowcase Project at Lambs Elementary School in North Charleston.[6]

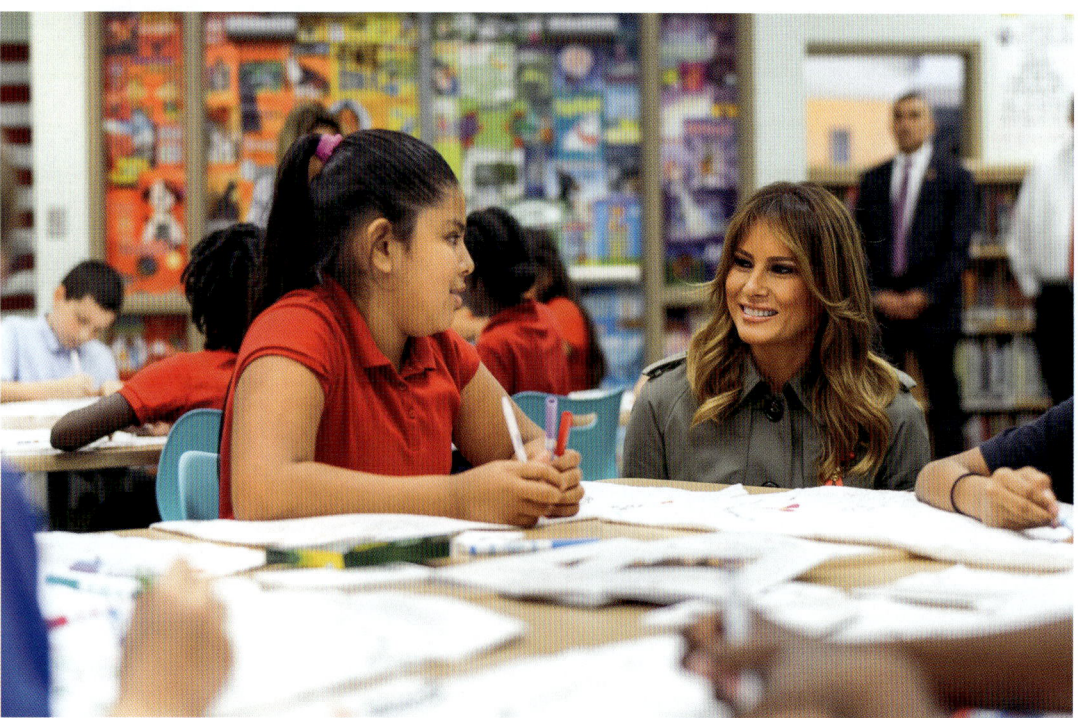

Right: Elegance breaks ground for the White House Tennis Pavilion![6]

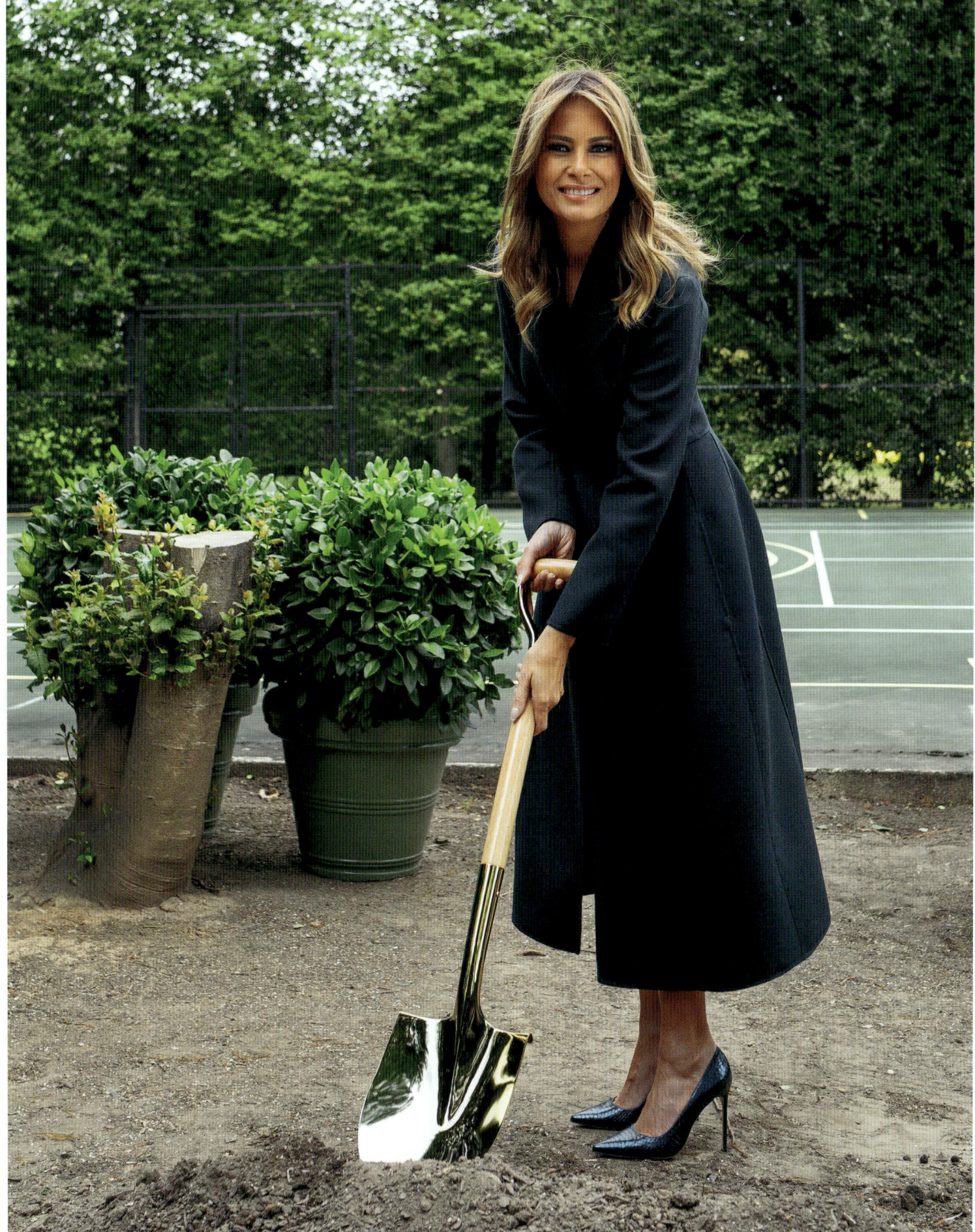

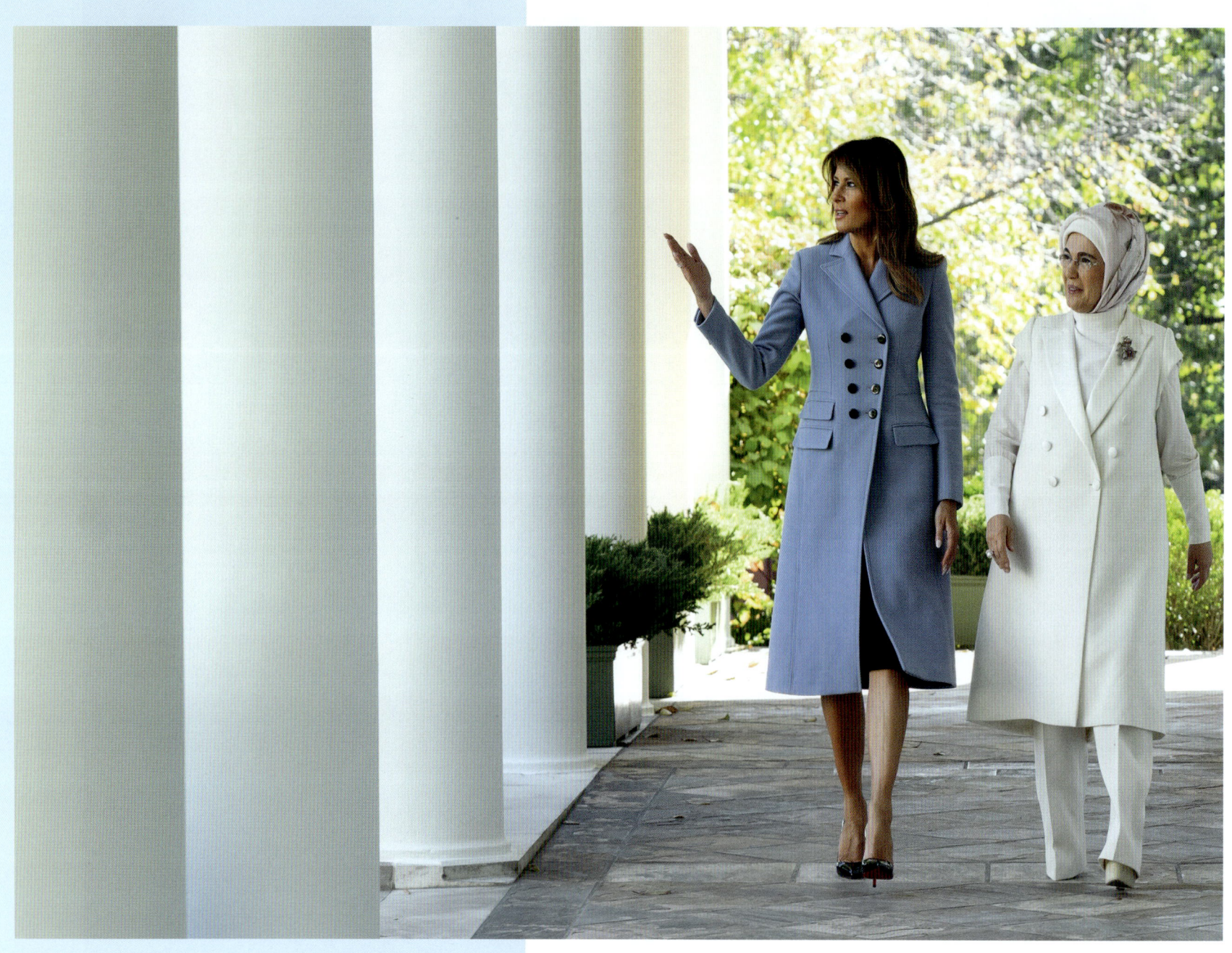

The First Lady walks with Mrs. Emine Erdogan, wife of Turkish President Recep Tayyip Erdogan Wednesday, November 13, 2019, along the Colonnade of the White House.[6]

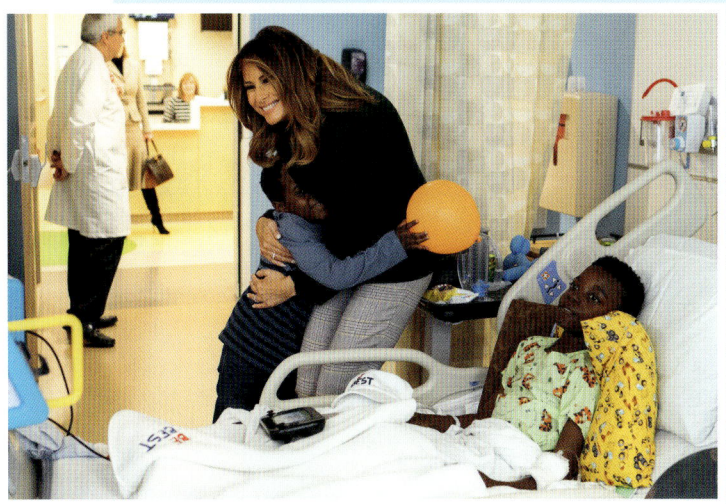

First Lady Melania Trump visits with patients and family members during a tour of the pediatric wing at Boston Medical Center.[6]

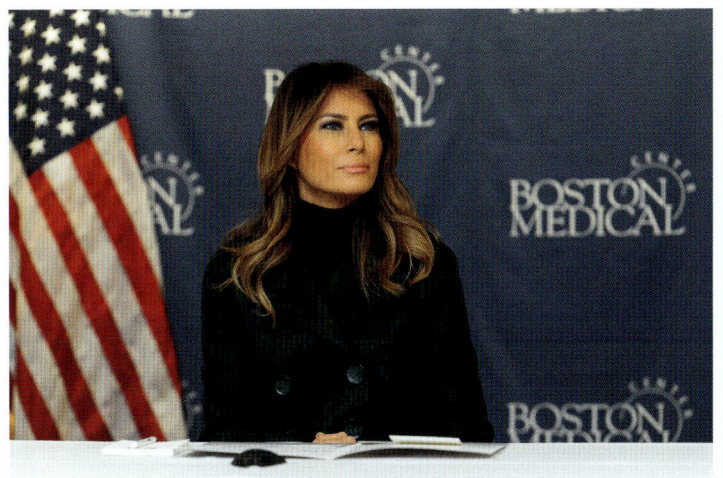

Melania Trump participates in a round-table on Boston Medical Center's Neonatal Abstinence Syndrome (NAS) Program.[6]

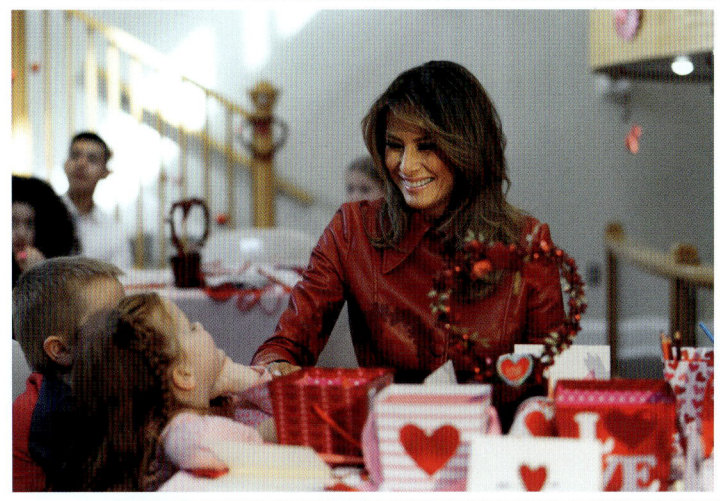

First Lady Melania Trump decorates cards with patients and their family members during a Valentine's Day visit to the Children's Inn at the National institute of Health in Bethesda, Maryland.[6]

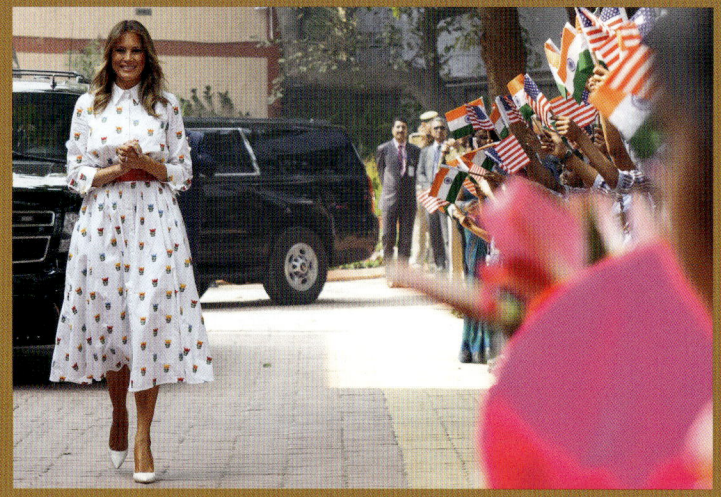

The First Lady is greeted by students as she arrives at Sarvodaya Co-Educational Senior Secondary School in New Delhi, India.[6]

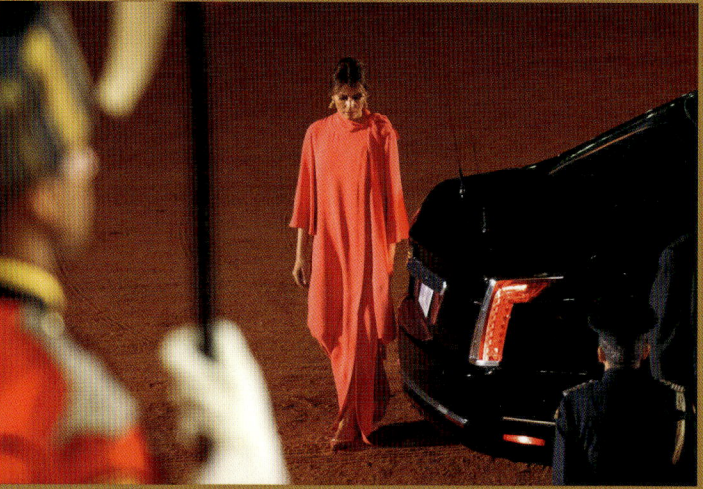

First Lady Melania Trump arrives to attend a state banquet at Rashtrapati Bhavan, the Presidential Palace in New Delhi, India.[6]

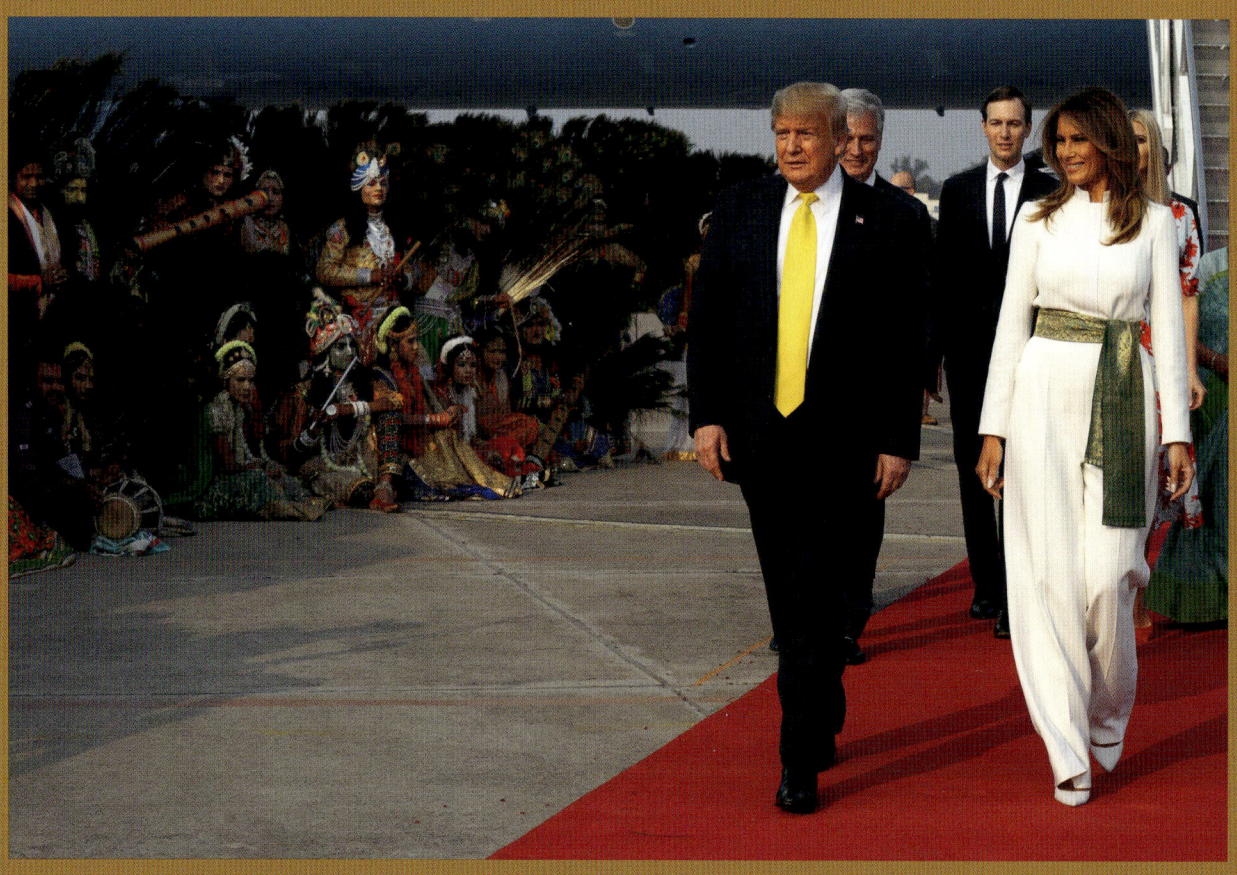

President Trump and the First Lady view cultural performances as they depart Agra for New Delhi.[6]

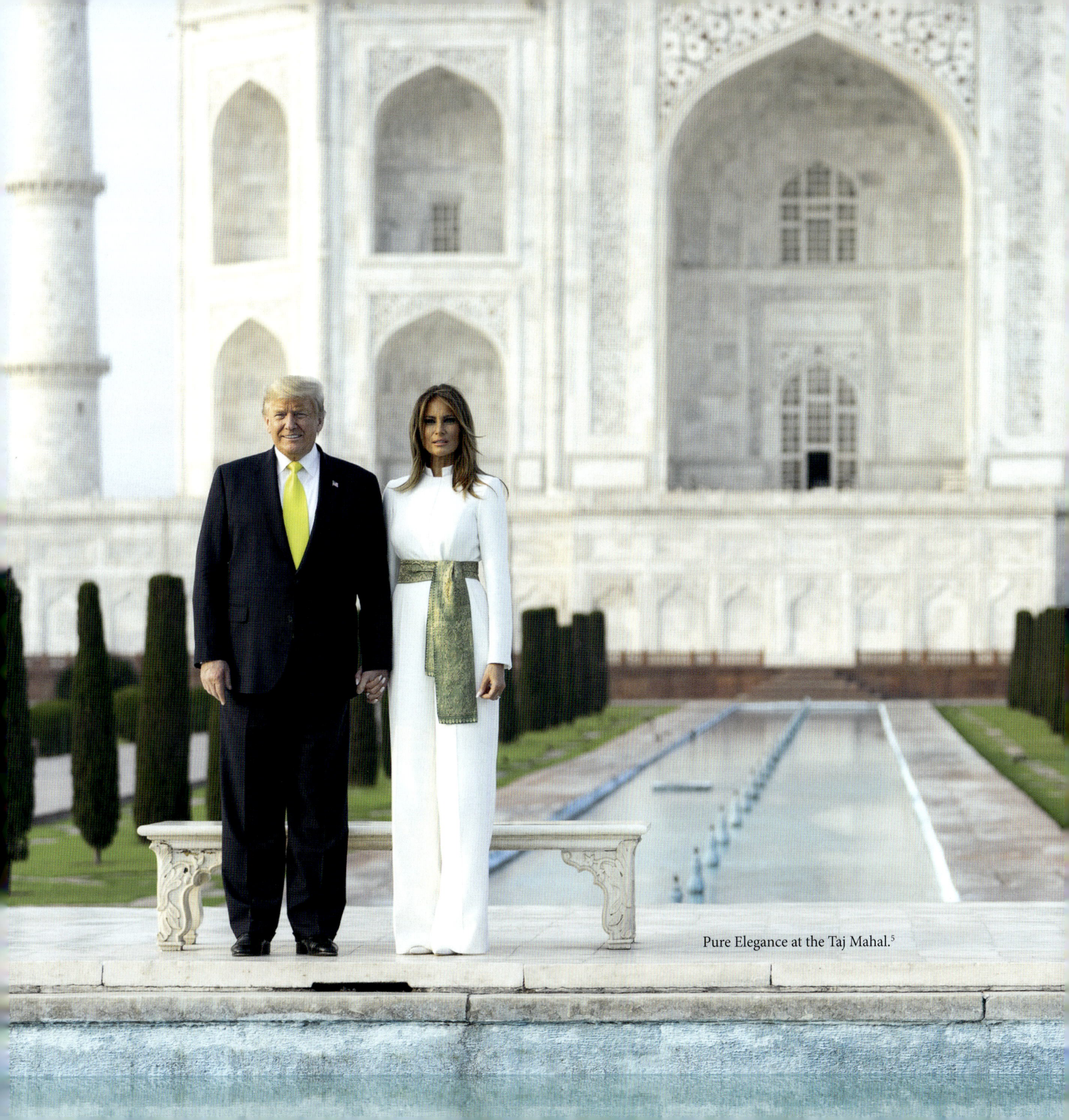

Pure Elegance at the Taj Mahal.[5]

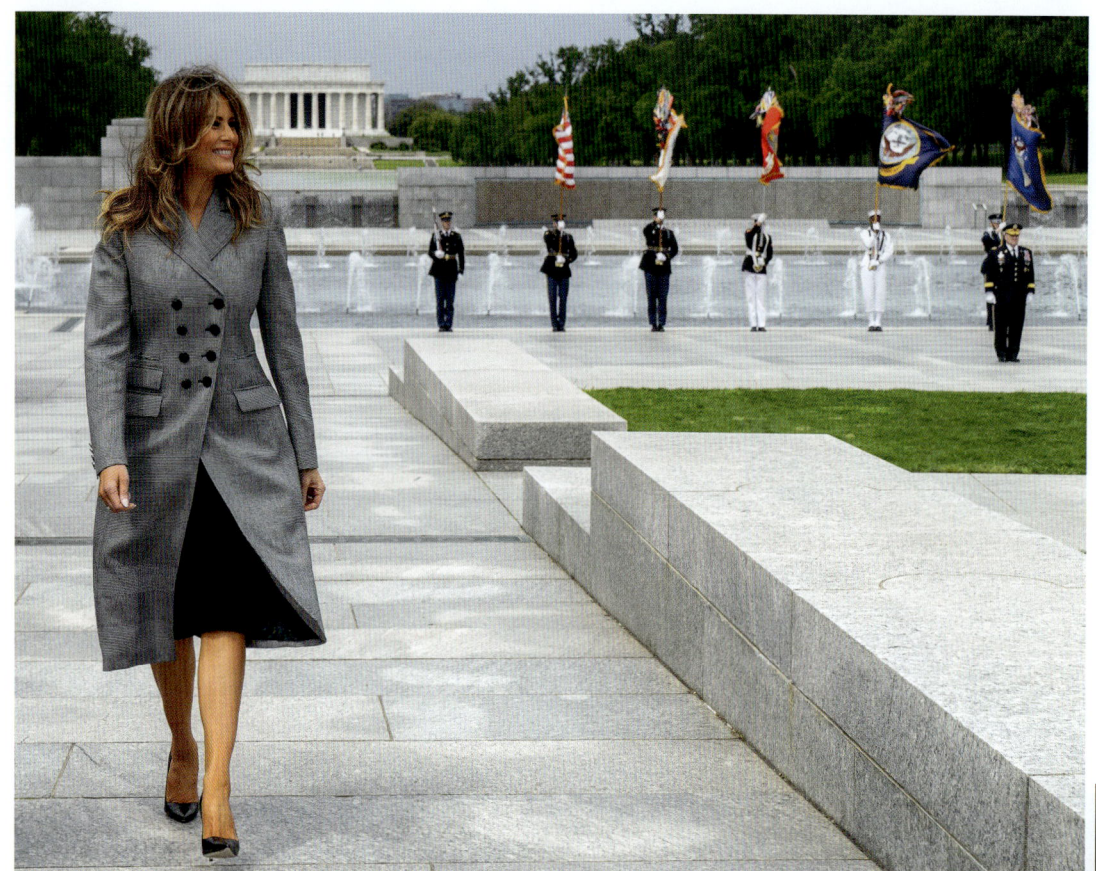

Elegance visits the World War II Memorial in Washington, DC, Friday, May 8, 2020, in honor of the 75th anniversary of Victory in Europe Day.[9]

First Lady Melania Trump participates in a Zoom call with first grade students for the second anniversary of BE BEST, May 2020.[6]

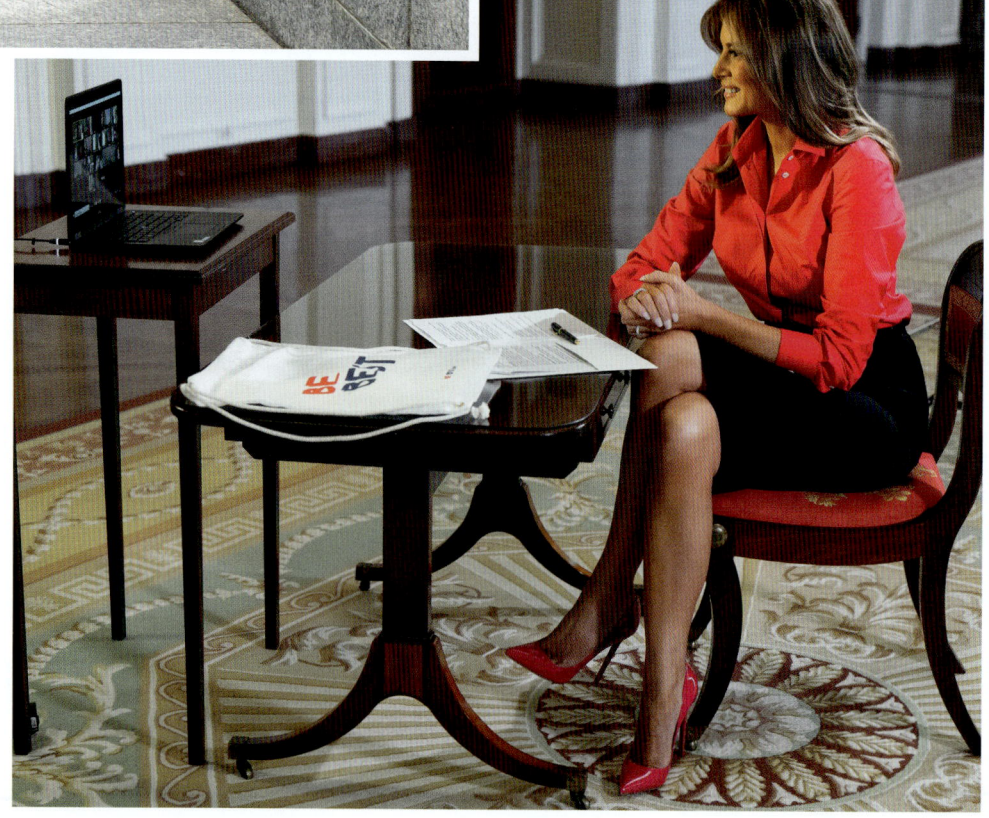

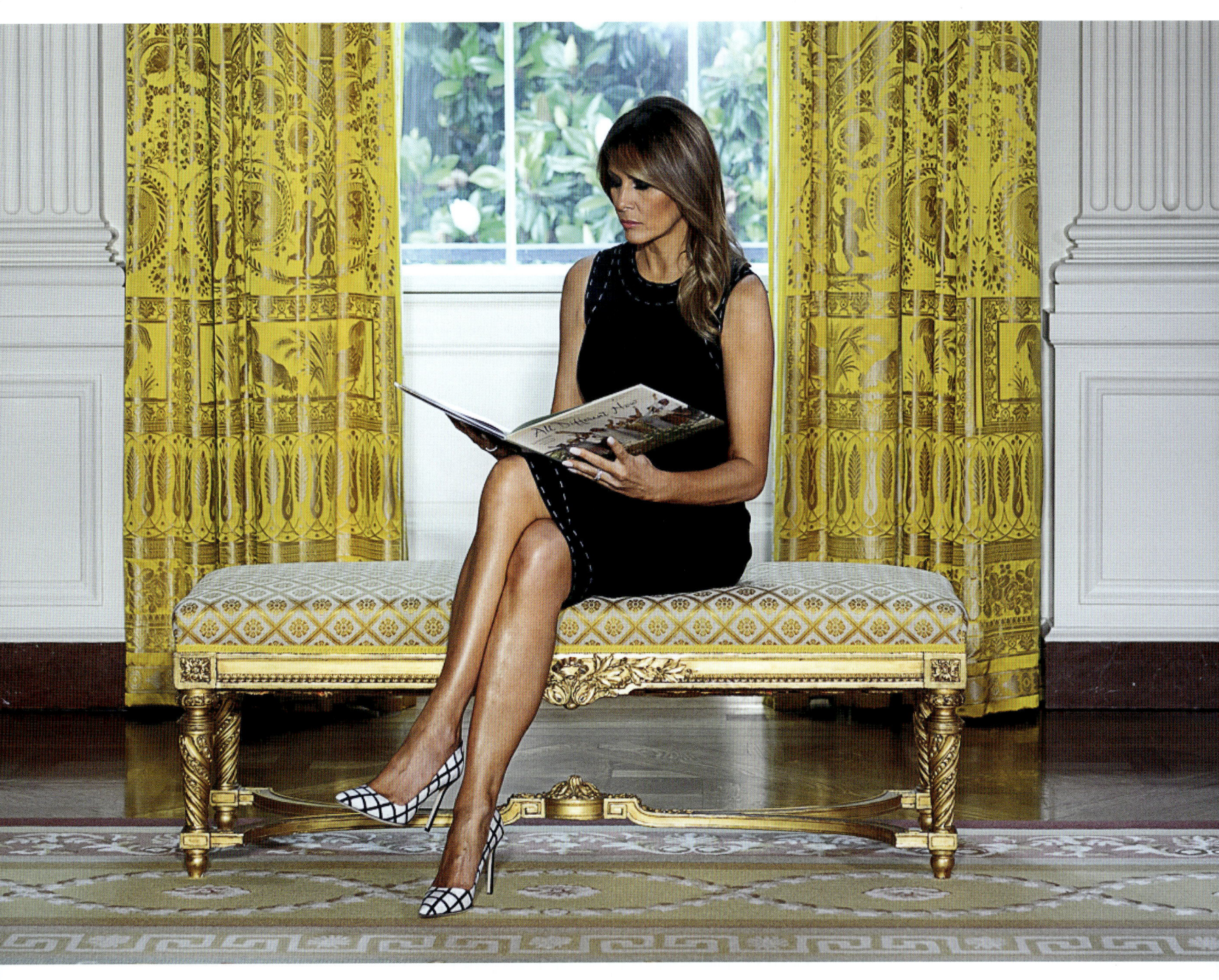

First Lady Melania Trump reads the book *All Different Now* by Angela Johnson during a video recording in the East Room of the White House, June 16, 2020, to be shared online in honor of Juneteenth.[6]

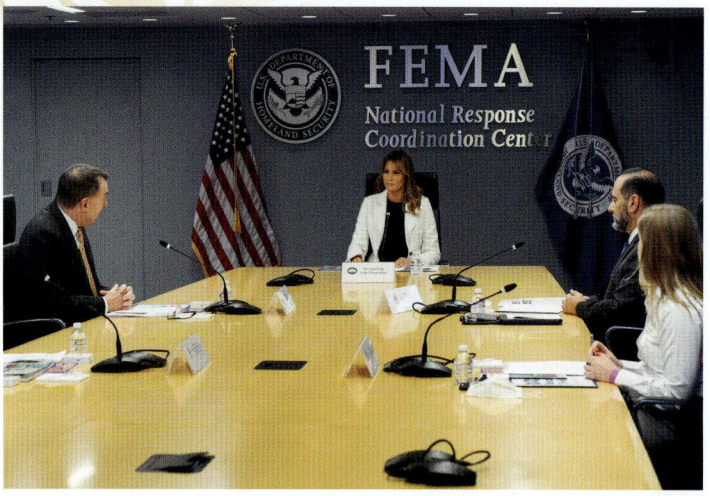

The First Lady participates in a briefing on youth hurricane preparedness with FEMA Administrator Peter Gaynor and American Red Cross officials.[6]

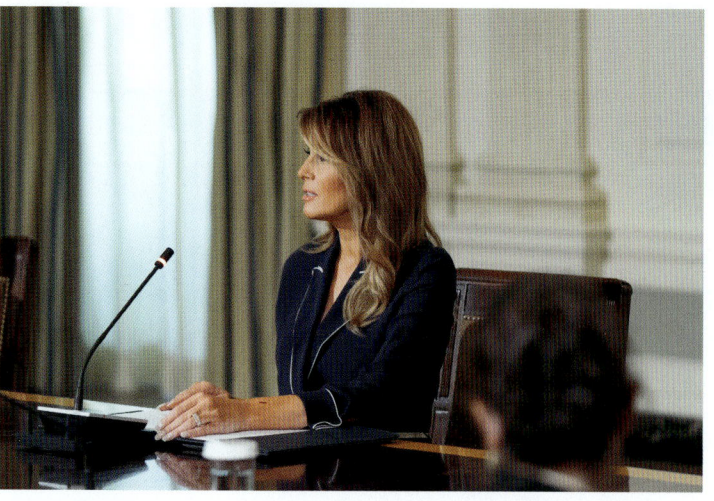

Melania Trump delivers remarks during a briefing on Protecting Native American Children in the Indian Health Service System.[6]

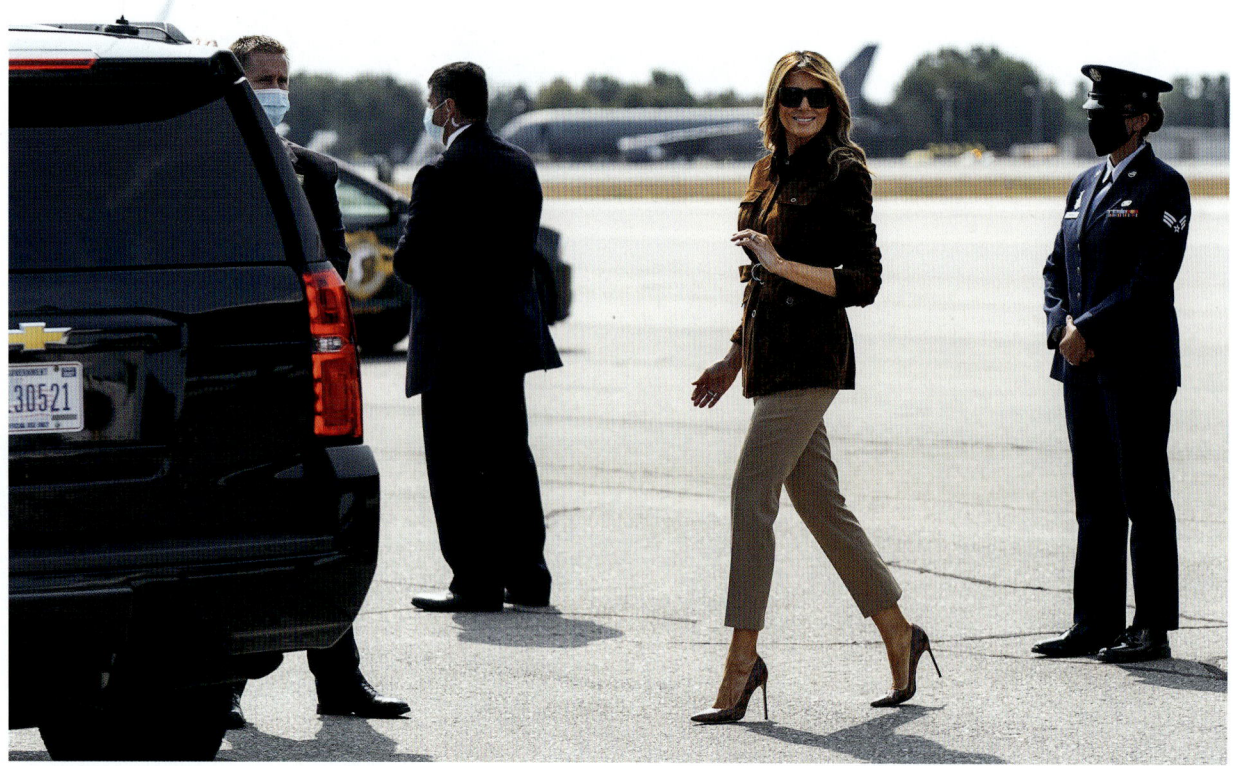

Elegance is all smiles as she arrives in Manchester, New Hampshire.[6]

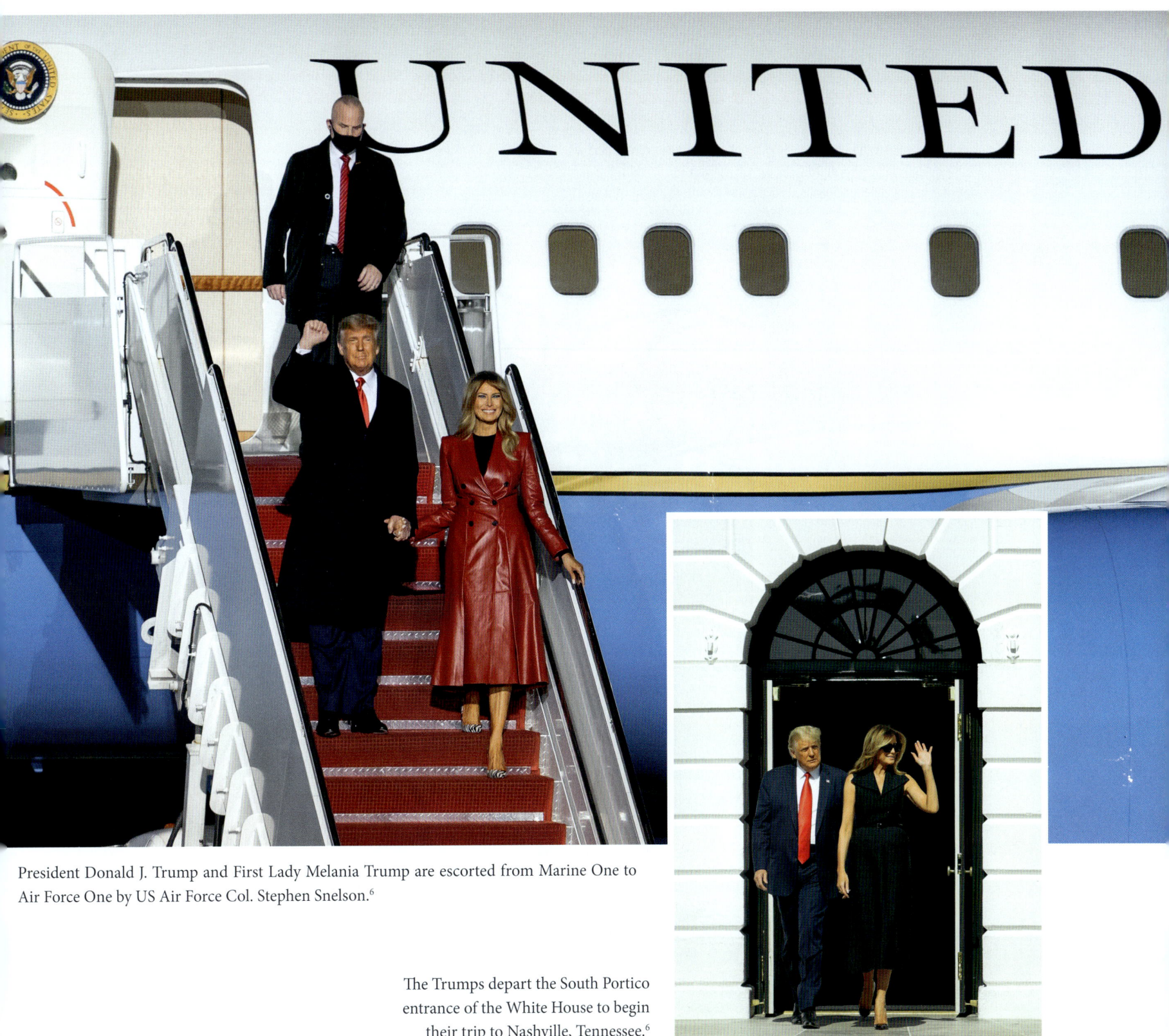

President Donald J. Trump and First Lady Melania Trump are escorted from Marine One to Air Force One by US Air Force Col. Stephen Snelson.[6]

The Trumps depart the South Portico entrance of the White House to begin their trip to Nashville, Tennessee.[6]

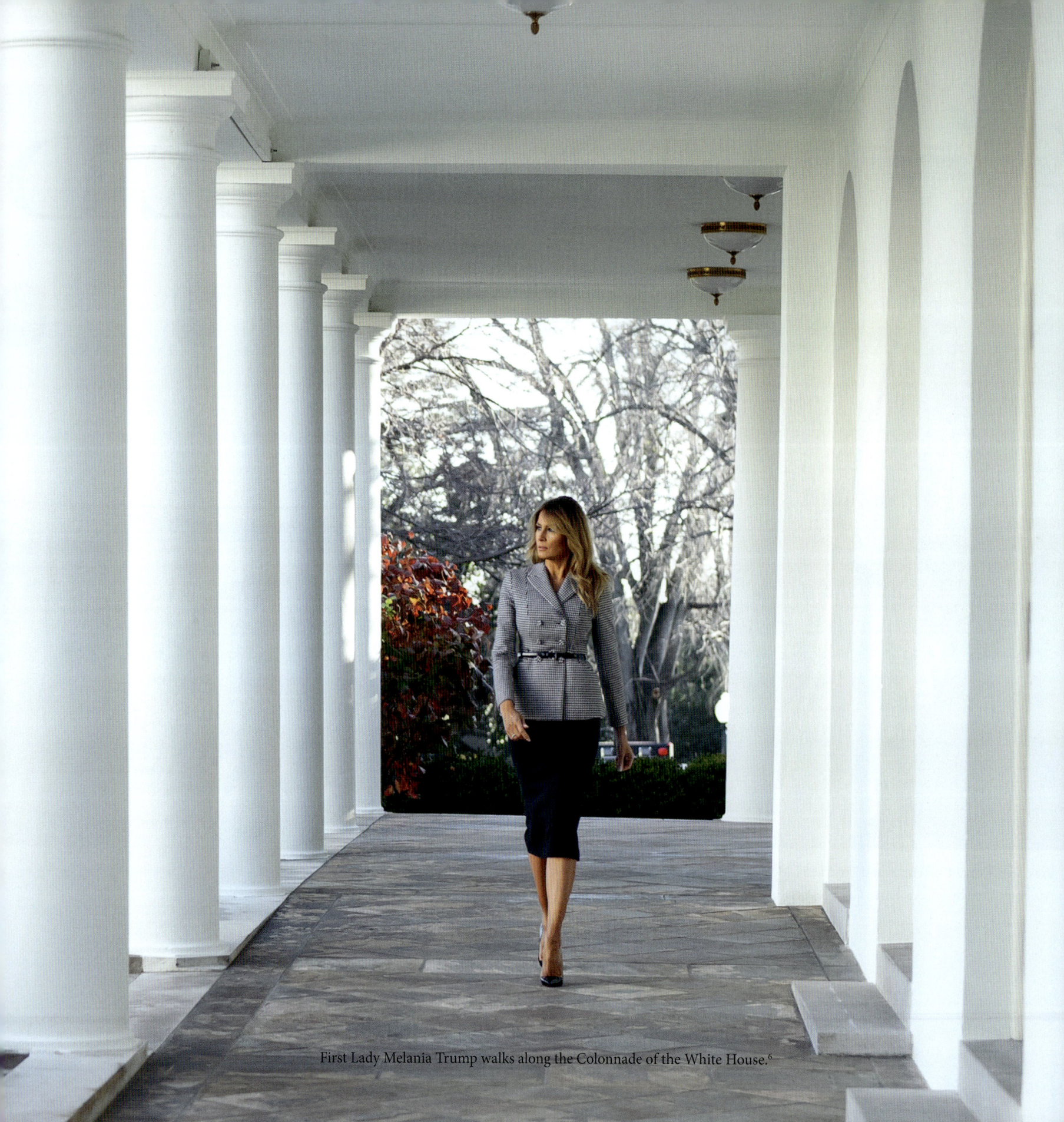

First Lady Melania Trump walks along the Colonnade of the White House.[6]

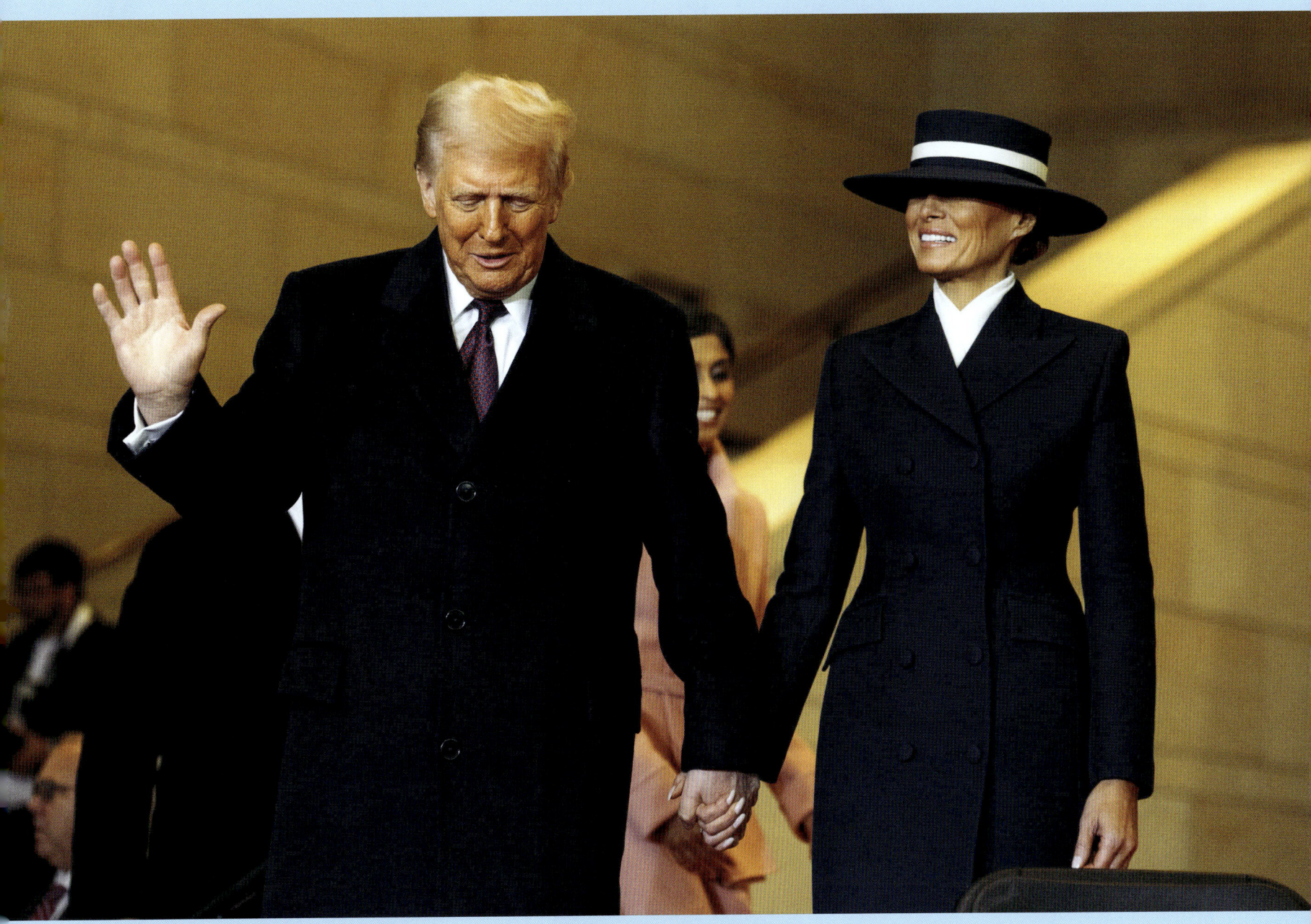

THE SECOND TERM

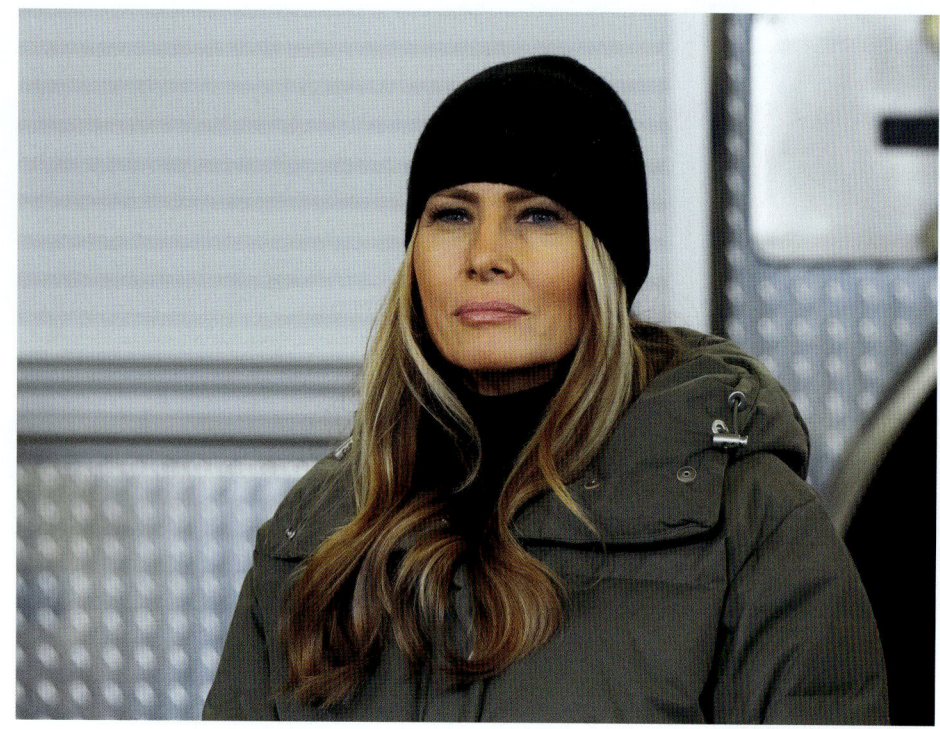

The President and First Lady visit North Carolina to survey damage from Hurricane Helene and assess recovery efforts.[6]

President Donald Trump and First Lady Melania Trump tour a fire-affected area in the Pacific Palisades neighborhood of Los Angeles, California.[6]

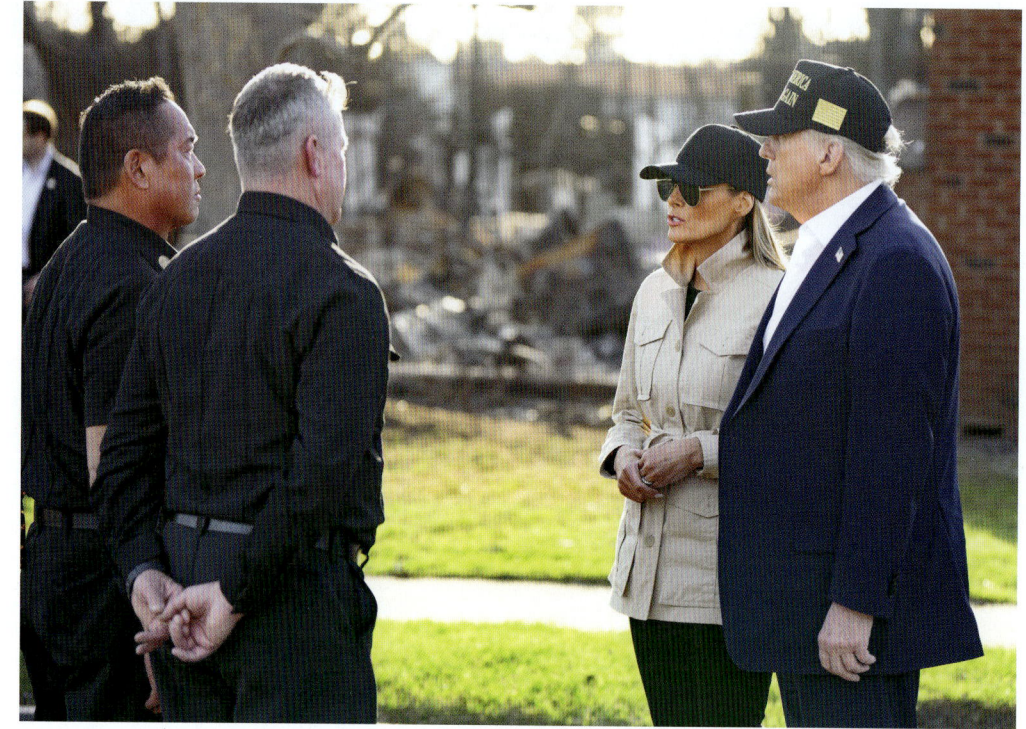

Right: Melania Trump exhibits power and poise for her updated official White House Residency Photograph.[8]

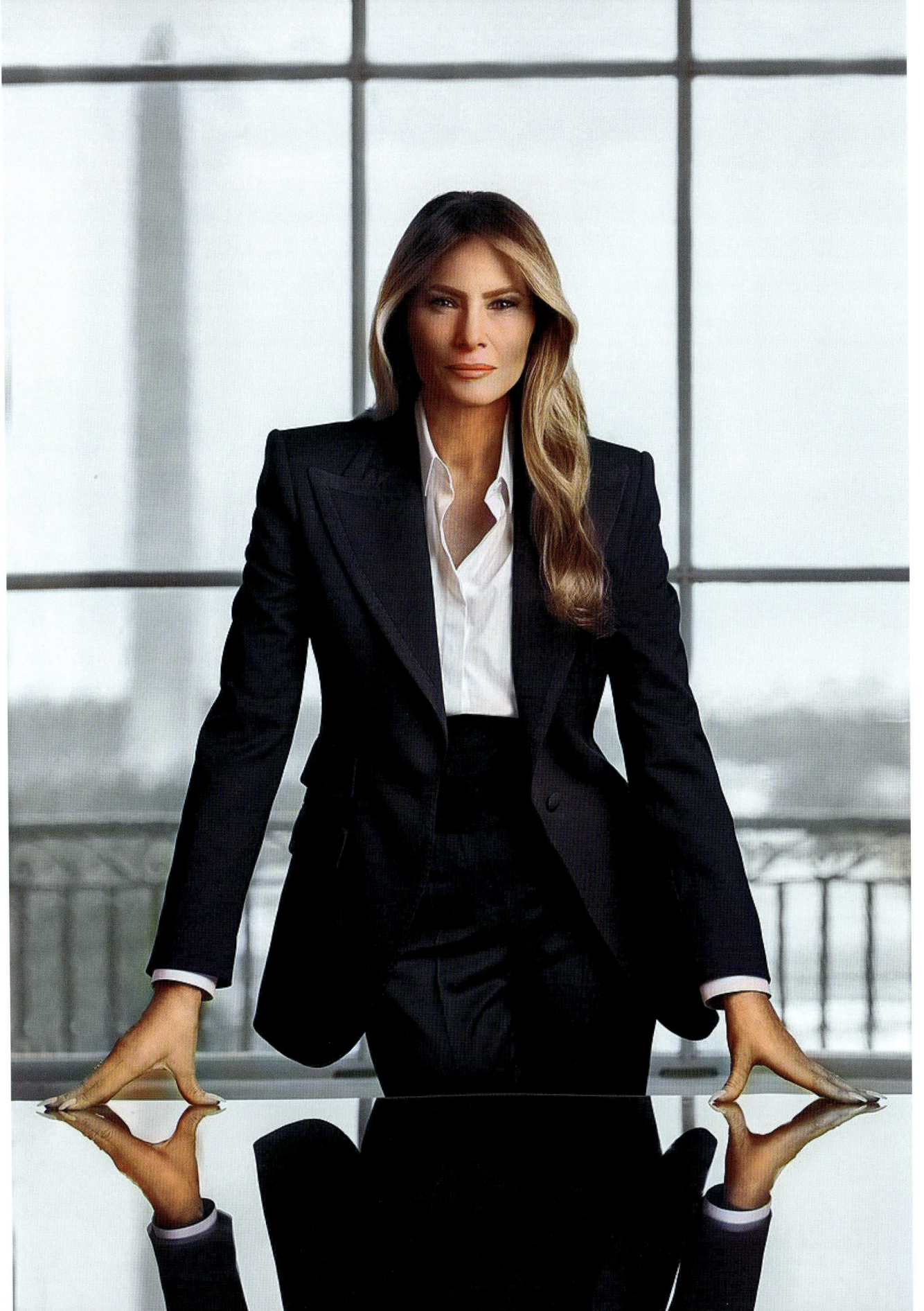

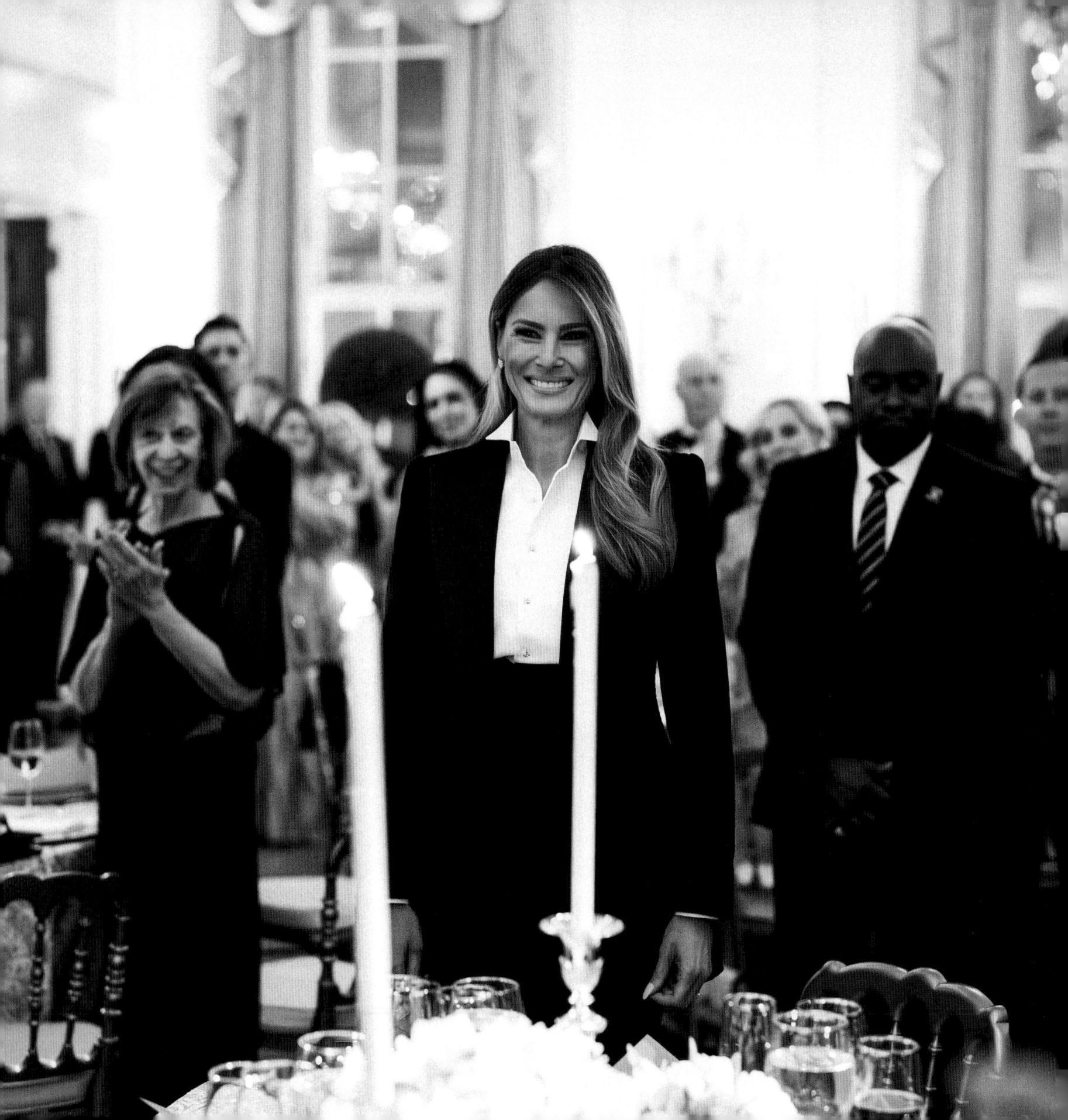

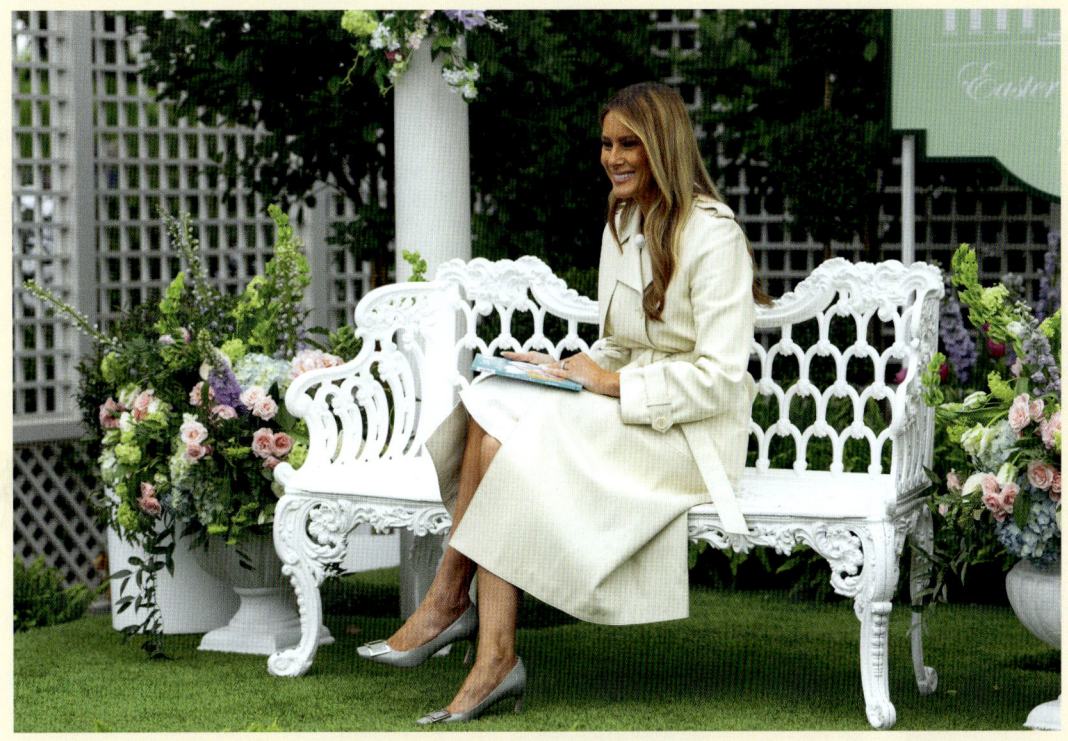

First Lady Melania Trump reads a book at the Reading Nook in the First Ladies Garden
during the White House Easter Egg Roll.[6]

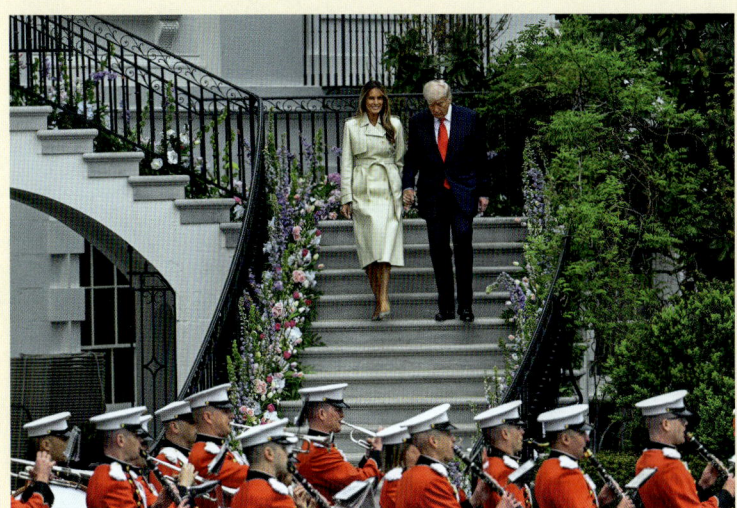

The President and First Lady arrive to the South Lawn to
participate in the annual White House Easter Egg Roll.[6]

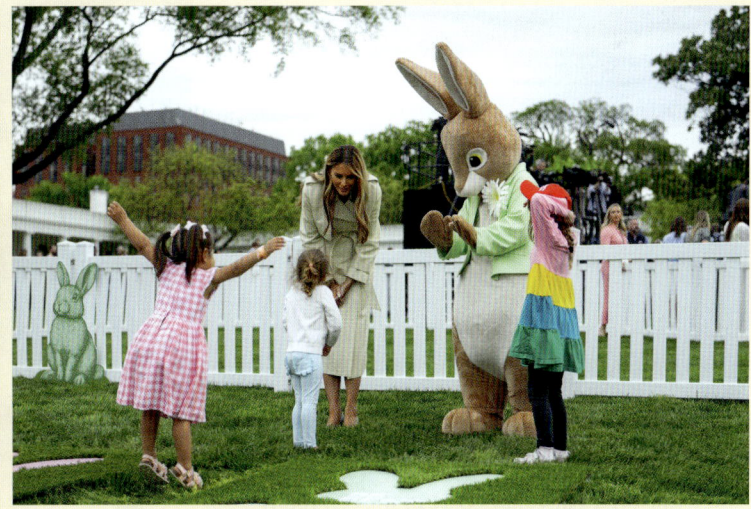

First Lady Melania Trump visits the Hop Scotch
activity at the White House Easter Egg Roll, Monday,
April 21, 2025, on the South Lawn.[6]

Left: Guests at the governor's ball acknowledge First Lady Melania Trump.[6]

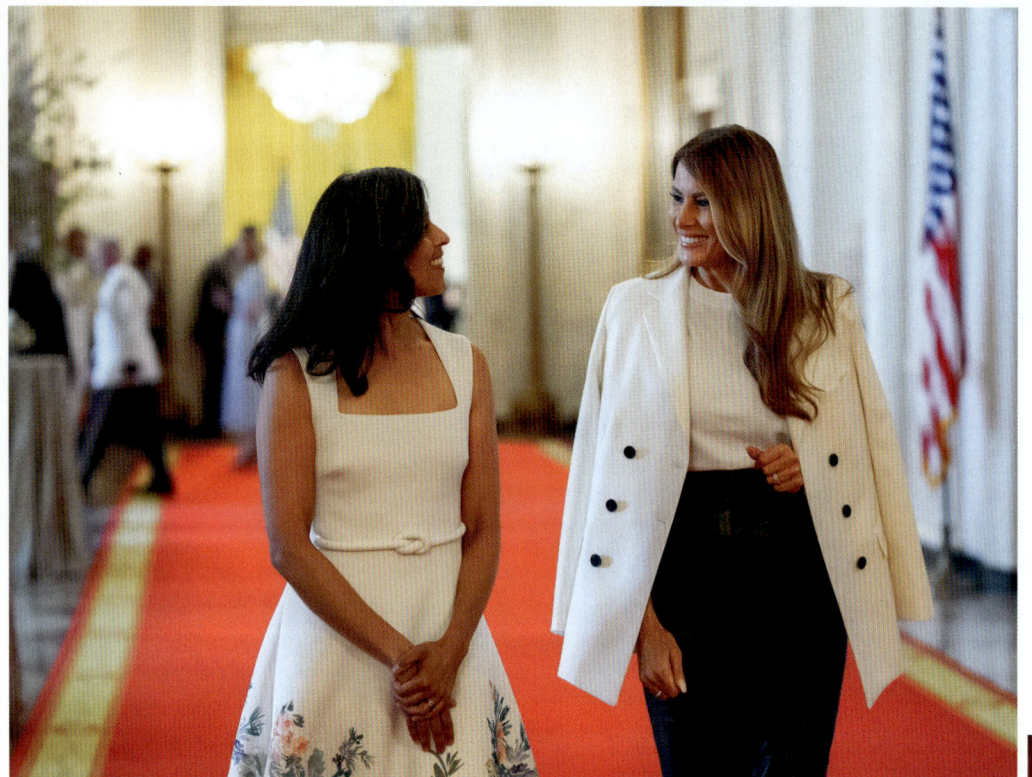

First Lady Melania Trump and President Donald Trump host a Celebration for Military Mothers event in the East Room, Thursday, May 8, 2025, at the White House.[6]

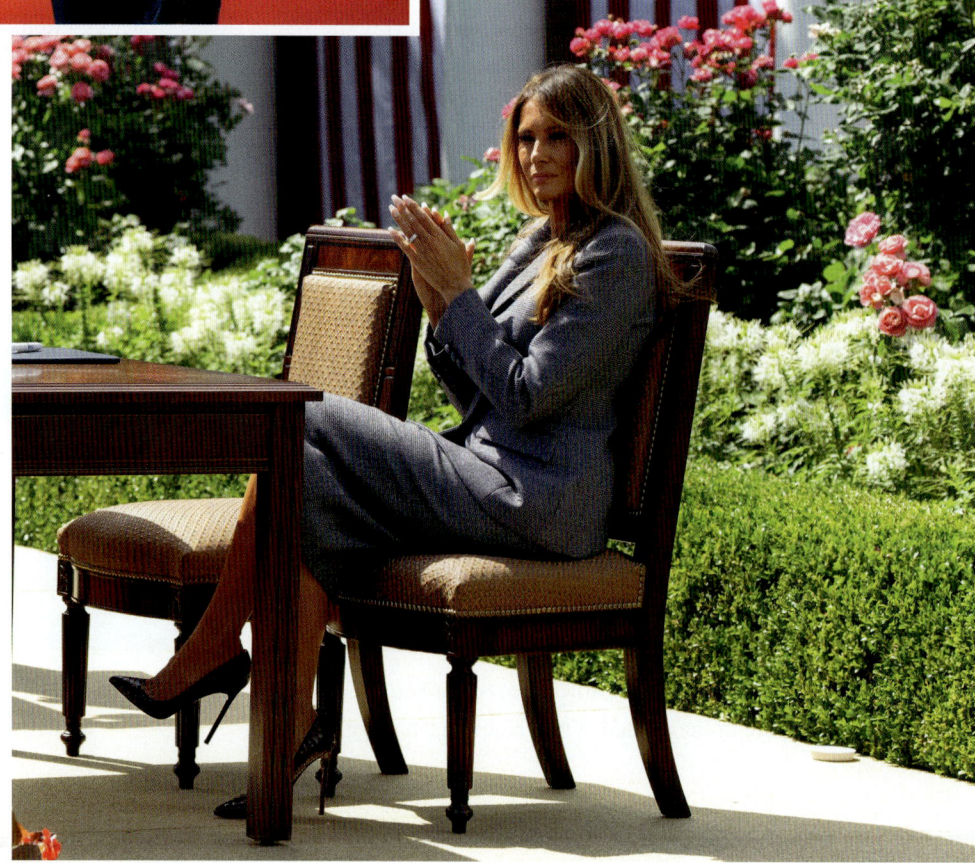

The First Lady takes part in the ceremony for the Take it Down Act in the White House Rose Garden, May 19, 2025.[6]

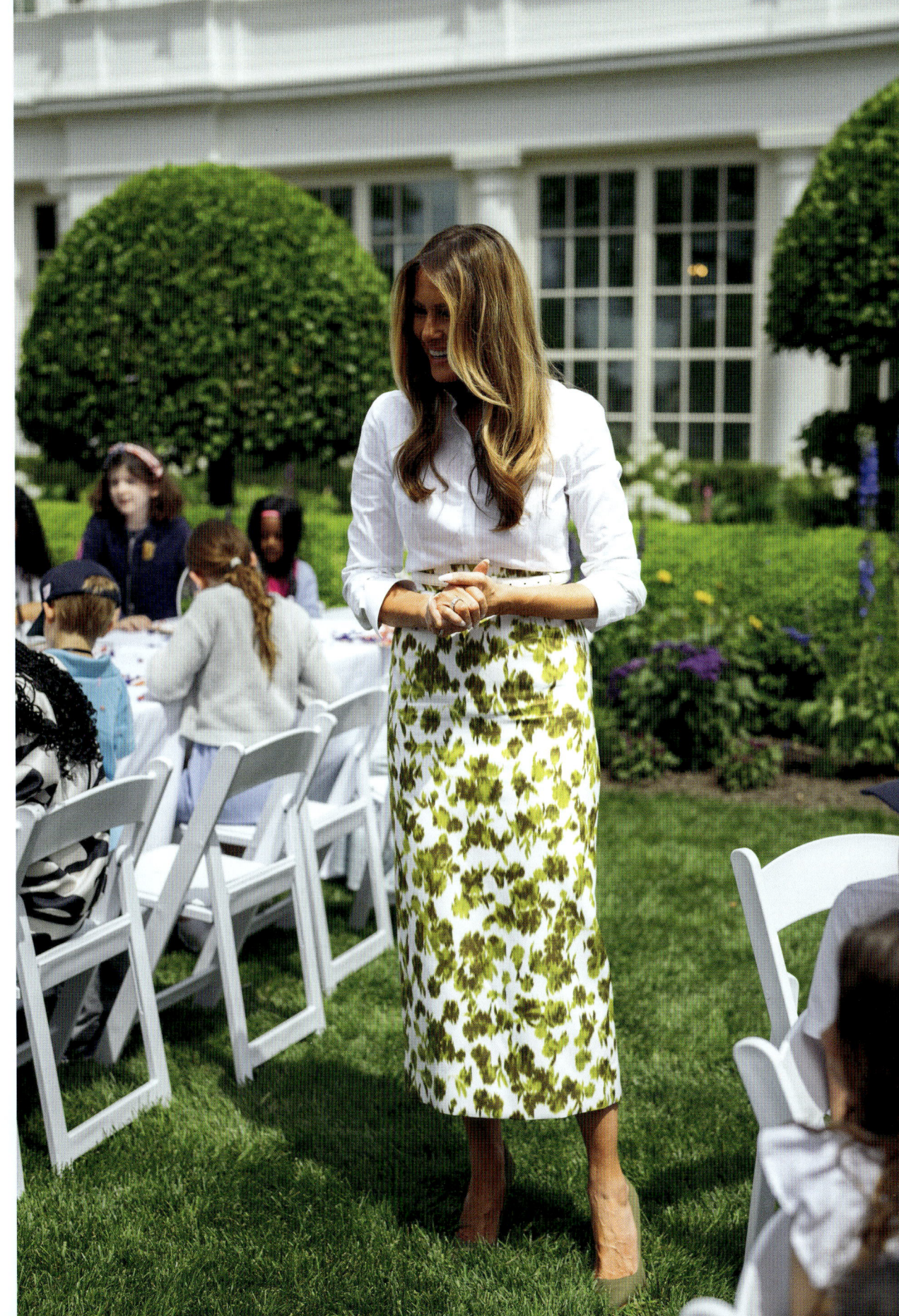

First Lady Melania Trump greets
parents and children at Take Our
Sons and Daughters to Work Day
on the South Lawn.[6]

First Lady Melania Trump participates in the Senate Spouses Luncheon at the National Gallery of Art in Washington, DC, Wednesday, May 21, 2025.[6]

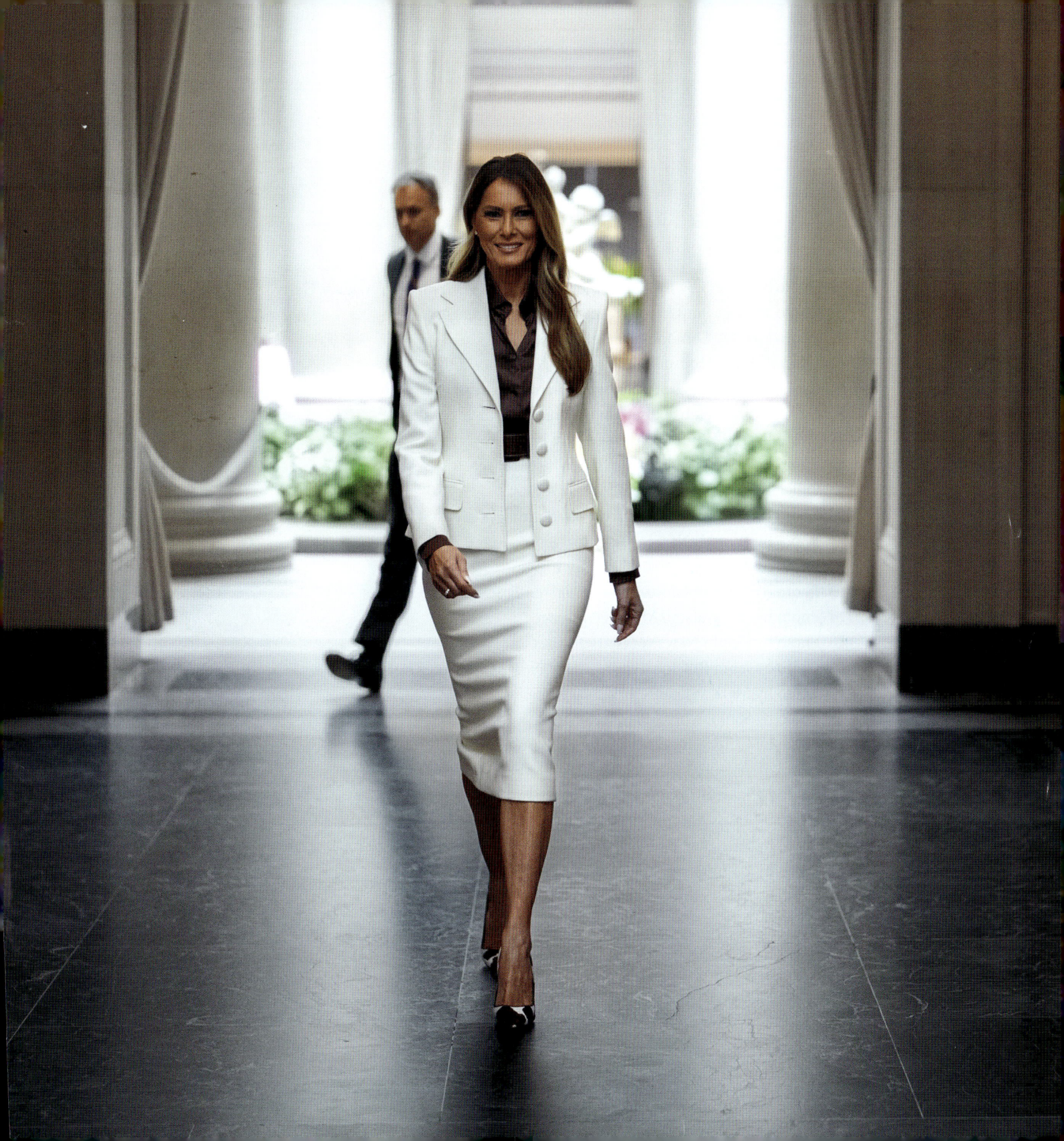

PHOTO CREDITS

ELEGANCE
— IN THE —
WHITE HOUSE

Melania Trump

2ND EDITION

BREANNA MORELLO

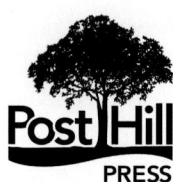

Post Hill Press
New York • Nashville
posthillpress.com

Published in the United States of America
1 2 3 4 5 6 7 8 9 10
Printed in Canada